Windows Vista® Security

O9-AHW-563

Checklist for ... ... ur Security Plan

A security plan is critical to your achieving the right balance between productivity and protection. The following checklist can guide you in putting your security plan together. After completing the checklist, you will have the data you need to build your security plan. Take the outstanding risks and utilize Vista or third-party tools to reduce those risks to a level that's acceptable to you.

- ✔ **Understand your system.** Perform a system inventory, identifying each system's hardware and software; interfaces (network and so on); how the system will be used; and what type of data will be on the system. Indicate how critical the availability of the system and data is.

- ✔ **Identify threats.** Write down the types of threats that might be presented to your system and data (viruses, spam, and so on).

- ✔ **Determine vulnerabilities.** From patches that need to be applied to having no redundant power supply, each system usually has some vulnerabilities. List the vulnerabilities that are present in your system.

- ✔ **List your current security safeguards.** List the safeguards that you have in place that address a particular threat or problem. For example, antivirus software is a safeguard against malicious code.

- ✔ **What are the chances of *that* happening?** Try to determine the chance of a particular event occurring. You might be surprised how this assessment helps determine how you proceed when defending against a particular threat.

- ✔ **Determine the real risk.** Quantify the real risk. Take into account the threats, vulnerabilities, and safeguards you have in place to protect against those threats as well as the chances of a particular threat occurring. What is the residual risk to you? After you understand the risks, you can move forward to protect yourself against those risks.

Security Tools That You Shouldn't Compute Without

The following list discusses five tools that you just do not want to go without. In Chapter 18, I describe these tools (and five more) in detail. Here are my favorite five.

- ✔ **Antivirus software:** This is absolutely critical to your security success. Make sure that you obtain software that's compatible with Vista, preferably from a Microsoft-registered participating vendor.

- ✔ **Spyware removal tools:** No one tool seems to catch it all. I suggest that you use a variety of spyware-removal tools to rid your system from this intrusive pest.

- ✔ **Firewall or other network protection:** A variety of personal firewall applications are available. The Vista Windows Firewall will likely have the functionality that most home and small office users need. Putting this tool or another third-party firewall utility to work is essential to the security of your system and data.

- ✔ **Online security newsletters:** You know the saying, "Knowledge is power." This couldn't be more true than when talking about the security of your system, data, and even personally identifiable information. If you're serious about your system, take the time to keep up to date on the latest security issues with these newsletters.

    ```
    www.sans.org/newsletters
    www.microsoft.com/technet/security/secnews/newsletter.htm
    ```

- ✔ **About.com's Identity Theft site** (http://idtheft.about.com): Protecting your personally identifiable information has never been more important than it is today. With identity theft being the fastest growing crime in America, you need to know the things that you can do to protect yourself.

Windows Vista® Security For Dummies®

Cheat Sheet

Quick Reference for Backup and Recovery Options

The following table provides a quick reference for the backup and recovery options available for Vista.

Backup and Recovery Options	Vista Version	Use	Data Type Preserved	Backup/ Recovery Time	Storage Media
System Restore Point	All	Protect OS from corruption	System configuration	Fast backup and recovery only	Backup within the OS itself; the only option is your hard drive.
File and Folder Backup	All	Backup of specific data	Application and personal data	Dependent on how much data is backed up and how it is done	Media must be large enough to handle how much data is backed up, but it can be as small as you want.
Complete PC Backup (System Image)	Business, Ultimate	Capture of all data on machine for use in rebuilding	All	Slow backup but allows for fast recovery compared with rebuilding the machine from scratch	Dependent upon how much data is within the image. Usually must be done on at least a DVD.
Shadow Copy	Business, Ultimate	Backup of open files and version control of files	Application and personal data	Fast backup and recovery	By default, reserves 15 percent of each hard drive volume, but both size and location can be configured.

For Dummies: Bestselling Book Series for Beginners

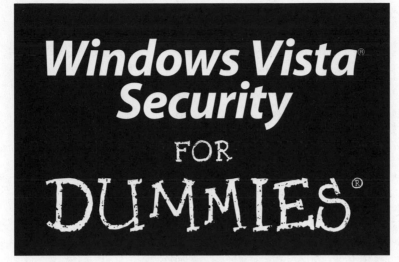

Windows Vista® Security

FOR

DUMMIES®

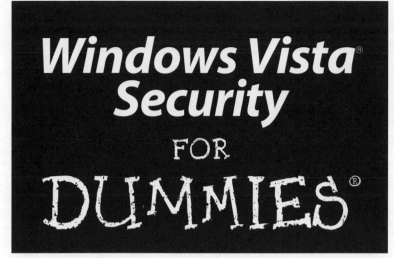

Windows Vista® Security FOR DUMMIES®

by Brian Koerner

Wiley Publishing, Inc.

Windows Vista® Security For Dummies®
Published by
Wiley Publishing, Inc.
111 River Street
Hoboken, NJ 07030-5774
www.wiley.com

WILEY

About the Author

Brian Koerner (CISSP, MCSE) is a former police officer who combined his law enforcement experience and technical skills for a career in information security. Brian is a Chief Security Engineer for a computer services firm, providing security expertise to some of the largest organizations in the world. He has conducted security assessments for compliance with security standards, regulatory mandates (such as HIPAA) and contractual obligations (such as the PCI Data Security Standard). He is adept in many Microsoft technologies as well as encryption and enterprise-security architecture. He has been trained in criminal procedure law, investigations, computer forensics, incident response, and more. Brian is an avid security researcher who is passionate about matters of security and privacy. He is an accomplished writer and speaker whose expertise related to information security, data breaches, and identity theft has been sought out by business and media organizations around the globe. He writes for About.com (`http://idtheft.about.com`), where he provides advice and tips to those concerned about or victims of identity theft and other crimes of fraud. Through this work, he has touched the lives and assisted thousands of individuals affected by these crimes. Brian has developed personal security-awareness seminars and identity theft workshops to help organizations educate their employees on how to protect their Personally Identifiable Information (PII) as well as proprietary business information. He's helped these organizations understand that they, too, must take seriously their role in protecting PII of their employees, customers, and partners.

Brian resides in upstate New York with his wife Cosimina and three children: Justin, Ashley, and Brianna. You can e-mail Brian at `idtheft.guide@ about.com`.

About the Co-Authors

As you might imagine, a book of this nature takes a significant amount of time to write. I was lucky enough to have two people that had the time, energy, and expertise to help when I came knocking.

Mike Borkin (GSEC, MCSE in NT and 2000), as both an end user and a security professional, has seen all the considerable changes in the Microsoft security philosophy in all the intervening operating systems from Windows 3.1 to Vista.

Currently, Mike's role in a Fortune 100 computer services firm makes him accountable for ensuring the security of Windows-based desktops and servers around the world. Since September 2005, Mike has worked with the Microsoft Technology Adoption Program to provide direction to Microsoft regarding Vista security and its features.

Of particular benefit to the reader is Mike's expertise in managing access in Windows operating systems and his related contributions to chapters on managing accounts, groups, and shares; advanced techniques for managing access; restricting the use of removable media; security policies and digital rights management.

Mike lives in the Detroit metro area with his wife Melissa. Mike would like to thank his family for generally putting up with him — except for Melissa, who doesn't have a choice. (I I)

Joe Howard (CISSP, CSSP) is a lead information-security architect who develops and implements corporate security policies and standards for Fortune 100 companies. As a leader in security strategy and direction, Joe has been exposed to many of the technologies and standards, including PCI, HIPAA, EAL, and Sarbanes-Oxley.

Joe is a proficient speaker and presenter for both government and corporate clients. He has authored white papers on security tactics and participated in RFC reviews. Formerly, he was a member of a government and corporate incident response team, security auditor, penetration tester, and white hat hacker. Joe has trained various government agencies in security awareness and developed several corporate security policies for large companies.

Joe contributed to the chapter on implementing IE 7 security features and the chapter on thwarting security risks.

Joe resides in Nashville, Tennessee, with his two children, Jacob and Lily, and a golden retriever named Ci-Ci.

Dedication

To my wife Cosimina, whom I am just as crazy about today as I was 17 years ago. Her pride in being a mother and understanding those things that are truly important has brought out the very best in me and our children. I can't imagine that she truly comprehends the magnitude of the inspiration that she provides me as well as our children, family, and friends with her fun-loving, positive attitude and tenacity — even through her hard-hitting, relapsing battles with multiple sclerosis. I dedicate this book to her and to our children — Justin, Ashley, and Brianna, whose support was paramount to my completing this book and from whom I continue to learn the true meaning of life each day.

Author's Acknowledgments

I would first like to thank Mike Borkin, who eagerly participated in all-night discussions and work sessions related to this book. I will finally be able to get some sleep. I would also like to thank Joe Howard for his willingness to jump in and help contribute to this work.

I must also thank Melody Layne, my acquisitions editor at Wiley, for contacting me and providing me this great opportunity. Without Melody and my project editor, Blair Pottenger, I wonder whether I would have really found the time to get this completed. Their encouragement and ability to keep this project moving was critical. I should also thank my copy editor, Teresa Artman, whose advice and ability to straighten out my English and keep me focused on the topic at hand were greatly appreciated.

I would like to give a special thanks to a friend, colleague, and technical editor, Christian Mayoros. His dedication and tenacity on assuring technical accuracy is greatly appreciated.

I must thank my family, for I am blessed to have people that care so much about me. Thanks to my mother and father, Marlene and Fred, who have always been there for not only me but my wife and children. Thanks also to my brother Phil and his wife Wendy; and my new nephew, Preston.

Of course, I owe a great deal to my wife Cosimina and our children: Justin, Ashley, and Brianna. Thank you all for your support, love, and dedication. You guys rock!

I must also remember my late brother, William Francis Koerner, who passed away when I was a teenager and who was a huge part of my life. He left me with many great memories that I will forever be grateful for.

Many thanks to those few true friends that you find in your lifetime that you can count on no matter what: Victor and Cindy Kandrotas, and Kym Grasby. Your unwavering support and loyalty over the last 20 years is admired and greatly appreciated.

A sincere thanks to those managers and team leads that have helped shape my craziness in one way or another, all of whom I also call friends — Katherine Diguilio, John Merkel, Mike Borkin, Gen Ramshaw, Randall Stroud, and Janet Quait. Thanks to those colleagues who inspired and put up with me: Christian Mayoros, Frank Carter, Alex Golod, Marc Mandel, and Paul Schooping. I have the deepest respect for your work ethic and tenacity, and I wouldn't hesitate to jump in the trenches of a project with any of you again.

Finally, for lack of time and space, thanks to all those whom I am unable to acknowledge who in one way or another contributed to my life, the information security field, or my career.

Publisher's Acknowledgments

We're proud of this book; please send us your comments through our online registration form located at www.dummies.com/register/.

Some of the people who helped bring this book to market include the following:

Acquisitions, Editorial, and Media Development

Project Editor: Blair J. Pottenger

Development Editors: Chris Morris, Linda Morris, Pat O'Brien

Acquisitions Editors: Melody Layne, Tiffany Ma

Sr. Copy Editor: Teresa Artman

Technical Editor: Christian Mayoros

Editorial Manager: Kevin Kirschner

Editorial Assistant: Amanda Foxworth

Sr. Editorial Assistant: Cherie Case

Cartoons: Rich Tennant (www.the5thwave.com)

Composition Services

Project Coordinator: Erin Smith

Layout and Graphics: Stacie Brooks, Melissa K. Jester, Stephanie D. Jumper, Ronald Terry

Proofreaders: Bonnie Mikkelson, Dwight Ramsey

Indexer: WordCo Indexing Services

Special Help: Brian Walls

Anniversary Logo Design: Richard Pacifico

Publishing and Editorial for Technology Dummies

Richard Swadley, Vice President and Executive Group Publisher

Andy Cummings, Vice President and Publisher

Mary Bednarek, Executive Acquisitions Director

Mary C. Corder, Editorial Director

Publishing for Consumer Dummies

Diane Graves Steele, Vice President and Publisher

Joyce Pepple, Acquisitions Director

Composition Services

Gerry Fahey, Vice President of Production Services

Debbie Stailey, Director of Composition Services

Contents at a Glance

Table of Contents

Introduction

. . . .

Computing is more and more an integral part of each of our lives, so securing our systems and personal information is paramount. Microsoft has made some very public promises that Vista is the most secure operating system (OS) to date. Such promises are certain to draw the attention of those who are intent on proving Microsoft wrong, and the true security strength of Vista will need to endure the test of time. Even still, Microsoft put forth considerable effort because the Vista OS offers some impressive security features and functionality. Although you will likely use some of these features with great enthusiasm, you might find others annoying and restrictive. That's to be expected when you try to stay safe, though: Security is a balance between productivity and protection. Your mission — with help from this book — is to choose the appropriate Vista security features that meet your needs.

About This Book

This book offers you instructions, tips, and advice on securing your Vista system and personal information. Much of the book is related to the security features and functionality of Vista, but I don't stop there. This book also will help you develop your personal security plan and deploy security strategies that reach beyond that which Vista offers. I cover third-partytools and resources that are not only helpful but are also necessary to achieve optimal digital security in a connected world. If you run Vista and are serious about protecting your system and personal information, this book is for you!

Conventions Used in This Book

This book uses the usual *For Dummies* style and conventions to provide you an entertaining and easy-to-understand experience.

I use the ⇨ symbol to provide a path for you to navigate through menu items. For example, choosing Start⇨All Programs⇨Maintenance⇨Backup and Restore Center provides you instructions on navigating to the Vista Backup and Restore Center utility.

Sometimes I lead you through a set of specific step to accomplish a task or change a setting, like this:

1. Click the Create Password button.

Any helpful results or nuggets that happen after that step follow in non-bold text, like this.

Where you see key names conjoined with a + sign, press those keys together. You know, like the stalwart Windows Ctrl+S for Save. Sometimes three keys make a combo, like the also-stalwart three-finger salute of Ctrl+Alt+Shift for reboot.

What You're Not to Read

This book is organized so you can easily find the information that's important to you. If a topic doesn't apply to you, you don't have to read it. And, you don't have to read the book in order, either. That approach might make sense for you, but hey — just jump to the chapter you want.

Foolish Assumptions

Although I should say that I made no foolish assumptions, the fact is that I did — namely, the following:

- You're an ambitious home or small office user who is familiar with the Vista OS.

- You have an interest in mastering the security features and functionality offered in Vista to help protect your system or personal electronic information in your home or small office.

- You have access to the Internet from your home or small office so that you can download tools or access additional resources outlined in this book.

How This Book Is Organized

This book is organized into six parts. Oh, and for fun, I throw in a couple of Appendixes.

Part 1: Vista Security Essentials

This part helps you build the right security foundation by covering the fundamental aspects of, um, security. I cover the new and improved security features in Vista and help you think about exactly what you need to secure. Read here how to develop a security plan that will help you not only survive but thrive when protecting yourself in the digital world.

Part 11: Controlling Access to Systems and Data

Controlling access to your system and personal data isn't about locking your system in a closet and guarding the door. Instead, you set only the level of access needed for users to be productive. When elevated access and privilege are provided unnecessarily, the risk exposure increases significantly. In this part, I cover Vista features and functionality that enable you to address risks associated with access and privilege to your system and electronic data. You can see how to use these features to optimally protect your system while still providing yourself (and others) the access they need to be productive.

Part 111: Preserving and Protecting Data

In this part, you can read about the Vista features for protecting your system and electronic personal information — not only which features to use for your specific needs, but also how to use them.

I also cover why backing up must be part of your security plan. Read how to map the Vista Backup and Recovery features to your system and data preservation needs so that you can achieve optimal protection.

For those who need a greater level of data protection, I also discuss when, why, and how to use the Vista encryption features: Encrypting File System (EFS) and BitLocker Drive Encryption.

Part IV: Guarding against Threats to Network Security

As great of a resource as the Internet is, being connected significantly increases your exposure to having your system or electronic data compromised. From viruses to spyware, falling victim to a phishing e-mail or that teenage hacker on the other side of the globe hacking your system to steal your personal financial information — and everything in between — network-related threats are a real problem that you must understand and address.

The good news is that in this part, I show you the Vista security features, techniques, and strategies that can help you mitigate your network and Internet connectivity risks.

Part V: Establishing Advanced Security Practices

This book wouldn't be complete if we didn't have a part that covered those advanced security practices that you can utilize to achieve an even greater level of security. Though perhaps not things that you will want or need to implement on every system in your home or small office, they certainly provide you a great deal of value when you have a system or data that does require that level of protection.

In this part, you learn about the associated risks with your data that resides on removable media. Data on the move is often overlooked, especially by those at home or in a small office.

You also learn about the many Vista local security policies and how you can use them to make your system and electronic data more secure. You not only learn what options Vista provides, but how to implement the security policies that make sense for you.

Part VI: The Part of Tens

In this part, I provide you some information and resources that will help you succeed in your journey to protect your system and electronic data.

Here, I highlight ten security risks, some of which even Vista doesn't necessarily mitigate. You can't overlook even those risks that are introduced by the new features, as well as all the new code, in Vista. I also provide you with must-have information as to what you can do to thwart these security risks and ensure optimal protection of your system and electronic data.

You can also read about ten additional security tools and resources that you just shouldn't compute without. These tools and resources go beyond what Vista provides and can help you protect your system, electronic information, and more. This is must-have information you just don't want to miss.

Oh, and because I'm in a generous mood, I also include two Appendixes: a glossary and a short chapter on the flavors of Vista and their security features.

Icons Used in This Book

This icon points out tips, tricks, and other advice that can help you understand a particular topic being discussed.

When I cover a particular point or topic that is worth remembering, I use this icon to highlight it for you. Committing it to memory will help you when you move forward in securing your system and electronic or personal information.

Pay particular attention when you see this icon. This icon points out potential negative consequences that might happen under specific circumstances. The good news is that knowledge is power, so read these as a heads-up on how to deal with these potentially dire situations.

Technical Stuff icons point out information of interest to those who desire a technical explanation. You don't have to read them, though, to understand the topic at hand.

An Author's Pick icon provides the reader with a recommendation from the author for a particular setting, configuration, or general security concept.

Where to Go from Here

This book provides you the foundation to use Vista security features so that you can adequately protect your system and electronic data. I don't stop there, though. The book also provides information that reaches beyond what Vista offers so that you can implement a comprehensive security strategy to protect your system and personal information now — and for some time in the future.

In particular, you can glean how to develop a security plan, come up to speed on the new and improved Vista security features, and use these features to meet your security needs. Perhaps just as important is that I talk about additional third-party security tools that you can use to further secure your system and data when Vista just isn't enough to meet your needs. And don't forget about those additional online security resources that will keep you in the loop on security issues and trends.

Part I
Vista Security Essentials

"Well, the first level of Windows Vista security seems good—I can't get the shrink-wrapping off."

In this part . . .

Anything built well starts out with a solid foundation. Whether it's a basement, a car frame, or even a book outline, the quality of the foundation often drives the end result of the product.

From covering Vista security features and understanding what you should protect (and why) to building a strong, comprehensive security plan, this part provides you the information you need to build and implement a personal security program to help you effectively protect your system and precious data.

Chapter 1

Getting Up to Speed on Vista Security

In This Chapter

▶ Seeing what new security features Vista provides

▶ Understanding what you should protect

▶ Filling up your security toolbox

▶ Common sense and security

Although the security of Vista will ultimately need to pass the test of time, it is obvious that Microsoft put forth considerable effort to develop a more secure operating system (OS). To the user, Vista improves on some familiar features found in previous OSes and offers a variety of new security features and functionality that do a fine job protecting your system and both personal and sensitive data.

In this chapter, I provide an overview of the features and functionality of these new and improved-upon security tools that Vista provides and also explain the various things that you should consider securing to give yourself optimal protection. You can find out about selecting those tools that make sense for you to fill your security toolbox so you can get the job done. To top it off, you also discover how to integrate a common-sense approach to security to help you protect your system, privacy, and sensitive information not just today — but for the future as well.

Seeing What's New in Vista Security

Vista is touted by Microsoft as its most secure OS to date and the first OS designed with the Security Development Lifecycle (SDL) methodology. Security Development Lifecycle is a software design methodology that promotes the Secure by Design, Secure by Default, Secure in Deployment, and Secure in Communications principles. These principles offer a more secure approach to software and systems development and deployment, and are indicative of the Microsoft commitment to security. Here, in a nutshell, are the principles:

- ✔ **Secure by Design:** This principle addresses the overall design and architecture of the application. The application is built upon solid security principles that take into account various threats and security vulnerabilities.

- ✔ **Secure by Default:** This is a principle that is used to reduce the attack surface of an application or system. By default, features or services that aren't needed are turned off, and applications aren't given any more authority than needed. As more features are needed, they can be enabled. However, by default, the system is as secure as possible.

- ✔ **Secure in Deployment:** This principle is related to keeping systems and applications up to date with OS or application patches to reduce any vulnerabilities.

- ✔ **Secure in Communications:** This principle relates to how an organization communicates security best practices. This communication plays a critical part in an organization's ability to have a secure computing environment.

The Vista OS consists largely of new code that was written under the auspices of this methodology, and any existing code leveraged by Vista was reviewed and revised to make it more secure. A variety of new features and functionality are available in Vista that assist the user in restricting user access, defending against spyware and malware, protecting against network related threats, and more.

The Vista User Account Control

Microsoft added a feature in Vista that provides some mitigation to a common mistake made by many users: namely, frequently using an account with elevated privilege to perform everyday tasks. Users mistakenly provide an account that they commonly use to log on to their system with the ability to modify system settings, change the Registry, install software, and more. What they don't realize is that this creates a substantial vulnerability if a malware program is executed in the context of such an account. The malware can then have authority to perform tasks and cause damage that it might not have otherwise been able to do.

User Account Control is essentially an intermediary that requests user consent prior to performing a task requiring elevated permission, such as changing system settings, installing software, and so on. In this way, it effectively treats every user as a standard user by default. Even if an account has the privileges to perform these elevated tasks, the user is prompted (see Figure 1-1).

For more on setting User Account Control, see Chapter 4.

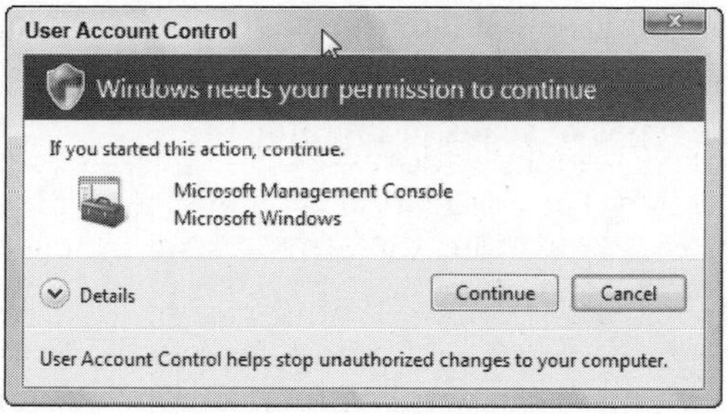

Figure 1-1:
The User
Account
Control
prompt.

Windows Defender

Spyware, a form of malware, has become one of the fastest growing external security threats in recent history, costing individuals and corporations considerable time and money. In its simplest form, spyware gathers Internet surfing habits and other information of user activity, without the user's knowledge, to be sold for marketing and advertising purposes. Outside of being considered by some as a violation of privacy, gathering this information consumes valuable CPU and memory resources of your computer, sometimes bringing your system to a crawl. Users often spend time and money to rid themselves of these intrusive programs to return their system to a normal working state.

The Microsoft answer to the spyware threat is Windows Defender (as shown in Figure 1-2), which is an easy-to-use and effective tool that can detect and deal with spyware both in real time and by means of on-demand scanning. Because Windows Defender is native to the Vista OS, you finally have a tool to deal with this growing problem without the need to purchase expensive third-party products. Some of the features in Windows Defender offer the following:

- ✔ **Easy-to-use interface:** Windows Defender provides an intuitive interface that is accessible via Security Center or independently.

- ✔ **Quick scan:** Defender affords you a quick and easy way to perform a scan of only those areas that most often hold spyware — such as specific areas of the Windows Registry and the Windows\System32, program files, and user directories — rather than scanning your entire system.

- ✔ **Full scan:** This gives you the ability to scan your complete system at the click of a button. The tool scans every drive and directory on your system.

- ✔ **Custom scan:** This option provides an interface for the user to customize a scan that better fits their needs. With a custom scan, you can select specific drives and folders that you want to scan.

✔ **Real-time scanning:** Windows Defender protects your system in real time so that if spyware infections occur, they can be detected and remediated.

Read about all these types of scans in Chapter 14.

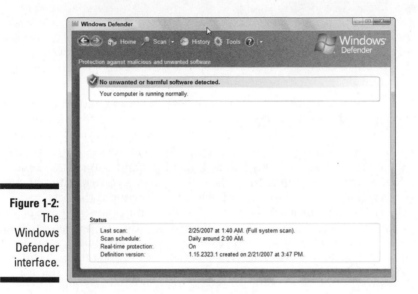

Figure 1-2:
The
Windows
Defender
interface.

Parental Controls

Like it or not, computing is becoming a fundamental part of our lives. Accesses to computer labs in elementary schools (and beyond) enable our children to become computer savvy at an early age. Students use computers to do research and homework, take quizzes, and communicate with their peers. Many would find it difficult to get through high school, even from purely an academic perspective, without access to an Internet-connected computer. Our children have a plethora of information available to them by a simple click of a mouse. Even though the Internet is a great resource, it does present certain risks. Now more than ever, our children have access to information and situations that may place them, or the data on our computers, in harm's way. Such situations have created a strong market for software products that monitor computer activity and block access to certain Web content, file downloads, and more.

Windows Vista offers the Parental Controls security feature (as shown in Figure 1-3) that provides monitoring and restriction capabilities to assist you in addressing this problem. Parental Controls provides the following capabilities:

- ✔ **The Vista Web Filter:** This function of Parental Controls allows you to block access to a specific Web site or specific types of Web content such as those rated as mature or for pornography, hate speech, drug-related, alcohol, gambling, weapons, and more.

- ✔ **File-download blocking:** Many know all too well the file-sharing sites that teens like to visit to download shared software, music, and movies. Such sites not only harbor illegally shared files but also serve as virus depots, infecting many of those unsuspecting people who download files. Parental Controls enables you to block a user from having the ability to download files from the Internet.

- ✔ **Time restrictions:** For those of you who worry about children getting out of bed in the middle of the night to chat online with their friends, Parental Controls allows you to grant or block access for certain users to the Internet during hours that you specify.

- ✔ **Gaming restrictions:** Parental Controls allows you to restrict a user's access to play a specific game or restrict a user's access based upon specific game ratings such as Early Childhood (EC), Everyone 6+ (E), Everyone 10+ (E10), Teen (T), Mature (M), or Adults Only (AO). Gaming access can also be restricted based on specific content, such as Alcohol, Blood, Gore, Cartoon Mischief, Crude Humor, Drug Reference, Fantasy Violence, Language, Lyrics, Mature Humor, and so on.

- ✔ **Monitoring capability:** Parental Controls allows you to monitor certain online activity of nonadministrative users. Reports can be viewed for the Top 10 Web Sites Visited, Most Recent 10 Web Sites Blocked, File Downloads, File Downloads Blocked, Logon Times, Applications Ran, Games Played, as well as certain e-mail, instant messaging, and Media Player events.

Parental Controls provides parents or a computer system's administrator some very nice features to monitor and restrict access of standard users. Parental Controls has functionality that has never been offered previously by an OS as well as perhaps enough functionality to circumvent the need to purchase third-party tools.

Wireless security enhancements

Wireless networking, which was once an expensive and relatively slow networking option, is on its way to becoming the preferred method of network connectivity for the home and office. Vista brings with it a variety of wireless networking enhancements, a few of which are related to security:

- ✔ Support for previous wireless protocols and the latest security protocols, including Wi-Fi Protected Access 2 (WPA2)

- ✔ Ability to define security polices to securely manage wireless connections at home or in the office

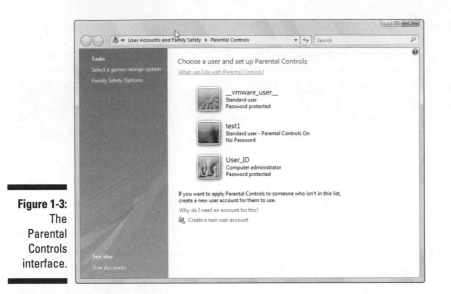

Figure 1-3:
The
Parental
Controls
interface.

Vista offers support for nonbroadcasting networks and even allows you to connect to a nonbroadcast network in your preferred list. However, don't be fooled into thinking that a nonbroadcasting network is more secure; sometimes, it is actually less secure. Even when you run the Vista OS and a nonbroadcasting network does not advertise its name (that is, the *service set identifier (SSID)* is set to a null value), some risk exists if other systems on the network are running Windows XP Service Pack (SP) 2. The problem is that systems running Windows XP SP2 will send a broadcast, even if your wireless network is configured as a nonbroadcasting network. Therefore, it is generally a bad idea to implement a nonbroadcasting wireless network as part of your security plan — security by obscurity is never a good idea.

Service hardening

Windows services are applications that provide OS functionality, are low-level application tasks, run in the background, and usually require no user interaction. Although services are essential to the operation of your system, they have historically presented a significant attack surface for malicious code writers. Service hardening is not necessarily a new security concept but has largely been the responsibility of the user — until now.

The Vista service hardening features are just one part of a multilayered security strategy that embeds security within the OS to reduce the risks associated with exploits that might target your systems. The real focus of service hardening isn't to prevent such attacks as much as it is to reduce the damage such an exploit can cause to your system if a service is compromised.

Vista service hardening provides security in the following key areas:

- ✔ **Least privilege service permission:** In previous Windows OSes, services ran largely under the local system account — which is, essentially, the most powerful account on your computer — even if they did not require such privilege. Vista allows services to run with the least privilege that they might require, such as Local Service or Network Service. Additional restrictions can be placed on a service to limit the areas of the Registry or file system that a particular system has the ability to write to.

- ✔ **Service isolation:** This allows a service to be *separated* (isolated) from other services or applications. Such isolation helps reduce the attack surface.

- ✔ **Firewall policy integration:** Vista allows firewall policies to now be applied to services. Because network-facing services are often the target of exploits, this feature can go a long way in limiting the attack surface of your system.

Vista provides a very comprehensive security approach to service hardening. With the exception of a few additional steps that can be taken to secure the Registry with regard to least-privilege permissions, Vista handles service hardening and requires no interaction by the end user.

For more on service hardening, see Chapter 7.

Internet Explorer 7

Although Internet Explorer 7 (IE7) is part of the Vista OS, it can be installed as a separate application independently from Vista. Microsoft has put a great deal of effort into making Internet browsing more secure and changes in IE7 certainly reflect that.

Internet Explorer 7 provides the following security features:

- ✔ **Protected Mode:** This defense-in-depth security feature restricts where files can be downloaded and executed, or the ability to invoke other programs without the user's consent.

- ✔ **ActiveX protection:** ActiveX are small, Microsoft application components that provide functions to the end user via their Web browser. Internet Explorer 7 provides security mechanisms that reduce potential risks of ActiveX exploits, such as ActiveX Opt-In and the ability to control ActiveX for a particular zone or site. Chapter 13 covers ActiveX security in more detail.

- ✔ **Cross-domain scripting protection:** Cross-domain scripting attacks have presented a significant security threat in previous versions of Internet Explorer and Windows OSes. Internet Explorer 7 forces scripts to run in their original context, even if they are redirected to run in another security domain, mitigating much of the risk associated with cross-domain scripting attacks.

✔ **Security status bar:** This feature allows you to differentiate an authentic Web site from one that is considered to be suspicious. The status bar also provides you with digital certificate information that can help you determine whether a site is trustworthy enough to make an e-commerce transaction.

✔ **Integration with Parental Controls:** Internet Explorer 7 integrates with Parental Controls security features, allowing more control over Internet browsing and downloading functionality.

✔ **Phishing protection:** The IE7 Phishing Filter provides some impressive functionality to protect you against an Internet phishing scheme that just might make you that next identity theft victim. Web sites that you visit are analyzed. If the site is a known phishing site or otherwise has characteristics that are commonly found in phishing sites, you will be warned of the potential danger.

✔ **Protection of personal data:** Internet Explorer 7 offers the ability for one-click cleanup of information entered in Web sites, browsing history, temporary Internet files, and so on that could potentially hold tracking or otherwise Personally Identifiable Information (PII) of the user.

✔ **URL display:** Crooks commonly attempt to mask a site for which they are directing you. One of the ways how crooks try to hide this is by displaying a pop-up without an address bar so that the URL of the site is not displayed. Internet Explorer 7 now requires an address bar in every window so that you can more easily identify whether the site you're being directed to is a trusted source.

For more on Internet Explore 7 security features, see Chapter 13.

Encryption with EFS and BitLocker

Now, more than ever, we use our computers to process or hold sensitive information. Whether our financial files, medical information, or private e-mail messages, this information has the potential to be the golden nugget to crooks trying to perpetuate identity theft or other crimes of fraud. To add to the problem, more of us are on the move, using portable computers that are more easily lost or stolen, ultimately putting our personal or corporate data at risk.

Vista offers the Encrypting File System (EFS) and BitLocker Drive Encryption to help you protect your sensitive information that is resident on your computer from theft.

✔ **Encrypting File System (EFS):** Offered in the Business, Enterprise, and Ultimate editions of Vista. Encrypting File System provides file and folder level encryption of user data. For more on Encrypting File System, see Chapter 9.

✔ **BitLocker:** Offered in Enterprise and Ultimate editions of Vista. BitLocker (as shown in Figure 1-4) provides data protection by preventing unauthorized users from accessing a lost or stolen computer. The entire windows volume — such as all user and system files — are encrypted. For more information on BitLocker, see Chapter 10.

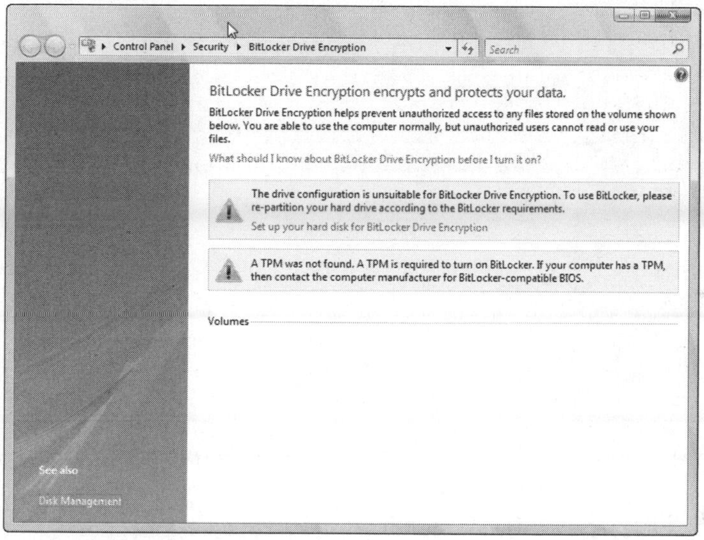

Figure 1-4:
The
BitLocker
interface.

Windows Security Center enhancements

Windows Security Center (WSC) made its first debut in the Microsoft Windows XP OS. It returns in Windows Vista with a similar look and feel but with some enhanced functionality. Windows Security Center (shown in Figure 1-5) continues to provide a single interface to manage multiple security functions, some of which are native to the Vista OS and some (such as third-party antivirus software) that are not. New WSC enhancements in Vista include the following:

✔ **Other Security Settings category:** Offers you the ability to monitor and manage IE security settings and User Account Control (UAC)

✔ **Malware Protection category:** Provides the ability to monitor and manage antivirus and anti-spyware settings

✔ **Manage multiple products:** Allows you to manage multiple firewall, anti-spyware, or antivirus products either native to Vista or third-party tools

✔ **Vendor resources:** Provides direct links to vendors of the products that you have installed to get updates or other fixes to remediate issues

For more on Windows Security Center, see Chapter 3.

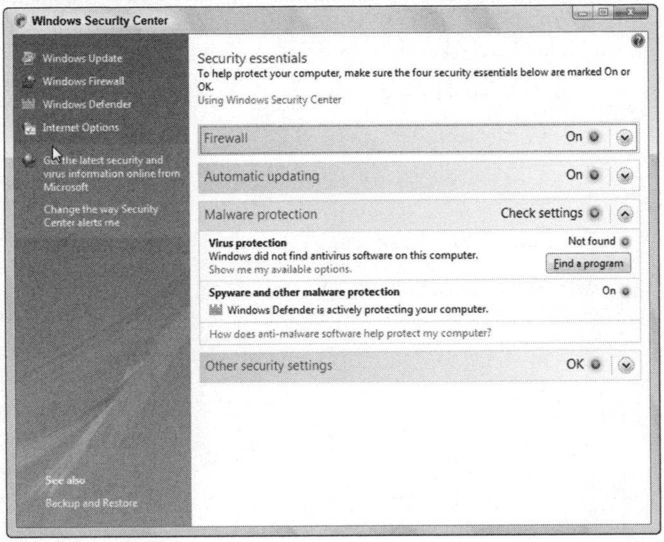

Figure 1-5:
The
Windows
Security
Center
interface.

Windows Firewall enhancements

Like WSC, Windows Firewall (as shown in Figure 1-6) also made its debut with Windows XP. It, too, returns in Vista as a significantly enhanced tool. The new Windows Firewall enhancements include the following:

✔ **Easily configurable through two different interfaces:** Windows Firewall is configurable via Security Center and also through the Microsoft Management Console (MMC) snap-in for those who want to implement some advanced settings. The advance settings provide a more resolute approach.

✔ **Filtering of incoming and outgoing traffic:** Vista Firewall, unlike previous versions, allows for outbound filtering.

✔ **IPsec integration:** This provides an advanced security-setting console that integrates IPsec and firewall management and allows for IPsec server isolation and other customizable IPsec settings.

✔ **Firewall profiles:** Although the previous version of Windows Firewall did allow for profile configuration, Vista Firewall provides for more profile options, such as Domain, Public, and Private Profiles for yet even more tenacious security than its predecessor. Such tenacity allows you, for example, to provide certain settings to your office connection yet quite different settings to your home connection.

For more on Windows Firewall, see Chapter 11.

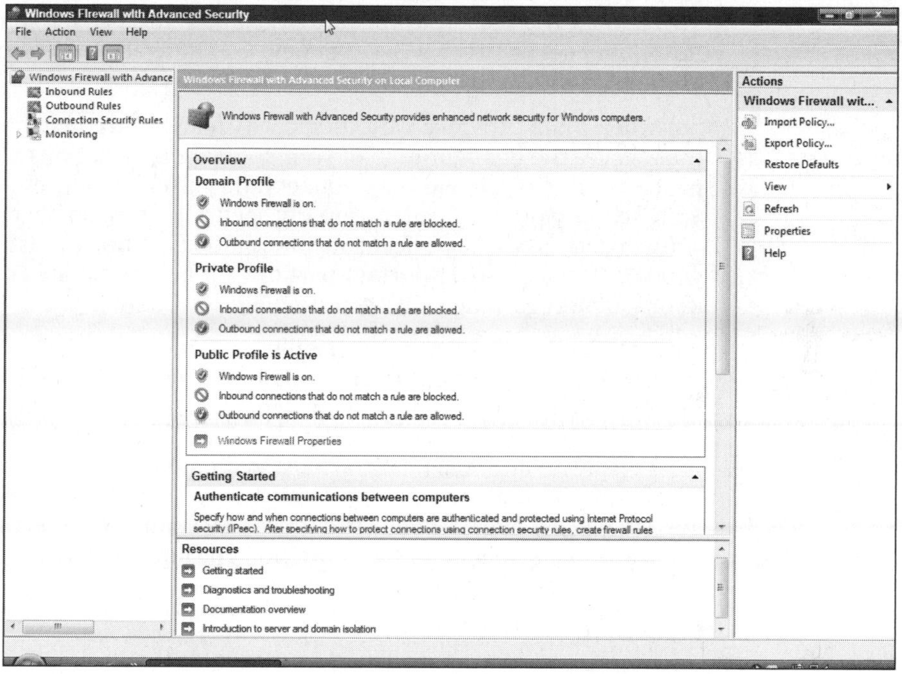

Figure 1-6:
The
Windows
Firewall
interface.

Knowing What to Secure

So you have available to you one of the most secure Windows operating systems offered by Microsoft to date. Now what? Although Vista has many security enhancements beyond earlier Windows OSes, it can't read your mind and magically protect those things that are so very important to you. Before you can implement the Vista security features that make sense for you, you must first understand what it is that you need or want to protect.

Hardware and software

When you think about what it is that you want to protect, it isn't necessarily intuitive that you might consider hardware and software — especially when thinking about it under the context of selecting security features in an OS. Even still, as you lay out your security plan and find out about Vista security features and functionality, keep in mind what value you place on your computing hardware and software. Consider the following relative to hardware and software security:

- **Hardware:** Protection against theft or damage from natural disasters isn't something that Vista can provide; however, as you develop your security plan (see Chapter 2), you need to be cognizant of hardware. Throughout the book (particularly in Chapter 18), I cover some of the third-party security tools that can help you mitigate some security risks associated with your hardware.

- **Software:** Vista provides various security features that enable you to further secure the configuration of your software applications and better protect your system and data from compromise. In addition, as part of your security plan, consider properly securing physical access to your software and associated licensing information. Although Vista can't help you with this, it is an important part of your security plan. For more information regarding your security plan, see Chapter 2.

- **Availability:** Protecting the availability of your system is ensuring that your hardware and software are available to you when needed. If you, like many of us, depend on your system to perform essential functions, then having it unavailable might not be a mere inconvenience but perhaps translate into real financial loss. Vista offers various security features that provide you some protection and ability to restore your system quickly in case of an OS or software failure. Various third-party tools are also available that can provide you some level of availability protection; see Chapter 18.

Personally Identifiable Information (PII)

Personally Identifiable Information (PII) is information that can be used to uniquely identify you, such as your name, address, driver's license, Social Security number, medical records, financial files, and more. Even if you might not fully understand how valuable your personal information is, crooks who perpetrate lucrative crimes (such as identity theft) will and do go to great lengths to harvest it. A piece of your information here, a piece there — pretty soon they have enough of your information to pretend to be you. Perhaps getting a utility service in your name, posing as you when receiving a traffic ticket, getting a credit card in your name, or even purchasing a car or house in your name! Sounds far-fetched? Think again — it happens every day.

For many of us this personal information, or bits and pieces of it, is often contained in various documents, spreadsheets, or other programs on our personal computers. After all, we have our computers so that we can be productive — do our taxes, our budgets, process medical claims, do online banking, and more. I'm not suggesting that you not use your computer this way, but I am suggesting that you take protecting your personal data seriously.

The market for your personal information has never been greater. Crooks who don't use it themselves can get a nice price for it on the black market, selling it on the Internet in just a matter of minutes. This means that you must protect your personal information that resides on your computer ferociously. Luckily, with the help of Vista and this book, you'll be able to do just that.

Sensitive information from work

You're not the only one that has sensitive information; corporations also have proprietary business information that is as sensitive to the business as your PII is to you. This proprietary business information might include, but is not limited to

- ✔ **Physical security:** As a trusted employee or business owner, you might have access codes to offices, safes, alarm codes, or other information related to physical security at your workplace saved on your computer.

- ✔ **Customer or sales information:** Employee computers commonly have sensitive contract information, customer databases, rate schedules, and sales and marketing information.

- ✔ **Vendor information:** Such data might be information regarding vendor supply terms, contact information, or other information that pertains to various vendors and suppliers that should not be public knowledge.

- ✔ **Employment-related information:** Such data might include payroll information, healthcare plan information, or personal information of other employees of a business.

- ✔ **Trade secrets:** Certain employees might have digital research data, patent, or design information on their computer systems that they want to protect from their competitors.

- ✔ **Company financials or assets:** This information could be the financials of the company, business tax information, departmental budget information, or information on other physical or intellectual assets.

As an employee or business owner, you might either now or later have sensitive information from work on your computer — and you need to understand how to secure it. With the help of Vista, perhaps some third-party tools, and this book, you will have everything that you need to amply secure this information.

Other information that can be used adversely

Here is the stuff of nightmares for a lot of us: an e-mail of a delicate or untoward nature that gets made public or falls into the wrong hands. You know, that e-mail you sent to a co-worker describing those annoying tendencies of your boss, or the document that you wrote to your significant other, or information on that Web site that you visited looking for a better job, or those off-color jokes that you've been e-mailing around the office.

Our computers might hold data other than that considered to be business propriety or PII. Yet, it might be information that is of a personal or private nature and, if made public, could cause us embarrassment or otherwise get us in hot water. Like other sensitive information, this information should be protected as well. Although its compromise might not lead to someone driving around in a car in your name, it certainly might adversely affect you if it were to become known to others.

Filling Up Your Security Toolbox

If you're going to effectively protect your hardware and software, PII, sensitive work-related information, or any other data that, if compromised, could have an adverse affect on you, having the proper tools to do so is critical. Just like carpenters, plumbers, and other craftsmen stock their toolboxes so that they can effectively practice their crafts, you, too, must fill your security toolbox with the proper tools to get the job done.

Understanding your requirements

As much as you want to jump in and get started filling up your security toolbox, understand what requirements you have. Not only will you select the right security tools to get the job done *today* — but perhaps for some time to come. When you understand your requirements, you can better prepare yourself down the road to address security threats as they present themselves. The following are some considerations in understanding your requirements:

✔ **Up-front work:** Before you can fill your toolbox with the right tools, you really need to understand your requirements. Much like that carpenter who needs to understand what type of work he will be performing so that he grabs the right tools to perform his craft, understand what it is that you want to achieve. Specifically, you must understand what it is that you want to protect. Whether your goal is to have the least amount of downtime, protect a particular document or file or protect your computer from being stolen, or all these things — understand your requirements so that you can select the proper tools to get the job done.

✔ **Criticality:** Not only do you need to understand what it is that you want to protect, but you also must understand how critical it is to protect it. Understanding the length to which you are willing to go in order to protect your system or data is essential in developing a security plan and selecting the right tools to meet your needs.

✔ **Security tolerance:** Security is often the opposite of convenience. You can do a great many things to protect your data, but too-stringent security controls can impede your ability to do certain things. In fact, Vista puts forth some security controls that will be considered by some folks as annoying. You can choose to use that security feature (put that security tool in your toolbox) or instead leave it out and opt for more convenience over security.

For more on security requirements, see Chapter 2.

Arming yourself with technical tools

Other tools you will have in your security toolbox are technical tools, which will play a large part in protecting your system and sensitive data from compromise. Vista offers a variety of security tools to assist you in appropriately protecting your hardware, software, and associated data. The majority of this book covers those Vista tools, but I also cover some additional third-party technical tools that you might need to consider when your requirements go beyond what Vista can provide. Here are some considerations when selecting the technical tools for your security toolbox:

✔ **Understand the tools that you have available to you.** Understanding all the tools that you have available to protect yourself is indeed important. This book provides you not with just the Vista tools that are available to you, but also with some third-party security tools that can provide some protections where Vista comes up short.

✔ **Understand what the tool protects.** Not all security tools are created equal. Some protect access, others assist with maximum availability, and even others might have entirely a different purpose. If you understand explicitly the protections that the tool provides, you can then make a better choice as to when and how to use it. I show you exactly what each Vista security tool can help you protect — and, just as important, what each can't protect.

✔ **Understand how to use the tool.** It isn't good enough just to know what tools are available and what it is that they protect: You must also know how to use them. I show you how to use each of the security tools in Vista, and provide you with some information on third-party tools if your requirements go beyond what Vista can provide.

Integrating Common Sense and Security

Not to be taken lightly or meant to be condescending in any way, but the fact is that almost every technical security control can be circumvented by some type of user behavior. At one point or another, you have likely either participated in or witnessed activity that caused security to be less effective than it otherwise could have been. My favorite is walking around the office noticing all the sticky notes on co-worker's monitors and keyboards with passwords scribbled on them for all to see.

Because security is often an inconvenience, you or people that you know will be tempted to exercise certain behavior that might not make the best use of the tools that you will find out about. Therefore, it is very important that you take the following into consideration:

✔ **Make security a frame of mind.** Take security seriously. Pay close attention to those things that you do that might put your system, PII, or sensitive information from work at risk. The more you make security a frame of mind, the better you will protect those things that are important to you.

✔ **Security is a process.** Understand that it takes more than thinking about security or technical security tools to make your system and data secure. Security is a process for which many things must come together if you are to truly achieve optimal security. This book help you bring all those things together so that you can ultimately have a security strategy that meets your requirements.

When you fill up your security toolbox with some of the new and improved-upon Vista security tools (and perhaps even a few third-party tools), don't forget to throw in a fair amount of a common-sense, security-minded approach to securing your system and data. Together, these things will provide you the ability to protect what' important to you, time and time again.

Chapter 2

Setting Up Your Security Plan

. . . .

. . . .

*I*n much the same way that a house must be built on a solid foundation, so must the security of your system and sensitive information. Without a comprehensive security plan, your effort to secure your system and any sensitive data will likely fall short of your needs. Falling short on security isn't to be taken lightly because inadequate security makes the availability, integrity, and confidentiality of your system and data vulnerable to compromise. That is, your system or data might not be available to you when you need it most, or important data could be altered, lost, or stolen.

The effect of any one of these scenarios varies from person to person and is largely dependent on how much you rely on your system and just how sensitive or important your data is. Maybe you suffer a mere inconvenience — or, maybe you suffer financial damages and become an identity theft or fraud victim. However, before you batten down the hatches and implement a myriad of security controls to protect your system and data, keep balance in mind. You want a security balance that reduces your risk to a comfortable level yet still allows you to accomplish what you need to be productive.

Many security practitioners fail to achieve this balance, locking down the hatches so tight that they impede productivity. Comparatively, many not-so-security-conscious users loosen security so that they won't be inconvenienced — placing themselves in harm's way to suffer consequences that they could easily avoid.

In this chapter, you discover a methodology that you can apply to the systems in your home or small office so that you can identify your applicable security risks. You develop a plan that appropriately addresses those risks and ultimately achieves a balance so that you're adequately secure and productive. You also begin to identify your threats, vulnerabilities, and risk so that you recognize methods and tools that can help you eliminate them.

Understanding the Risk

When trying to achieve a security balance that reduces risk while accomplishes what you want, start by recognizing and quantifying your system's and data's risk. I cover how to determine risk in greater detail in the upcoming section, "Assessing Your Systems' Security Risks." However, let me take a moment and explain the basic concept of risk and why it's so important to understand.

Risk is the likelihood of a particular event happening that will have a negative effect on your system or data. In the information security world, many complex models and methodologies can assess a system for risk, most of which are beyond this book's scope (and unnecessary for you to understand). What you must understand is exactly how a particular risk to your system or data can ultimately affect you.

For example, what if a particular spreadsheet were lost or stolen? If the information contained in the spreadsheet is inconsequential and losing it has little or no effect, implementing a plethora of security controls to protect that spreadsheet doesn't make much sense. However, if that spreadsheet contains medical and financial information that can't be replaced or leaves you vulnerable to identity theft or other fraud crimes, your risk is much higher. For the latter example, it just makes sense to implement the necessary security controls to reduce the chance and effect of a lost or stolen spreadsheet.

Generally speaking, the more productive that you are with your computer, the greater the risk your system likely presents to you. Say you have a system that your children only use to play games — you don't use it to do your bills, send or receive e-mail, process or hold any sensitive data; and it's not even connected to the Internet. That system presents very little risk to you. However, if you use your system to manage your finances and medical information, process e-mail, and have a constant broadband connection to the Internet, that represents a greater risk to you.

If sensitive data is compromised, you could suffer data loss or even become a victim of identity theft or fraud. Your job is to understand the level of risk that your system(s) present and accordingly put in place the proper controls to reduce those risks to a level that you find acceptable. True, you can never eliminate all risks that your systems present. Still, you can follow a fundamental process so that you can make those risks less painful.

Assessing Your Systems' Security Risks

Assessing your system is only part of your security plan. Nonetheless, this assessment is a very critical part, indeed. To protect yourself from the evils of the digital (or not-so-digital) world, you must first understand what you're protecting yourself against. This sounds simple; however, assessing systems' risk is an art as much as it is a science. Many organizations use complex methods to achieve consistent results. The good news, though, is that you don't have to use a complex method for your home or small office. Instead, you can follow a fundamental process loosely based on resources from the National Institute of Standards and Technology (NIST). This road map is a simplified, yet effective, approach to help you implement an appropriate level of security for your needs.

The premise is the same whether you're at home or in a large enterprise environment: Assess your system(s) to determine the outstanding risk and then reduce that risk to an acceptable level. Understand, however, that risk assessment is an ongoing effort. Threats that you don't need to worry about today might rear ugly heads tomorrow. Monitoring your environment so that you can react when you're exposed to certain risks is critical to protecting your systems and data. Before going farther, follow my road map to better understand where you're going.

Understand your system

Your system comprises hardware and software configurations that have some effect on your system security. Applications often need to be patched, and a network configuration certainly has security implications. Additionally, understanding your system includes knowing what data it holds or processes, who uses it, and how it will be used. For example, will the system hold your financial and medical information, or will it be used only for gaming? Understanding these variables is critical for protecting your system or data from loss or compromise.

Identify threats

After you have a solid understanding of your system, you can begin to see what threats you should be concerned about. For example, if you use your system to process e-mail, browse the Internet, or perhaps publish Web content, the threats that you need to be concerned about include viruses, worms, spyware, and so on.

Identify system vulnerability

Because you use and configure your systems differently, one system may be more vulnerable to a particular threat than another. Therefore, identifying a particular system's vulnerabilities is critical to crafting an effective security plan that truly meets your needs.

Identifying vulnerability is different than identifying a threat. *Vulnerability* is a particular weakness in your system (such as a patch that has not been applied) that a particular threat might take advantage of.

Identify what you have in place (Or can put in place)

What tools do you have in place to minimize your risk? Perhaps you use antivirus software or a network router, or practice safe surfing to reduce vulnerability from a particular threat. At this point, you won't likely know all the safeguards you have at your disposal. Keep reading to see how Vista, third-party tools, and best practices can reduce your risk exposure.

Assess the chance of a security breach

Gather enough data to make a reasonable determination of the likelihood of a particular event occurring. This isn't fortunetelling: It's an important part of your security plan. If you can quantify the likelihood of an event happening, you have a better understanding of how to deal with it appropriately. In other words, focus your efforts on those things that are more likely to happen and don't waste time and effort on events that aren't likely to occur.

Know the true effect

The angst over a compromised system your children use to play games is different than that for a compromised system that holds your financial and medical data. Understanding the difference is critical. Don't spend time and money protecting a piece of data that has little or no effect if it's compromised. When you make this analysis, consider three general areas: loss of integrity, availability, and confidentiality. In upcoming Table 2-4, you can catalog risks as well as what measures you have in place to prevent those risks. There, take the time to really think about the effect if a particular event occurs.

Determine the risk

Determining the risks that you're faced with combines the following:

- Thoroughly understanding the likelihood of a particular event occurring
- The effect if the event occurs

> ✔ What measures you have in place to help reduce the chance of the event occurring — or its effect, if it does occur

After you understand these things, you can quantify a particular risk.

Taking action to reduce risk

After you determine the risk, it's time to take action and deal with it. Perhaps you simply accept the risk and move on. Or, you find the risk significant enough that you need to reduce it to an acceptable and appropriate level.

The information that you gather in this chapter will help you determine what security features to implement to meet your security needs. For example, if while going through the next section, you find a particular system that holds sensitive data, you want to pay particular attention to Chapter 9 (which covers Encrypting File System [EFS]) and Chapter 10 (which covers BitLocker). You can then make a better determination about which of these encryption tools you might want to use to protect your sensitive data. Likewise, if you don't have a system that uses wireless network connectivity, skip Chapter 12 (which covers locking down wireless).

Understanding Your System

Understanding your system is a key component to your security that is often overlooked or not fully comprehended. To truly be secure, you need to understand the architecture of your system. That way, you can begin to see where your system might be vulnerable. This step is absolutely essential. Study both the hardware and software configuration of your system, who uses this system, and how the system is being used — including the types of data that are processed or stored on that system.

Even in a home or small office, all systems aren't created equal. One system might present very little risk, yet another might hold sensitive medical and financial data (and possibly the keys to your kingdom). And don't forget about multiple-user systems. Many folks simply acquire an understanding of a particular system under their immediate control. If you have multiple systems in your environment that are used by others (such as employees or children), take the time to understand each of those systems and their associated risks. When you develop a thorough understanding of each system in your environment, you'll be better prepared to comprehend any associated risks and to take the steps necessary to protect yourself from the things that can go wrong.

To that end, I suggest that you take an inventory of each system. You can use Table 2-1 as a reference for performing the inventory. I included some examples (in italic) in the table to assist you.

Table 2-1	System Inventory	
Category	*Inventory*	*Notes*
Name or description	*Joe's system in office*	
Hardware	*Dell 820, network storage device*	
Software	*MS Office 2007, TurboTax*	
Interfaces	*Network card: Internet, USB storage*	
Data on system	*My résumé, TurboTax files*	
Who uses the system	*Dad, kids*	
What the system is used for	*Internet, budget, process prescriptions, taxes*	
How important this system is	*Critical; can't tolerate system data being unavailable for long periods of time*	
How sensitive this data is	*Sensitive; financial and medical information*	

Hardware and software

System configurations for your home or small office will likely vary a bit: for example, different hardware platforms; or different hardware components, such as wireless network cards, attached storage, and so on. Very often, software installed on one system might not be installed or configured in the same way as another.

Additionally, software (such as BIOS and applications) often needs updating — some, specifically security related. When you gather an understanding of your hardware and software configurations, you'll be better prepared to recognize what components may require such updates.

Use an inventory, such as that in Table 2-1, to keep track of what software is installed on each system. Don't forget to revisit this inventory to keep your software updated as needed.

Interfaces

Understanding the interfaces of a system is very important to achieve optimal protection, regardless of whether the system is on a network, is attached to the Internet, or is a storage device where sensitive data is kept. Understanding the interface of these can certainly affect how you secure that particular system. Make sure that you indicate these interfaces in Table 2-1 for reference.

System usage and what type of information is on it

It's essential to understand how a particular system is used and what type of information the system might hold or process if you're to have the slightest chance of appropriately protecting it.

Accomplishing this understanding isn't a trivial task, and many larger organizations fall short of achieving such an understanding. For a home or small office, accomplishing this isn't nearly as difficult; however, it requires a fair amount of work and tenacity.

A good starting point is to use Table 2-1 (shown earlier in this chapter) or something similar to perform a periodic inventory of the systems in your environment. Indicate how the system is used and the type of data on the system. This is an excellent exercise that is likely to call your attention to some important data that's not being protected or preserved.

If you have systems that your teenage children or employees in your small office frequently use, you might not know exactly what information is held or processed by that system. You can imagine how difficult protecting a system or its data might be if you don't have an understanding of what you need to protect. Whether at home, in a small office, or even as part of a large organization, one of the biggest challenges is to consistently understand what types of data are held or processed by a particular system. And regardless of what information is on a system today, tomorrow, a user could add or remove that information and make your inventory invalid or out of date.

Identifying Threats

Identifying threats is being aware of the needs of a particular type of system, or of when a system is used in a certain way. The National Institute of Standards and Technology (NIST) defines a threat as "the potential for a particular threat-source to successfully exercise a particular vulnerability." You can see from this definition that a threat doesn't necessarily translate into risk if no vulnerability exists for that particular threat to exploit. However, at this point, your job is simply to identify the threats that you should be concerned about. NIST has developed a complex method of doing this; however, using a more simplified variation of this methodology is more applicable for a home or small office system. Look at it as brainstorming to identify the threats that apply to your environment after you have an understanding of your systems' configuration, how they will be used, and what type of information might reside there.

To understand what threats to be concerned about, you must understand what a threat-source is. Think of any circumstance or event that has potential to cause harm to your computer or data. Threat-sources can be categorized in three areas — human, natural, and environmental.

- **Human threat-sources** are caused by (yep, you guessed it) humans. These include actions that are of purposeful, malicious intent as well as those happenings that could occur from a user's unintentional actions.

- **Natural threat-sources** are often called *acts of God,* such as a flood, tornados, lightning, and so on. Comprehending natural threat-sources often triggers you to think of security controls that would help you preserve your data if such an event occurs.

- **Environmental threat-sources** are power failure, pollution, and so on. Like natural threat-sources, these can typically affect your system and data from an availability perspective and might prompt you to think of those security controls that will address availability (and preservation) of your system and associated data.

So get your brainstorming session kicked off! Table 2-2 lists some of the more common threats to a home or small office, but see whether you can add to these. Table 2-2 is broken into three columns: threat-source, threat manifestation, and applicable systems.

In the threat-source column, list those things that might affect you. I put down a few that are common. I suggest that you elaborate on them and come up with those that apply to your environment.

Table 2-2	Potential Threats	
Threat-Source	*Threat Manifestation*	*Applicable Systems*
Disaster (fire, flood, hurricane, and so on)	Loss of entire system or data	All
Power failure	System shutdown, no availability, potential loss of data	All

Threat-Source	Threat Manifestation	Applicable Systems
Network/Internet/e-mail	Spam, worm, Trojan horse	
User error	Deletion or modification of data, system files, and so on	
System failure	Loss of data or availability	
Disgruntled employee	Stealing or destroying corporate information	
Hackers/crackers	System intrusion, social engineering	

There are no wrong answers when listing potential threats in your environment. Brainstorming areas of concern will help you think of ways to protect your systems and associated data more thoroughly.

Vulnerability Identification

Vulnerability is a weakness that exists in a computer system in an environment. Perhaps the OS or applications don't have up-to-date patches, or a user has access to data that he doesn't need. Whatever the case, identifying these vulnerabilities and understanding what (if any) threat-sources can exploit those vulnerabilities is a critical component to effectively determining risk.

The information security world has many complex methodologies for determining vulnerabilities. You can use vulnerability sources to help you identify system bugs that pertain to specific types of systems, OSes, and other types of software packages. You also use scanning tools to scan systems to identify any weaknesses. However, for a home or small office, you can take a much simpler, yet still effective, approach. Identify those vulnerabilities that you have in your environment to determine the risks and then take appropriate steps to address them.

Table 2-3 outlines some examples of vulnerabilities that might exist on systems in a home or small office environment. Again, feel free to add any that you think of that pertains to your particular situation. Table 2-3 is only a list of some examples to help start your brainstorming session.

Table 2-3	Potential Vulnerabilities	
Vulnerability	*Notes*	*Applicable Systems*
OS	System OS doesn't have all up-to-date patches	
Other software	Application patches not up to date	
Viruses	Antivirus software isn't installed or up to date	
No power backup	Could lose data in power failure	
Unnecessary access to data	Access not needed; user could accidentally delete data	

What Safeguards Do You Currently Have in Place?

When you determine the risks in your home or small office environment, understand what you already have in place to reduce risk that these threats present to you. Use Table 2-4 to list the threats in your environment as well as the controls in place to deal with those threats. More often than not, you have a variety of controls already in place to help minimize your risk. I include some examples to help you identify what you have in place — and think of others you might want to implement.

I suggest that you take some time and develop a comprehensive list to serve as part of the foundation for securing your system and associated data. You'll likely find that when you start compiling this list, you start to drift into a security mindset, thinking of what's already in place — and what you've neglected. My examples are in italic.

Table 2-4	Current Safeguards		
Threat-Source	*Safeguard*	*Applicable Systems*	*Notes*
Access	*System requires login, don't let children use my computer.*	*Dad's office system*	*System is used only by Dad and has work-related info. Access needs to be restricted.*

Threat-Source	Safeguard	Applicable Systems	Notes
Sensitive data (Budget)	BitLocker, access control, weekly inventory to understand what data is on system	Family office system	Budget information is stored on this system.
Viruses	Antivirus software, Windows Defender	All systems	
Power outage	UPS* backup battery	Dad's office system	
Data loss	Identify important data, perform backups regularly	Office computer; daughter's system	

*UPS: Uninterruptible Power Supply

Telling the Future: What Are the Chances of That Happening?

If I had a nickel for every time I heard someone ask, "What are the chances of that happening?" I'd have quite a chunk of change. Perhaps the information security field constantly thinks in those terms. It doesn't bode well to insist that organizations spend a lot of time and money to solve a security problem that will likely never occur. There's some sort of expectation that security issues be quantified to some extent so that the business can make an appropriate decision on how to deal with certain risks. Generally, this is *risk management* — a practice that you, too, should follow. Trying to determine the likelihood of something occurring might resemble fortunetelling, but it's a worthwhile effort so that you don't spend a bunch of your time and money addressing a security issue that really isn't much of a problem.

For some threats, determining the likelihood of an occurrence may be very easy. Other threats, however, aren't as easy to predict. That's where occurrence prediction becomes more of an art than a science. Fortunately, for a home and small office, quantifying threat likelihood is something you can easily do. Table 2-5 presents a guideline developed by NIST, which is often used by organizations to assist in determining the likelihood of a particular threat occurring.

Table 2-5	Threat Likelihood (As Outlined by NIST)
Level of Likelihood	*Criteria*
High	Threat-source is highly motivated and capable, and safeguards to prevent are ineffective.
Medium	Threat-source is moderately motivated and capable, but safeguards in place impede exploitation of vulnerability.
Low	Threat-source isn't motivated or capable, or controls prevent or highly impede exploitation of vulnerability.

Understanding the Real Impact

Standards in the information security industry (particularly those defined by NIST) go to some length to describe how the magnitude of impact should be defined. Most of that is beyond this book's scope; however, I do believe setting a level with a standard definition of impact is good. The three things you typically need to consider while determining the effect of a certain event are availability, integrity, and confidentiality.

✔ **Availability:** *Availability* is very much what it sounds like — having your system and data available to you when you need or want it. Tolerance of unavailability varies from user to user and depends largely on how you use your system(s). After looking at each system in your home or small office and understanding how you use that system, you can then understand how its availability (or lack thereof) might affect you. Maybe you're okay with some systems being down and unavailable for days, whereas others might need to always be readily available. Whatever the case, understanding this is critical in developing and implementing any strategy that will protect you adequately.

✔ **Integrity:** *Integrity* typically refers to the unauthorized or improper modification of your data or system. In most regards, it's irrelevant if the modification was made intentionally or unintentionally. For example, if a user accidentally modifies or deletes your budget spreadsheet, you suffered a loss of integrity for that specific piece of data. It doesn't matter whether the loss was intentional or from a simple user mistake. You need to protect yourself not only against purposeful, malicious acts but also against user error. The effect is the same.

✔ **Confidentiality:** *Confidentiality* of your data is simply protecting your information from unauthorized disclosure to others. The effect of compromised confidentiality varies depending on the type of data, and perhaps from who compromised it. If your Personally Identifiable Information (PII) is compromised on the Internet, you risk becoming an identity theft or fraud victim. If, however, your budget spreadsheet is compromised by your children, that's likely to be less of an issue. Compromising your data's confidentiality needs to be seriously considered when you're determining the effect that threat could potentially have.

I could come up with a definition of each level of impact for you; however, different things concern and motivate different people. Therefore, I provide Table 2-6 as a starting point, but I suggest that you modify it so that the definition signifies exactly what is important to you and is accurately reflected in the definition of that particular level of impact.

Table 2-6	Levels of Impact
Level of Impact	*Definition Criteria*
High	Results in incurring serious financial impact; or significantly causes harm to person, reputation or interest
Medium	Results in moderate financial loss; or causes harm to person, reputation or interest
Low	Results in loss of some tangible asset; or might noticeably affect your reputation or interest

As shown in Table 2-6, the definition criteria are related to the financial affect that a particular threat might have. Financial impact is likely to be a concern to many, but it might not be the most important concern or motivator to some. You can replace the definitions with what's important to you. Define the levels of effect to reflect your own concerns and motivators.

Determining the Risk

The tasks I walk you through in the earlier sections of this chapter help you get to this point — namely, where you can determine the real risk and make some decisions to reduce that risk to an acceptable level. In a home or small office, you can determine risk by taking two things into account:

- The probability that a threat is likely to occur
- The impact that a threat would have if it were to occur

For example, say you have a medium or high likelihood that a threat will occur, paired with a medium or high impact if it does occur. Rate the risk accordingly: either medium or high. Although determining risk can involve using a matrix and calculating a risk score, you can accomplish this for a home or small office by taking these things into account and making a decision that makes sense for you.

Use Table 2-7 as a guideline to addressing those risks.

Table 2-7	Guidelines for Dealing with Risk
Risk Level	*Actions to Mitigate*
High	Should definitely take measures to mitigate risk
Medium	Should take corrective actions, but might need time to do so
Low	No action might be needed but should be considered

Establishing Your Security Plan

After you better understand the threats, vulnerabilities, and risks that exist, establish a plan to reduce those risks to an acceptable level that allows for a safe computing environment.

Taking action to reduce the risks

Use *safeguards* — also known as *security controls* — to help reduce the risk in your environment to an acceptable and appropriate level. Safeguards range from technical (such as a firewall or antivirus software) to nontechnical (such as changing user behavior to prevent exposing a system and data to risk).

You likely don't necessarily know all the Vista security features and functionality that can assist you in reducing risk in your environment. The good news is that you will if you work your way through this book. You'll discover the safeguards offered by Vista as well as a few third-party tools. Although this book focuses mainly on technical safeguards, you also find out about preventive and detection safeguards. In the end, you'll have plethora of options that will enable you to protect your systems and data for some time. All you need to do is to take action and implement those safeguards.

Table 2-8 illustrates a few of the safeguards that you might use to address a particular risk or problem. It even shows you where in the book a particular safeguard is addressed. This table isn't a mini index; instead, it illustrates a few safeguards that Vista offers to deal with some common risks or problems. In the earlier section, "Assessing Your Systems' Security Risks," you can read how to determine the threats, vulnerabilities, and ultimately the risks in your environment. With a better idea of those things, while you progress through the book, you'll recognize the things that can help you address those risks. Take a look at Table 2-8 to get an idea of some of the safeguards that can assist with common security problems.

Table 2-8	Security Safeguards	
Problem (Risk)	*Safeguard(s)*	*Chapter Location*
OS/application patches	Auto updates Vendor Web sites	3, 18
Virus/spyware	Antivirus/anti-spyware Windows Defender	3, 11, 14, 18
Disclosure of sensitive data	BitLocker EFS Access controls	6, 7, 9, 10
Access to data	Permissions Isolation	6, 7
Network threats	Firewall OS configuration settings	11, 12, 13
Data loss	Vista Backup and Restore Center Third-party products	8, 18

A little about how users introduce security risks

Do users introduce an element of risk to your home or small office computing environment? The answer is a resounding, "Yes!" The human element always presents certain risks to security, whether at your home, a small office, or a Fortune 500 organization. In fact, it's the human element that is most exploited and perhaps presents the most risk. For example, you can use technical controls to force strong password policies, but if you walk around your office, you're likely to find users who have their passwords written on sticky notes pasted on their monitors or tucked away under their keyboards. This example illustrates how the behavior of users can render even a very capable and valuable technical control almost useless. Your security plan cannot rely only on the controls offered within Vista but must also include those things that can address users' behavior in your particular environment. Here are a few examples:

- ✔ **Don't give users access they don't need.** Although this can also be addressed with controls within Vista, I suggest going farther. If others in your home don't need access to the system that you use for your budgeting or that may otherwise hold sensitive data, don't allow it.

  If you don't have multiple systems so that you can segregate usage, I suggest directing users to avoid specific data that they don't need access to. This might seem somewhat trivial, but doing so may help reinforce a policy of least privilege.

  Users don't need access to everything — only those things that pertain to their functions. A compromise might not be a malicious event but rather a mistake by a user who had access to data that they didn't really need access to. Of course, in addition to providing such direction, reinforce it with technical controls if possible.

- ✔ **Educate your users.** User education is a key component to the success of any security program, whether it's in a large organization or your home and small office. While you gain an understanding of security, share that knowledge with those around you. Many security incidents can be avoided with the proper security awareness training. Educating your spouse, children, friends, family, or co-workers on matters of security and privacy is always worth the effort.

- ✔ **Have users take ownership.** Security is everyone's job. You can't do it all by yourself, so the more that you can have the users in your home or small office accept some ownership the better off everyone will be. Get them involved in security. Spend some time talking to them and listening to their ideas: You might be surprised by what they come up with. Have them help with inventorying the systems in your environment, particularly the ones that are under their control. Therefore, they can locate the data that's important to them and communicate it to you so that it can be appropriately protected.

Chapter 3

Dispensing Security from Windows Security Center

*W*indows Security Center (WSC) made its debut with Windows XP Service Pack 2 (SP2), offering users a central interface that alerts them when certain security settings need attention. It even went as far as to offer some recommendations as to how to fix a problem when it was detected, but it fell short of providing the user a clear and intuitive path. In the end, it was very much up to the user to figure out how to fix the problem that WSC cited. Even still, WSC was a hit with many users. WSC presents users with a dashboard where they can view security settings, such as Firewall, Automatic Updates, Virus Protection, and Internet Options.

During the development of Vista, quite a bit of hype and controversy surrounded the new and improved WSC. Microsoft piled the hype on WSC almost as much as on Vista itself. Third-party vendors screamed foul because they believed that Microsoft was imposing WSC on users and not allowing them to integrate their products with WSC. When the smoke cleared, however, third-party vendors could integrate with WSC and the features and functionality in the Vista WSC. In this chapter, you find out how to dispense security for your Vista system by using the new and improved WSC.

Windows Security Center Essentials

Windows Security Center comes with a handful of new and improved features and functionality. WSC is a dashboard for Vista users where they can manage their PC security settings. In previous Windows versions, users were alerted to a problem but provided with unclear suggestions as to what could be done to fix it. However, the Vista WSC is improved, not only providing alerts when something goes awry but also integrating with security features (even those from participating third-party vendors) and providing a path to remediation. This easy-to-use interface actually helps you fix the problem while it continually manages security settings.

To access WSC, follow these steps:

1. **Choose Start⇨Control Panel.**

   Control Panel appears.

2. **In default view, choose Security⇨Security Center. In classic view, choose Control Panel⇨Security Center.**

   The Windows Security Center interface appears. (See Figure 3-1.)

Microsoft went to some effort to improve upon the WSC that was first offered with Windows XP SP2. The Security Essentials Notification pane is very much the same. However, check out the left pane (the Options pane) of the WSC window. There, you can find an area in which you can access each of the essential security tools. Not only are you provided a dashboard (the Notification area) where you can view the status of these tools, but now you can also use WSC as a single interface to manage and configure these tools. The Security Essentials Notification pane alerts you of the status of each of the essential security tools.

Options pane   Security Essentials Notification pane

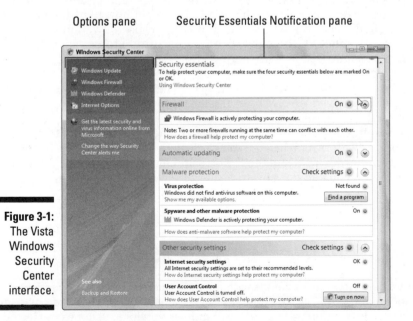

Figure 3-1:
The Vista Windows Security Center interface.

Managing Firewall Settings

In Chapter 11, I describe in greater detail the features and functionality of Windows Firewall. Here, I describe how you can use WSC to monitor and manage your firewall settings.

Monitoring, alerting, and remediation

From WSC, you can monitor the on and off status of Windows Firewall, or even perhaps a firewall from a participating Independent Software Vendor (ISV). The Notification area is the right pane of the WSC window. In Figure 3-1, see the Firewall section. The firewall status is shown as On (green) or Off (red). Click the Turn On Now button to enable the tool immediately for optimal protection.

In the Windows XP SP2 WSC, the user was provided a recommended way of turning Firewall back on, but you had to go through multiple menus. The Vista version is much more intuitive.

Using WSC Options menu to manage Firewall

In the Options pane of WSC is a link for Windows Firewall. If this is the firewall tool that you use, manage and configure your firewall settings from WSC interface. Clicking the link initiates the Windows Firewall applet found in Control Panel, as shown in Figure 3-2.

Being able to access Windows Firewall from WSC puts the firewall right in front of you so you are more apt to read about it and use it to protect your system and sensitive information.

You can also access Windows Firewall from the *Microsoft Management Console (MMC)* tool, which is covered in Chapter 11. The MMC tool offers more options for configuring Windows Firewall settings than the Windows Firewall applet that you access through Control Panel or WSC. A link to Windows Firewall is a very useful WSC feature. Still, the MMC tool offers more choices when configuring Windows Firewall, which offers you better protection.

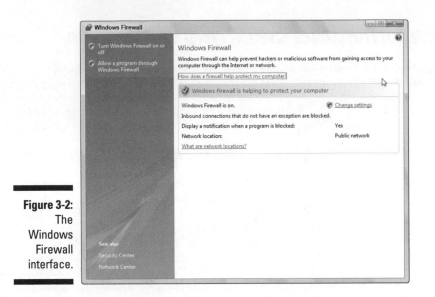

Figure 3-2:
The
Windows
Firewall
interface.

Use the MMC tool when configuring Windows Firewall. Chapter 11 provides the detail as to the differences of both tools and how to use the MMC tool to configure Windows Firewall settings. For those times when you need to change settings available from the basic Windows Firewall applet, using the WSC interface can be quick and easy. Just don't rely on it exclusively. When you need to roll up your sleeves and get into the nitty-gritty details of configuring Windows Firewall, understand that the MMC with the Windows Firewall snap-in is a better choice.

Configuring Automatic Updating

Automatic Updating provides you an automated way of updating your operating system (OS) and some applications with software updates, many of which have a tendency to be security related. Of course, you need an Internet connection because your OS has to contact the Microsoft mother ship to download the needed updates. Because updating your system and applications is critical to securing your system and any personal or sensitive data, Automatic Updating is a great tool. If you choose to not take advantage of Automatic Updating, you can still update your OS and applications manually. That being said, if you forget to monitor your updates, you could leave your system and data vulnerable.

Monitoring, alerting, and remediation

You can monitor whether Automatic Updating is enabled from the WSC Notification pane. It's simple: If Automatic Updating is On, the panel is highlighted in green. Life is good. Likewise, if Automatic Updating is Off, the panel is highlighted in red, indicating an alert status. Click the Change Settings button to enable Automatic Updating immediately and better protect your system.

Managing Automatic Updating

In the Options pane of the WSC window is the Windows Update link (refer to Figure 3-1) that you can click to manage Automatic Updating settings:

- **Check For Updates:** Click the Check For Updates link to manually check for updates. This works just like when Automatic Updating in enabled. Windows Update checks the Microsoft Update Web site for software updates for your OS and other selected software. If updates are available, the Windows Update interface indicates this. Figure 3-3 shows updates that are available for the system. Notice in that figure the Important Update that's available — which should be installed. When a system has an Important Update awaiting installation, the Install Updates for Your Computer panel is highlighted in yellow. If this were a Critical Update, the panel would be red.

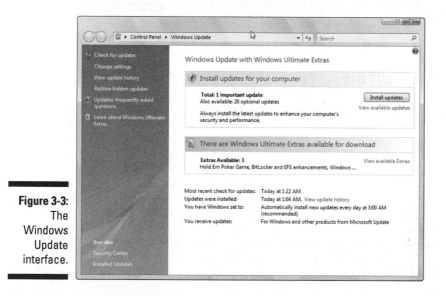

Figure 3-3:
The
Windows
Update
interface.

- ✔ **Change Settings:** Click the Change Settings link in the Options pane of the Windows Update applet (see Figure 3-3) to enable Automatic Updating and schedule a time and frequency of your choosing. You can also turn off Automatic Updating here.

However, if you disable Automatic Updating, the onus is on you to keep your system up to date. Manually updating is sometimes a very tedious task. And, if you don't perform it consistently, you can leave your system and your data at risk.

You can also configure additional options here, such as having the application provide recommended updates (those updates that Microsoft recommends for your system) and using the Microsoft Update service to provide updates not only for Windows but for other Microsoft products as well.

By default, these settings are enabled. I recommend that you keep them that way.

- ✔ **View Update History:** Clicking this intuitive link provides you a history of what updates were applied to your system, their status, their type, and when they were installed.

WSC Malware Protection

Windows Security Center provides a Malware Protection panel in the Security Essentials Notification pane that addresses two areas of importance: Virus Protection; and Spyware and Other Malware Protection.

Monitoring, alerting, and remediation

To illustrate the monitoring and remediation functionality of the Malware Protection panel, I did not install antivirus protection software on a test system. In Figure 3-1, the Malware Protection panel alerts if the system doesn't have any virus-protection software installed and sports a Find a Program button you can click to help you find an appropriate virus-protection program for you to install. Clicking that button takes you to the Microsoft Web site, where you can choose and purchase one of its approved vendors to purchase Vista-compatible virus-protection software.

If you have virus-protection software installed but the software isn't up to date, the WSC Malware Protection panel alerts you and provides a remediation path as well.

Virus Protection options

Providing that your system does have virus-protection software installed, the Options pane of the WSC window offers a link to your virus-protection software, providing (of course) that the software vendor is a participating ISV and its software can integrate with the WSC interface. You can then easily manage your virus-protection software from the WSC interface.

Windows Defender options

The Options pane of the WSC window (refer to Figure 3-1) also provides a link to Windows Defender, which is the Microsoft answer to spyware and other malware protection. Windows Security Center can provide you easier access to manage your Windows Defender settings.

Clicking this link runs a scan of your system and opens the Windows Defender console. From there, you can manage the many Window Defender settings that can help you protect your system from spyware and other malicious software.

I cover Windows Defender in depth in Chapter 14.

Accessing Other Security Options with WSC

Windows Security Center also provides Other Security Settings, which includes Internet Security Settings and User Account Control (UAC; refer to Figure 3-1). These tools offer a variety of ways to monitor and manage your system to help better secure it.

Internet Security Settings

Internet Options, located in the WSC Options pane, offers a variety of security and privacy settings that you can use to better secure your system from a variety of network and Internet-related threats. In Chapter 13, I take an in-depth look at implementing these settings to limit your security exposure. Here, take a look the WSC interface options for monitoring and managing your Internet Options settings.

In the Security Essentials Notification pane of WSC, under the Other Security Settings section, is a panel provided for Internet Security Settings. Here, you can monitor whether all Internet security settings are set to their recommended levels. If these settings are set to the recommended levels, the panel indicates an OK status. If they're not set to the recommended settings, you see a red status color.

Internet Options comprises a vast amount of settings: namely those at Internet Properties⇨Security Settings – Internet Zone, as shown in Figure 3-4. If you select a setting that's not recommended, it's tagged Not Secure and is highlighted in red.

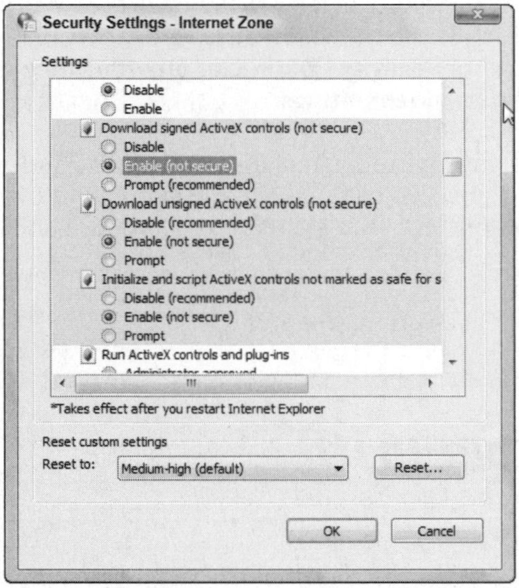

Figure 3-4:
Security
Settings –
Internet
Zone.

Also, the Internet Security Settings panel in the notification pane of WSC will be red and indicate Check Settings status instead of OK. Click the Restore Settings button to make changes. Intuitively, clicking Restore Settings reconfigures settings that are deemed Not Secure by the application and resets them to their recommended state.

An OK status for Internet Security Settings in WSC doesn't necessarily indicate that your Internet settings are as secure as they should be. Internet Options comprises a vast amount of settings, many of which are security related. Although WSC monitors critical security settings in the Internet Zone, WSC doesn't monitor some settings in Internet Options that are important to the security of your system. In Chapter 13, I discuss those settings in greater detail.

User Account Control

User Account Control (UAC) is a new addition to Vista and provides an additional layer of security. In many regards, UAC is ingenious in how it takes care of serious security problems when malicious programs execute with sometimes-elevated privilege. For some people, however, UAC seems like a constant nagging security feature that drives them to quickly search for a way to turn it off.

Whatever side of the fence you're on, the Security Essentials Notification pane of WSC does provide monitoring of the On or Off status of UAC. If UAC is On, the panel is green. If UAC is Off, the panel is red.

Unlike many of the other Security Essentials monitored in WSC, there is no integration with the UAC application interface. WSC provides only monitoring of the UAC application's status and nothing more. However, having a dashboard indicator to quickly determine whether UAC is On or Off allows you to assess your security as it relates to UAC.

Other things to know

As you can see in Figure 3-1, the Options pane has several options to use with tools that are be essential to the security of your system: Windows Update, Windows Firewall, Windows Defender, and Internet Options.

Also in the Options pane of the Windows Security Center window are links to other options that may be of interest to you. I discuss these options in the following sections.

Get the latest security and virus information from Microsoft

Click the Get the Latest Security and Virus Information from Microsoft link in the Options pane of the WSC window to go on an Internet journey to up-to-date security and virus information from Microsoft. Specifically, the first stop in this journey is the Microsoft Security Central Web site. Here, you can find a plethora of information about protecting your system and data, such as tips and guidance on home security, information on security updates, and tools you can use to remove malicious software. Look for the other Microsoft resources relevant to a particular topic you're interested in.

This Web site is a resource that I recommend you take the time to familiarize yourself with.

Changing how WSC alerts you

Windows Security Center has configurable options to customize how you want to be alerted. Click the Change the Way Security Center Alerts Me link in the Options pane of the Windows Security Center window to find these options. As illustrated in Figure 3-5, you can select the following options:

- **Yes, Notify Me and Display the Icon (Recommended):** This is the recommended setting from Microsoft. When you enable this, a yellow alert icon appears in the Notification area as well as a balloon comment indicating the issue. Some users find these alerts rather annoying, especially for issues that they're aware of. Even still, using this setting assures you that you will be made aware of any deviation of the recommended security settings in WSC.

- **Don't Notify Me, But Display the Icon:** Choose this setting if you don't want all the nagging but do want to be made aware of security setting deviations in WSC. Enabling this setting doesn't give you pop-up notifications but does show an alert icon if something is amiss.

- **Don't Notify Me and Don't Display the Icon (Not Recommended):** This settings is for users who are so confident of their system's security stature that they don't want any WSC alerts.

  For you users who are really on top of your security and check it manually daily, this setting might be appropriate. However, if you're not truly on top of your system's security, disabling both the notification and the displaying of the icon on the tray will likely be a recipe for disaster.

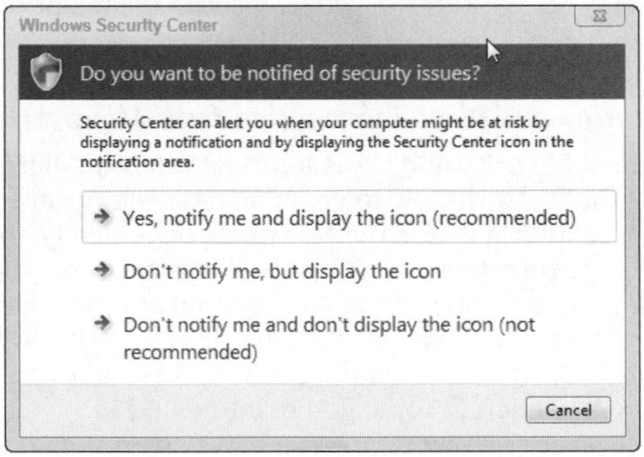

Figure 3-5: WSC Notification options.

Windows Security Center

Do you want to be notified of security issues?

Security Center can alert you when your computer might be at risk by displaying a notification and by displaying the Security Center icon in the notification area.

→ Yes, notify me and display the icon (recommended)

→ Don't notify me, but display the icon

→ Don't notify me and don't display the icon (not recommended)

Cancel

Part II
Controlling Access to Systems and Data

"You know, Jekyll, this is a single log-on ID system. There's no need for multiple identities anymore."

In this part . . .

Implementing an appropriate level of security is a delicate dance between protection and productivity. One step too far in one direction, and users have a level of access to your system and data that they don't need — introducing you to a plethora of unnecessary risks. Two steps the other way, and users can't perform essential tasks — and thus lose productivity.

In this part, I look at how to use Vista security features to control access to your system and sensitive data. You can read about User Account Control (UAC); Rights Management; and managing accounts, groups, and shares. For those who are interested in advanced technical principles, hold on as I dive into controlling NTFS permissions, the Advanced Sharing Interface, and more so that you can further control access to your systems and data.

Chapter 4

Administering User Account Control

● ●

● ●

*V*ista *User Account Control (UAC)* reduces the exposure and attack surface of your computer's operating system (OS) by forcing all users to run in *Standard User mode.* This new gatekeeper reduces the opportunity for a malicious program to hijack a session with elevated privilege because UAC serves as an intermediary.

If UAC is enabled, all user accounts in Vista run in Standard User mode. This means that when a task is performed that requires administrative privilege, such as installing an application or modifying certain system configurations, Vista notifies the user and requires authorization, such as

✔ An acknowledgement to continue executing the task

✔ Entering of administrative credentials (Over-the-Shoulder Credentials; OTS)

User Account Control is a significant security improvement over previous Windows versions, but it's the most annoying and intrusive security feature in Vista. Many users try to either modify its behavior to be less intrusive (which makes it less protective) or turn it off completely. I'm not sure that Microsoft achieved the right balance between security and productivity. It will be up to the Vista user base to accept or reject this feature and all its security value.

Understanding Life As a Standard User

Vista UAC helps reduce your attack surface and total cost of ownership. Working in Standard User mode isn't really all that bad, and Microsoft did make some effort in Vista to decrease the number of tasks that require administrative privilege.

Don't succumb to the temptation of choosing less-secure settings just to make them less intrusive and bothersome. Although UAC might be intrusive, annoying, and a royal pain in your side, it provides you a great amount of security. The recommended settings in this chapter give you the information that you need so you can optimally secure your system.

In Windows XP, users really had no idea of exactly what functions they could or could not perform as a Standard user. In Vista, though, you can perform a variety of functions that you can't perform in Windows XP. Table 4-1 illustrates some of what tasks you have permission to do as a Standard user or an administrator.

Windows XP: The bad old days

If you used Windows XP and had only general user permissions on your computer, you likely understand the frustration that such limited privilege can muster. However, being productive as a general user was a challenge. And, to make an already difficult situation worse, you really weren't sure what you did or did not have the permission to do. There was no warning nor any indication of what task you couldn't perform. Sure, you could learn from trial and error — usually, at an inopportune time. Relying on the local system admin (or whoever actually had the appropriate permission to help you do what you needed to do) was, at best, inconvenient. At worst, life as an ordinary user just wasn't good.

If you were lucky enough to be part of Windows XP Power Users Group, you had a little respite from those daily challenges. You could perform some system tasks, such as installing applications or making certain changes to configuration settings without needing full administrative privilege. You didn't have to call your local administrator for every task, but you couldn't do a fair amount of things.

Because of the difficulty in getting the users the right privileges to be productive, many users at home, at a small office, and even in large enterprise environments ended up having full administrative privilege on their systems. This privilege increased security risk and total cost of ownership of your system. Malicious programs could execute in a user account without the user's knowledge — and if the account had elevated privilege, so did the malicious software. Thus, a malicious program could change system-level settings and all kinds of neat stuff to wreak havoc on a system and perhaps in a network environment. It also meant that a user could unintentionally alter system-level settings, oftentimes making their system unstable and needing some type of intervention.

Table 4-1	User Types and Common Tasks
Standard User	*Administrator*
Change time zone.	Change time, date, and time zone.
Establish local network and wireless.	Install/uninstall applications and updates.
Back up and restore personal files.	Configure Parental Controls.
Configure Accessibility Options.	Open and configure Firewall.
Configure Power Management settings.	Modify UAC settings in local Sec policy.
Sync mobile devices.	Modify user account type.
Change personal password.	Add or remove a user account.
Use remote desktop.	Schedule automatic tasks.
Modify background and display properties.	Configure Automatic Updates.
Play and burn CD/DVD media.	Browse to another user's profile directories.
Create a Virtual Private Network (VPN).	Install ActiveX controls.

Knowing what you can't do

If you can't perform a particular function in your current user context, Vista displays a Shield icon in the operation that you're attempting to perform.

For example, as shown in Figure 4-1, the Shield icon located on the Change Date and Time button indicates that the user doesn't have the proper authority to change the date and time of this particular system.

Admin Approval mode: When Standard User mode isn't enough

Admin Approval mode provides a clear distinction between an operation performed with administrative privilege aznd one being performed with Standard user privilege. That is to say, a Standard user in Vista can't perform certain functions, such as installing software and running certain tasks. To perform these functions, a user needs elevated privileges, many of which are those privileges assigned to an administrator.

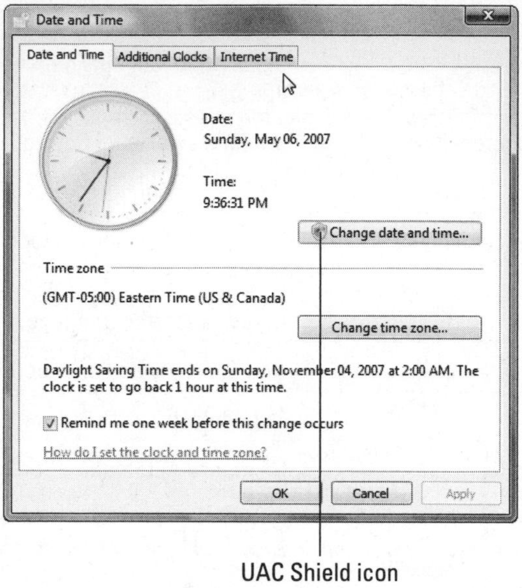

Figure 4-1:
The Vista
UAC Shield
icon.

UAC Shield icon

This is great for security because it helps reduce the threat of a malicious program being able to covertly execute tasks under the context of an account with elevated privilege. UAC and Admin Approval mode, if configured appropriately, ensure that each user is logged on to the machine with Standard user privilege, even if that user is an administrator.

When a task requires administrative-level privilege, Admin Approval mode serves as intermediary and prompts the user with a notification that running the task requires elevated privilege, as shown in Figure 4-2. This notification is called an *elevation prompt.* The user is required to take the appropriate action, depending on how UAC is configured. If the appropriate action is taken, elevated privilege is granted through an administrative token.

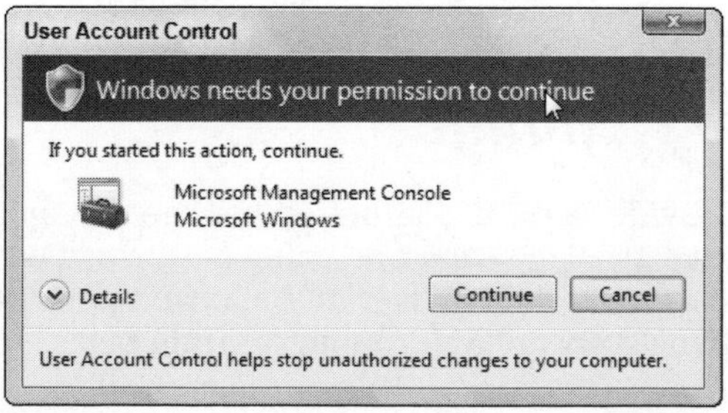

Figure 4-2:
The UAC
Admin
Approval
mode
notification
prompt.

Although UAC and Admin Approval mode can help you reduce the threat of a malicious program covertly executing under the context of an account with elevated privilege, it doesn't completely prevent the problem. Users can get desensitized to prompts and just click Continue without fully understanding the consequences. When you're prompted with the UAC notification prompt that a task is going to be performed, make sure that this task is what you want to do — and not a malicious program trying to perform a task on its own. Think before you click Continue from habit. Also, because now a Standard user really can perform a larger variety of tasks than in previous Windows versions, you might not need all users on your system to have administrative privilege.

A variety of settings can control the behavior of Vista Admin Approval mode. The upcoming section, "Managing UAC with Local Security Policy Settings," describes in detail the settings that can affect the behavior of this feature. By default, this feature is turned on, and the notification shown in Figure 4-2 will be displayed.

Over-the-Shoulder Credentials

What happens when a user without administrative privilege tries a forbidden task? It depends on how you configure the UAC security policies on a Vista system.

By default, the user will be prompted for OTS. For the task to continue, the user is prompted to supply the credentials of an account with administrative-level authority.

Figure 4-3 illustrates a Vista Standard user, attempting to perform a task that requires administrative privilege, being prompted for credentials. The user needs to know the local administrator account and password to perform these functions.

You can also configure this feature to simply deny the task instead of prompting the user for credentials. See the upcoming section, "Managing UAC with Local Security Policy Settings," to read about the configurable settings for this feature.

User Account Control

🛡 Windows needs your permission to continue

If you started this action, continue.

    Microsoft Management Console
    Microsoft Windows

To continue, type an administrator password, and then click OK.

User_ID

Password

Insert a smart card

⌄ Details   OK   Cancel

User Account Control helps stop unauthorized changes to your computer.

Figure 4-3:
The UAC
Over-the-
Shoulder
Credentials
prompt.

Evaluating a user's need for access

Every person in your home or small office probably doesn't need the highest level of privilege. Therefore, your assignment is to determine the level of privilege that the users in your environment might need. Whether that's only yourself, or other people in your home or small office, you make the decision.

Security is a balance between productivity and protection. To help you determine the balance appropriate for you, consider the following:

✔ **More authority** means more risk and higher total cost of ownership.

✔ **Less authority** sometimes means less productivity.

✔ **Understand the functionality that you're likely to need.** You need to understand all the tasks that might need to be performed, such as software installation, configuration changes, and printer installation. After you understand the tasks that need to be performed, you can figure out who needs to perform them and how often. You can then decide what type of permissions the users might need and how UAC can help control any elevated privilege.

You can have multiple accounts that have different levels of privilege. That way, you don't have to use an account with more privilege than is necessary at any particular time.

Managing UAC with Local Security Policy Settings

Although perhaps not on a daily basis, configurable settings are available that control UAC behavior. These settings can be managed by altering the security policies for Admin Approval mode for built-in administrators:

- ✔ **Behavior of the elevation prompt for Standard users**

- ✔ **Detection of application installations and prompt for elevation**

- ✔ **Elevation of only those executables that are signed and validated**

- ✔ **Elevation of only those UIAccess applications that are installed in secure locations**

- ✔ **Running all administrators in Admin Approval mode**

  If you disable this setting, you essentially disable UAC for your system.

- ✔ **Switching to the secure desktop when prompting for elevation**

- ✔ **Virtualizing file and Registry Write failures to per-user locations**

The applicable security policies can be found by opening the Local Security Policy editor snap-in. Here's how:

1. **From the Start menu, choose Control Panel.**

2. **Depending on the view that's set in Control Panel, choose one of the following:**

   - *Default View:* Choose System and Maintenance➪Administrative Tools.

   - *Classic View:* Choose Administrative Tools.

3. **Click Local Security Policy.**

   After the Local Security Policy editor is opened, the policies are listed in the right pane. Find the UAC-related policies. Figure 4-4 illustrates the Local Security Policy editor snap-in and the available settings related to UAC.

Admin Approval Mode for Built-in Administrators

This UAC setting determines behavior for

- ✔ The built-in administrator's account

- ✔ Users who have local administrative privilege on the system as part of the local administrator group

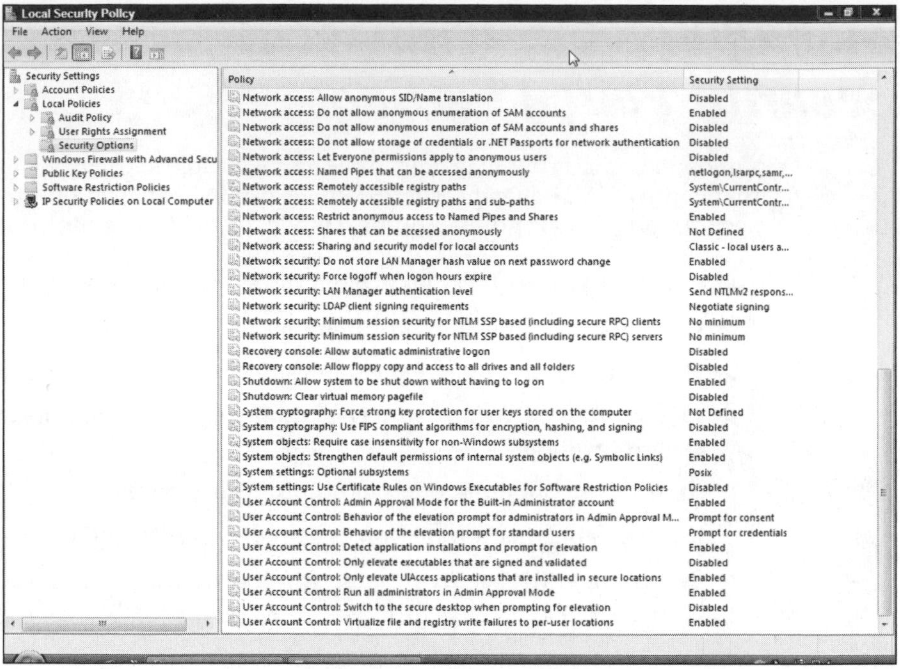

Figure 4-4:
Use the
Local
Security
Policy editor
to modify
UAC
policies.

This setting has two options:

✓ **Enabled:** If this setting is enabled, the built-in administrator account is logged in with Admin Approval mode. Therefore, any operations that require elevation of privilege will prompt the user to either permit or deny the operation.

✓ **Disabled:** If this setting is disabled, the built-in administrator logs on to the system in XP-Compatible mode. All the applications and operations performed by the administrator will be run with full administrative privilege.

By default, this setting is Disabled. In the right pane of the Local Security Policy (refer to Figure 4-4), if you select the policy that you want to modify, you see the window shown in Figure 4-5 to make the modification.

Enabling this setting can be annoying to those administrative users that likely believe that they don't need such an interference, but enabling this setting offers a great deal of security value. Say, for example, that a system is infected with a virus or other malicious code. When the administrator logs on to the machine, the code attempts to perform certain undesirable operations that require administrative authority — of course, without the knowledge of the user. Because Vista now runs even an administrative-level user as a Standard user, performing that operation requires an elevation of privilege. This setting helps determine whether intermediary steps need to be performed by the user prior to granting this elevation of privilege or whether this elevation of privilege is granted automatically.

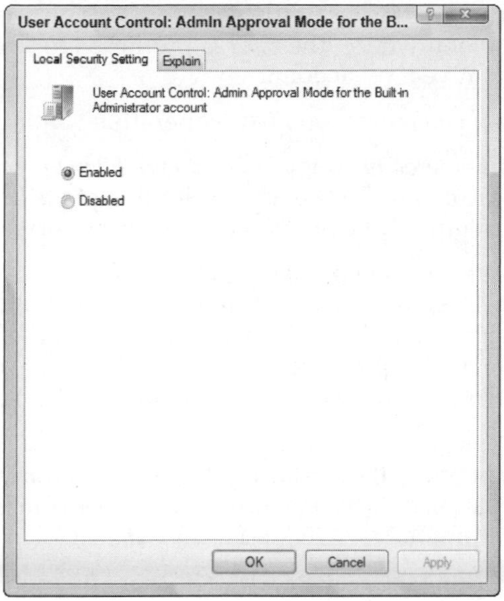

Figure 4-5:
Admin
Approval
mode
settings.

If this setting is enabled, you are then requiring an intermediary step prior to privilege escalation, and you can use User Account Control: Behavior of the Elevation Prompt for Administrators, in Admin Approval mode, to specify exactly what that step (or better) is the required behavior.

I recommend that you enable this setting and appropriately configure the associated setting: that is, User Account Control: Behavior of the Elevation Prompt for Administrators, in Admin Approval Mode, which you can read about in the following section.

Behavior of the Elevation Prompt for Administrators in Admin Approval Mode

This UAC setting determines behavior of the elevation prompt for administrators on the system. These configurable options are available for this setting:

✔ **Prompt for Consent:** If this setting is selected, for any operation that requires an elevation of privilege, the user is prompted for authority to continue the operation. If the user elects to permit the operation, the operation continues with the highest available privilege.

This is the default.

✔ **Prompt for Credentials:** If this setting is selected, for any operation that requires an elevation of privilege, the user is prompted to enter a password to an administrative-level account:

- *If the credentials entered are valid,* the operation continues.

- *If the credentials entered are not valid or do not have the proper authority to perform the operation,* the user is notified of the Logon Failure error and will continually be prompted to enter the correct password.

I find this setting quite effective in that the user is already an administrative-level user, so he is essentially entering the password for the account that he's already logged into. If the user walks away from the system and doesn't lock the screen, this provides an additional layer of security to prevent someone else from just walking up and performing an elevated operation.

✔ **Elevate without Prompting:** If this setting is selected, for any operation that requires an elevation of privilege, the user can perform that operation without being prompted for credentials or consent.

I do not recommend using the Elevate without Prompting setting. I would be the first to agree that UAC (and in particular, this setting) can be annoying, but it serves as a very important gatekeeper that helps prevent a malicious program (such as a virus or Trojan horse) from performing operations on your system that require administrative privilege. If you enable Elevate without Prompting, you essentially turn off this gatekeeper.

In the right pane of the Local Security Policy (refer to Figure 4-4), selecting the policy that you want to modify brings up the window shown in Figure 4-6.

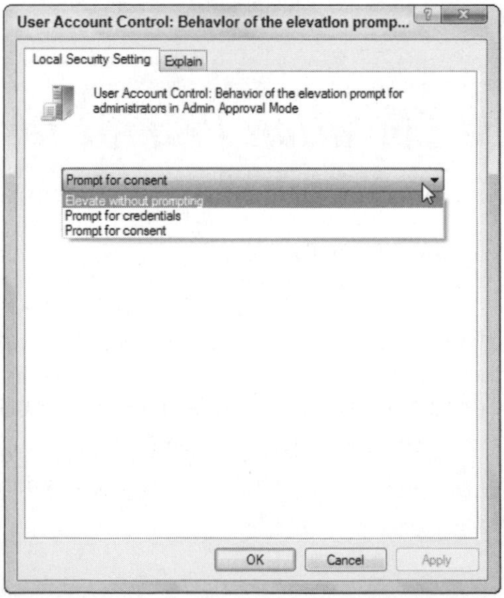

Figure 4-6: Administrators in Admin Approval mode settings.

If you configure this setting so that the user is prompted for credentials and the user has knowledge of an administrative level account, the user can perform that function. Even though the user is an administrator, the user will operate in Standard User mode and will have to take a specific action to perform certain tasks.

The Prompt for Consent setting is most likely adequate if you're at home or in a small office where you don't have a lot of people around with access who could walk up to your system if you happen to forget to lock the screen when you're away for a bit. This setting is likely the appropriate balance between protection and productivity because it provides prevention of a malicious software program executing a task without the knowledge of the user, yet the user can quickly select permit and move on. The Prompt for Credentials setting does provide more security, but it's likely to be annoying to users and is a bit of overkill. Therefore, I recommend configuring this setting to Prompt for Consent.

Behavior of the Elevation Prompt for Standard Users

This UAC setting determines behavior of the elevation prompt for Standard users (those users that have no elevated privilege and are part of the Users Group on the local system). By default, all Vista users are made members of the default group named *Users Group*. This group is assigned certain permissions; when users are added to a group, they inherit those permissions. Chapter 6 provides more detail on this topic.

This setting has two configurable options:

- ✔ **Prompt for Credentials:** If this setting is selected, for any operation that requires an elevation of privilege, the user is prompted to enter a password to an administrative level account.

  - *If the credentials are valid and the account has the required level of authority to perform the operation,* the operation is executed.

  - *If the credentials are not valid or the account does not have the proper level of authority to perform the operation,* the user will be notified of the Logon Failure error and will continually be prompted to enter the appropriate credentials.

  Prompt for Credentials is the default in the Vista Home version.

- ✔ **Automatically Deny Elevation Requests:** If this setting is selected, any operation that requires an elevation of privilege results in an Access Denied error message.

Automatically Deny Elevation Requests is the default in the Vista
Enterprise version.

In the right pane of the Local Security Policy (refer to Figure 4-4), selecting
the policy that you want to modify brings up the window shown in Figure 4-7.

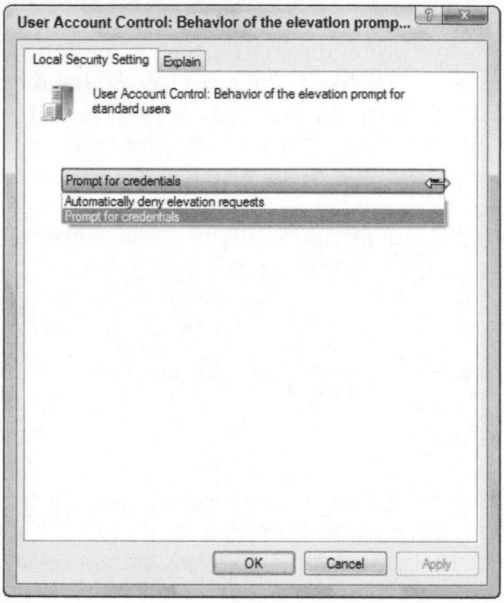

Figure 4-7:
Elevation
Prompt
settings for
Standard
users.

If you configure this setting so that the user is prompted for credentials and
the user has knowledge of an administrative-level account, the user can perform that function. The user normally operates in a Standard User mode and
has to take a specific action to perform certain tasks. The system will be
more secure. And, with knowledge of the administrator account, the user can
operate at a higher level of authority — and, perhaps, productivity. Of course,
risks come with this as well. If you don't want the user to perform those tasks
and the user becomes privy to the administrative account information, he
can then perform a wide variety of administrative tasks.

By contrast, if you configure this setting so that the user is automatically
denied any elevation request, you can have a more secure system and control those things that the user can perform. The user won't be able to perform those operations that need administrative privilege.

This setting will be different for each user. Determine which users must be
able to perform advanced operations to be productive:

  ✔ **If a user doesn't need to perform those operations:** Configure this setting
    to automatically deny elevation requests. (This is the default in the Vista
    Enterprise version.)

✔ **If the user likely needs to perform advanced functions, do the following:**

- *Set this setting to Prompt for Credentials and supply them with the appropriate credentials.* This is the default in the Vista Home version.

- *Educate the user on properly handling those credentials.* Although perhaps not as big an issue at the home or small office as it might be in a larger environment, take this seriously.

Detect Application Installations and Prompt for Elevation

This UAC setting determines behavior of application installation detection for the entire system. Here are the two configurable options for this setting:

✔ **Enabled:** If this setting is selected, any application installation that requires an elevation of privilege to install is detected and prompts the user with the elevation prompt.

By default, this setting is Enabled for the Vista Home version.

✔ **Disabled:** If this setting is selected, any application installation that requires an elevation of privilege isn't detected, and the user isn't be prompted with the elevation prompt.

By default, this setting is Disabled for Vista Enterprise.

Typically, larger environments that use other installation technologies, such as the Microsoft Systems Management Server (SMS) and Group Policy, don't use this feature.

In the right pane of the Local Security Policy (refer to Figure 4-4), selecting the policy that you want to modify brings up the window shown in Figure 4-8.

Many times, malicious programs (such as viruses, Trojans, and spyware) will install programs on your system. When enabled, this setting will alert you that such an installation is occurring and will require some intervention on your part. Specifically, when an installation occurs that requires elevation of privilege so that it can install appropriately, you will be prompted to allow the elevation. Only if you allow the elevation will the installation be able to continue.

Enable this feature if you're in a home or small office and not using any delegated installation technologies, such as Group Police Software Install or SMS.

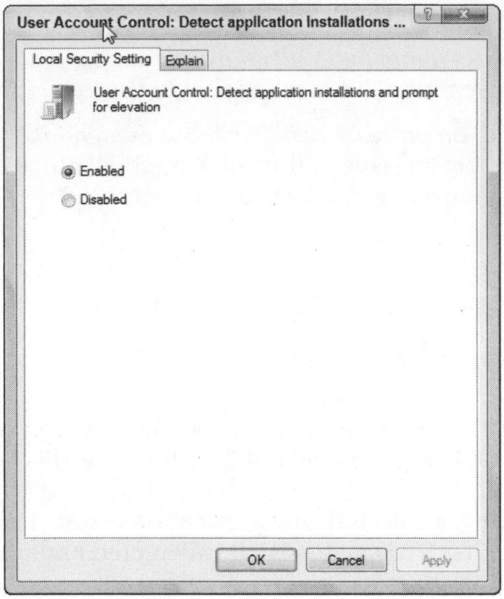

Figure 4-8:
The Detect
Application
Installations
setting.

Only Elevate Executables That Are Signed and Validated

This UAC setting assists in the enforcement of PKI signature checks on any interactive application that requests elevation of privilege.

This allows administrators in a large enterprise environment to control the admin application-allowed list through the population of certificates on the local system.

This setting has two configurable options:

- **Enabled:** If this setting is selected, only signed executables are permitted to run.

  The system validates that PKI certificate chain for an executable.

- **Disabled:** If this setting is selected, both signed and unsigned executables would be run.

  By default, this setting is Disabled.

In the right pane of the Local Security Policy (refer to Figure 4-4), selecting the policy that you want to modify brings up the window shown in Figure 4-9.

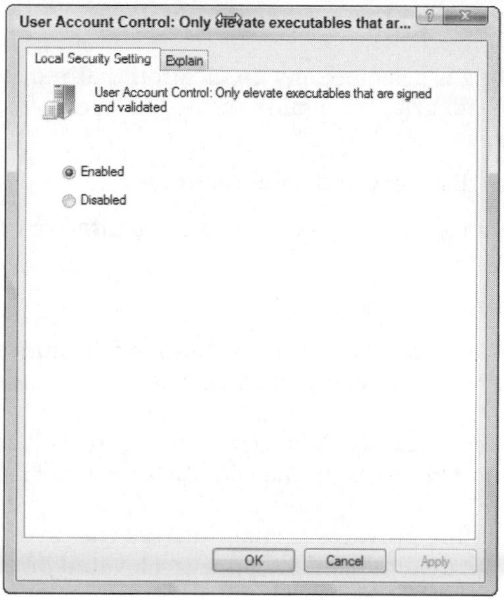

Figure 4-9:
Elevate
Executables
settings.

This setting, if enabled, provides an extra layer of security in that only signed and validated executables will run on your system; this reduces the likelihood of a user running malicious programs. However, enabling this setting can be somewhat limiting because all software is not necessarily signed. For example, I went to the Microsoft Web site and downloaded some third-party Sidebar gadgets. The programs were not signed, so if this setting were enabled, I wouldn't have been able to install them.

The security guy in me recommends that you enable this feature because it provides an extra layer of security. However, enable it only if you can handle the restrictions that it will impose. If you can't — and many won't be able to — keep it disabled and take other precautions, such as

✔ Knowing the source of the application

✔ Scanning the file for viruses, spyware, and other malicious software

Only Elevate UIAccess Applications That Are Installed in Secure Locations

This UAC setting enforces the requirement that applications requesting execution with a UIAccess-integrity level must reside in a secure location on the file system.

The two configurable options for this setting are

- ✔ **Enabled:** If this setting is selected, any application that requests execution with a UIAccess-integrity level must reside in a secure location on the file system, such as

    - `\Program` files directory and subdirectories
    - `\Windows\System32\r-_Program Files` directory and subdirectories

    This setting is Enabled by default.

- ✔ **Disabled:** If this setting is selected, the application will launch with UIAccess integrity even if it doesn't reside in a secure location.

In the right pane of the Local Security Policy (refer to Figure 4-4), selecting the policy that you want to modify brings up the window shown in Figure 4-10.

The security value this setting provides is ensuring that the program isn't modifiable so that it can be manipulated to run with elevated privilege.

This setting is enabled by default. Although it's a very complex security setting, it does protect against malicious software that attempts to run covertly with elevated privilege. Therefore, I recommend leaving this setting enabled.

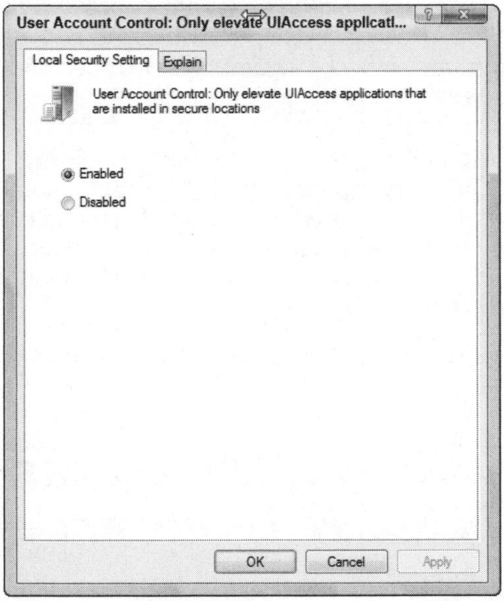

User Account Control: Only elevate UIAccess applicati...

Local Security Setting | Explain

User Account Control: Only elevate UIAccess applications that are installed in secure locations

◉ Enabled
○ Disabled

[OK] [Cancel] [Apply]

Figure 4-10:
Elevate
UIAccess
settings.

Run All Administrators in Admin Approval Mode

This UAC setting determines the behavior of UAC policies for the entire system — and, in particular, if all users (including administrators) are run in the context of a Standard user.

If you disable this setting, you essentially disable UAC for your system.

The two configurable options for this setting are

- ✔ **Enabled:** If this setting is selected, UAC runs all users — including administrators — as Standard users.

  By default, this setting is Enabled.
- ✔ **Disabled:** If this setting is selected, all UAC-related policies are disabled, including Admin Approval mode.

In the right pane of the Local Security Policy (refer to Figure 4-4), selecting the policy that you want to modify brings up the window shown in Figure 4-11.

Keep this setting enabled even if you find UAC a bit intrusive. Disabling this setting significantly reduces the overall security of the OS. If UAC is too annoying, you're better off by modifying other settings to make UAC behavior a little less intrusive than shutting UAC off completely for administrators.

The case for a secure desktop

Many users find switching to Secure Desktop as quite an annoyance that provides little value. Some say that its only purpose is to keep their attention on the elevation prompt so that they must address it. That is part of the reason for this feature, but it's not even nearly the complete picture.

Secure Desktop is meant to prevent anything from running in the background while an elevation prompt is occurring. For example, take a malicious program that tries to impersonate an elevation prompt. Malicious code writers realize that users are tired of the prompt and also that many users will continue with the operation without really even reading the prompt to understand what the operation even is:

- ✔ If a malicious program ran in the background *and* impersonated the elevation prompt *and* this setting was disabled, the user could be tricked into executing an operation within the malicious code.

- ✔ If this setting were enabled, such spoofing could never occur because the user would not be allowed to interact with the fake elevation prompt interface, but would interact with the real UAC interface that is launched during the installation of a program. Although this might seem far-fetched, it could be quite common.

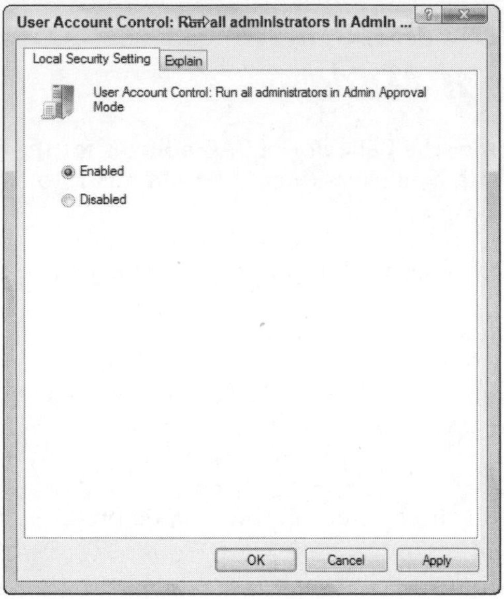

Figure 4-11:
Administra-
tors in
Admin
Approval
mode
settings.

Switch to the Secure Desktop When Prompting for Elevation

This UAC setting is specifically responsible for restricting any access to the desktop when a user is prompted for elevation.

When Secure Desktop is activated, the desktop is dimmed, and users are forced to look at the prompt right before their eyes — and do nothing else but address it.

The two configurable options for this setting are

✔ **Enabled:** If this setting is selected, when a user receives and elevation prompt from UAC, the background is dimmed, and the user is restricted to only the prompt. The user cannot continue to work nor access anything on the desktop.

By default, this setting is set to Enabled.

✔ **Disabled:** If this setting is selected, the user can continue to work even with an elevation prompt from UAC. Users can't perform that function being requesting, but they can interact with the desktop and perform other functions that don't require privilege elevation.

In the right pane of the Local Security Policy (refer to Figure 4-4), selecting the policy that you want to modify brings up the window shown in Figure 4-12.

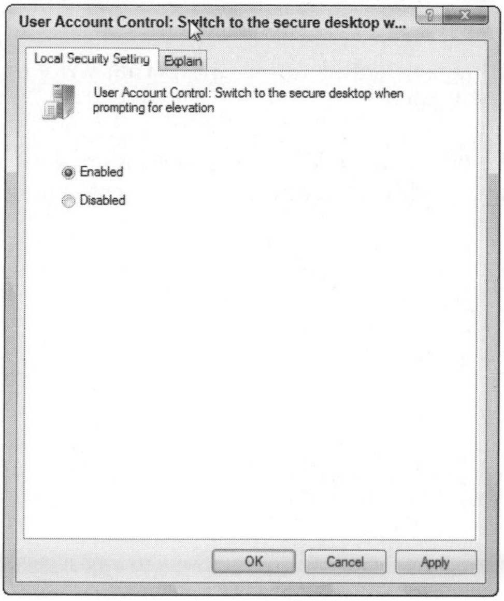

Figure 4-12:
Secure
Desktop
settings.

I recommend enabling this setting. The only downfall is that you can't ignore an elevation prompt and work in the background.

Virtualize File and Registry Write Failures to Per-User Locations

This UAC setting enables redirection of legacy application Write failures to defined locations in both the Registry and file system in an attempt to mitigate older applications that ran as administrator.

This setting controls compatibility for applications that aren't UAC compliant. The application can work without putting the security of the system at risk. When a legacy application attempts to write to a protected directory on the system, this setting forces it to store the virtualization in the user's profile, providing it with some protection from the system and other users so that the application cannot be manipulated in an unsecure way.

The two configurable options for this setting are

✔ **Enabled:** If this setting is selected, the runtime redirection of application Write failures to the defined user locations for both the file system and Registry is enabled.

By default, this setting is Enabled.

✔ **Disabled:** If this setting is selected, applications that write data to the protected locations will fail.

In the right pane of the Local Security Policy (refer to Figure 4-4), selecting the policy that you want to modify brings up the window shown in Figure 4-13.

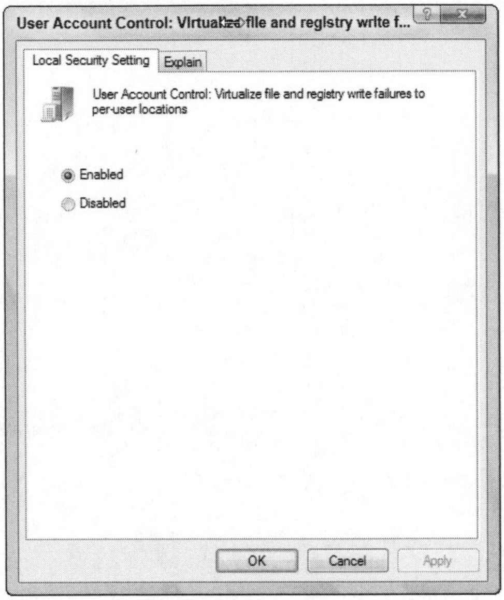

User Account Control: Virtualize file and registry write f...

Local Security Setting | Explain

User Account Control: Virtualize file and registry write failures to per-user locations

⦿ Enabled

◯ Disabled

OK   Cancel   Apply

Figure 4-13:
The virtuali-
zation
settings.

Keep this setting enabled (the default setting). If you disable this setting, legacy applications usually don't work with UAC.

Chapter 5

Protecting Your Data with Rights Management Service

*H*ave you ever sent an e-mail to someone, who then forwarded it to the wrong person? Have you ever backed up confidential financials to a CD or DVD and then lost the disc? Would you like to put a timer on someone's ability to view the confidential information that you send so that after a certain date, it's no longer accessible?

The ability to protect data no longer in your control is something that security people have wanted for a long time. Microsoft responded with *Rights Management Service (RMS)*. The RMS client integrates directly into Vista: If you're part of an RMS infrastructure, your applications can take advantage of this.

In this chapter, I discuss what RMS is and isn't; how RMS works in an environment; and finally, how RMS integrates with Vista applications so you can control how others use your data.

What Is RMS?

Rights Management Service is a back-end solution in Windows that allows you to protect digital information after it's no longer in your control. For example, most people are familiar with a *Portable Document Format (PDF)* file — a protected document created and published with Adobe software. When an author creates a PDF, he decides what the reader can do with the file: reading it, writing to it, and printing it.

If you've ever been frustrated because you weren't allowed to print a document downloaded from the Internet, you can blame the creator of the file. Microsoft RMS takes this basic concept of protecting what a user can do with data and extends it to specify which users can do it and for how long.Rights Management Service provides these capabilities by encrypting the file via a 1024-bit key, and then managing access to the file through eXtensible Rights Markup Language (XRML) certificates and licenses.

Using RMS within Vista requires that your machine is part of an RMS infrastructure and that your user account is a Trusted Entity. A detailed description of the RMS infrastructure is beyond the scope of this book, but you can easily find it at the Microsoft Web site.

Why you might need to use RMS

Rights Management Service provides what Microsoft calls *persistent protection* of electronic data. That is, the protection isn't reliant on the access control permissions that only apply to where the data resides. Instead, the access control for the data is embedded into the file — wherever the file travels, the permissions that you specify travel as well.

Protecting the data at this level means that even if a hacker gets into your system and steals your files, he can't do anything with them unless they can break an encryption scheme that's considered to be unbreakable at this time.

Federal regulations are applicable to certain business segments, such as the Health Insurance Portability and Accessibility Act (HIPAA) for healthcare providers, and Sarbanes-Oxley for financial and accounting disclosures. In addition to these federal regulations, most states have passed laws stating that any information that is personally identifiable to a customer must be kept in encrypted storage. Because violations of these laws and regulations can cost you money, using RMS protection can help.

How RMS client integrates your machine

An RMS infrastructure provides a document author, or anyone assigned sufficient rights through RMS, the ability to manage that document. In this context, the term *document* also refers to e-mail messages. This assignment of rights isn't limited to when you create the document, however.Rights Management Service allows you to manage these rights long after you no longer have direct control of the data itself. To understand why this works, you need to understand how the creation actually occurs:

1. The first time an author protects information, the RMS server provides a client-licensor certificate for the RMS client on a machine.

This only occurs once for a client machine and enables the machine to create RMS-protected data while the machine is offline. This client-licensor certificate is the public part of a public/private encryption key pair.

2. In an RMS-enabled application, an author creates a protected document.

   The author uses the RMS-enabled application as he normally would; however, before he "publishes" the information, the author defines the usage rights and conditions for that document.

3. The RMS-enabled application and the RMS client on the machine create a publishing license for that document and encrypt the file.

4. A user obtains the encrypted data from the author.

   The author can send the encrypted e-mail or put the protected file on a network share. (Or, it could be stolen by someone hacking into the author's system.)

5. The user attempts to open the encrypted data in an RMS-enabled application.

   The RMS-enabled application calls to the RMS server, which validates that the user is a trusted entity and issues a use license for that user. If a user isn't a trusted entity, RMS doesn't issue a use license, and the application can't decrypt the information. The same holds true for trying to open the file in an application that isn't RMS-enabled.

6. The RMS-enabled application decrypts the file and opens it as normal, but enforces the rights and conditions defined in the use license.

   When the user tries to perform some function, such as forwarding an e-mail or editing a Word document, the RMS-enabled application checks the use license before allowing the action. The application also checks whether certain conditions, such as expiration of rights, have occurred; then the application takes the appropriate actions.

RMS management features

RMS administrators can specify some options on the backend that can affect what happens at the client level. These include the following:

- **Rights Policy Templates:** These templates are configured for the document author. The author can select one of the templates when creating the rights assignment. This template assigns the current policy to the document but also passes policy changes to the document user so that the permissioning is consistent.

- **Exclusion Policies:** These policies are implemented on the server to deny license requests by specific users, or even applications. Exclusion policies affect only new requests for use licenses, however.

> ✔ **Revocation Lists:** These lists are distributed to RMS clients when requesting use licenses and invalidate the certificates for the specific user or computer included in the list. This means that no further RMS-related operations could occur for the revoked entity.

Microsoft Office Information Rights Management (IRM) Capabilities

Your next step is to install applications that can use RMS to protect the files that you create from within them. Although any application can become RMS-compliant if the developer integrates the capabilities, RMS is so new that not many programmers outside Microsoft have started to take advantage of it yet. Microsoft, however, has made integration between the Office suite (including Word, Excel, Outlook, and PowerPoint) and RMS a priority.

This integration between RMS and Office is *Information Rights Management (IRM)*. The IRM protections that began with Office 2003 extend into Office 2007. Here's a distinction between RMS and IRM: IRM is available via the Microsoft Passport service even if RMS isn't available (although it's not as robust). IRM allows an author to restrict a user authorized to read a document from performing any or all the following actions:

- ✔ **Forwarding e-mails**
- ✔ **Copying content**
- ✔ **Capturing restricted content through the Windows Print Screen command**

    Third-party screen capture applications will still work.

- ✔ **Modifying content**
- ✔ **Printing**
- ✔ **Faxing**

IRM and Outlook

By far, e-mail is how most information leaks today. People reply to and forward messages without even thinking about the content. In addition, these messages are usually unencrypted and can be intercepted and read by anyone. IRM, within Outlook, attempts to address these issues by integrating RMS protections into your e-mail client.

Outlook allows only for a Do Not Forward policy, which has a blanket permission that prohibits forwarding, printing, or copying a message's content. Outlook integrates the IRM protections on the message itself rather than the MSG version of the file, so the protection is available only within the message. This might not seem like a big deal, but it does affect attachments.

✔ **Attaching a document with a managed file extension:**

- *If the document with a managed file extension isn't already rights-managed,* the protections placed on the e-mail message are added to the document.

- *If the document is already rights-managed,* the protections specified by the author will prevail.

For example, if a user attempts to open a Word document attached to your rights-managed message, Word respects the restrictions placed upon that file.

Table 5-1 lists IRM-managed file types and extensions.

✔ **Attaching a document with an unmanaged file extension:** If you attach a document that isn't managed by IRM (including MSG files), these documents won't have the IRM protections integrated into the document permissions. For example, if a user opens the file within Outlook, he could do whatever he wishes with the data (including forwarding the attached message).

Table 5-1	IRM Managed File Types and Extensions
File Type	**Extension**
Excel macro-enabled add-in	`.xla, .xlam`
Excel macro-enabled template	`.xltm`
Excel macro-enabled workbook	`.xlsm`
Excel non-XML binary workbook	`.xlsb`
Excel template	`.xlt, .xltx`
Excel workbook	`.xls, .xlsx`
Office theme	`.thmx`
PowerPoint macro-enabled presentation	`.pptm`
PowerPoint macro-enabled show	`.ppsm`
PowerPoint macro-enabled template	`.potm`

(continued)

Table 5-1 *(continued)*

File Type	Extension
PowerPoint presentation	`.ppt, .pptx`
PowerPoint show	`.pps, .ppsx`
PowerPoint template	`.pot, .potx`
Word document	`.doc, .docx`
Word macro-enabled document	`.docm`
Word macro-enabled template	`.dotm`
Word template	`.dot, .dotx`
XML paper specification	`.xps`

IRM and documents

Document protection is more robust than what is available for e-mail. Document protection not only allows you to assign different permission levels for the entire document, but it also allows you to assign permissions based on user or groups (if integrated with Active Directory; AD). How you specifically access the permission interface from within your application depends upon the version of Office you're using. However, unlike file permission, you access document protection within the Office application.

Here are the three basic permissions in Office available to an author:

- **Read:** Users assigned this permission can open the document and view it but can't edit, print, or copy it.

- **Change:** Users can view, edit, and save changes to the document but can't print it.

- **Full Control:** Users assigned this permission have all the rights of the original author of the document. This includes being able to set permissions on the file.

In addition to the basic permissions, you can specify other rights and conditions for the file. These include

- **File Expiration Date:** Until the date specified, all users assigned rights can access the file with the permissions specified. After this date, only users with Full Control can open the file.

✔ **Print Content:** All users can print the document. *Note:* In the preceding bullet list, you can read in the basic permissions discussion that users with either Read or Change access aren't allowed to print.

✔ **Allow Users with Read Access to Copy Content:** Users with only Read authority can copy content from the protected document to another source.

✔ **Access Content Programmatically:** This allows programs running under a user's context to access the content of the protected file.

Finally, here are additional management options that you can specify for the file:

✔ **Request Additional Permissions From:** This option allows you to specify an e-mail address (by default, the author's address) for users requesting additional permissions for the file. Requesting additional permissions is an option presented to the user via each Office application.

✔ **Allow or Deny Read Permissions from Earlier Versions of Office:** This option allows you to specify whether the file should include additional information that allows users who don't have RMS-enabled versions of Office to view the file through a browser.

✔ **Require a Connection to Verify a User's Permission:** By default, the RMS-enabled application checks for the use license only the first time when a user opens the file. Requiring a connection to verify a user's permission checks for the use license each time a user attempts to access the file.

Rights Management add-on for Internet Explorer

The Rights Management add-on for Internet Explorer (IE) provides a way for users to view rights-enabled documents through a Web browser. If the author allows this on a particular file, a rights-managed HTML version of the document is embedded into the full document itself. The rights specified within the permissions of the file are still applicable to either the standard or HTML version of the document.

To access the rights-enabled document, point your browser to the path of the document. Naturally, your browser opens the HTML version of the document. Similarly, the Rights Management add-on for IE is also required if you use Outlook Web-Access (OWA) to access RMS-protected e-mail across the Web.

Digital Rights Management (DRM) versus RMS

Digital Rights Management is a way to protect commercial, copyrighted digital media, such as music or video. Specified by industry groups, and supported by Microsoft, this technology is a way to protect commercial revenue streams against piracy. Because RMS also allows authors to place protections on digital information, they're similar in nature — but not the same.

RMS is an enterprise rights-management solution for data contained in all kinds of documents. RMS uses an RMS server infrastructure (along with other Windows server technologies, such as AD) to provide support of a protection scheme that can differentiate between authorized and unauthorized users. However, DRM doesn't allow this kind of protection scheme and is generally not specified from within your environment.

Drawbacks to RMS

RMS provides some very promising capabilities that allow you to protect your data regardless of where it travels. However, RMS isn't a perfect technology, and you should understand its weaknesses before attempting to use it.

- ✔ **RMS requires significant back-end capabilities.** To implement it correctly, an RMS infrastructure requires a significant amount of planning; several servers; and possibly, integration with an AD structure.

- ✔ **The ability to read the file is dependent upon at least one connection with the proper RMS infrastructure.** If you're sending a rights-enabled document to someone who isn't in your network, you must provide that person with network access (usually over the Internet) to an RMS server. Otherwise, the receiver won't be able to open the document.

- ✔ **Managing permissions at low levels can be complicated.** You can address this somewhat by using templates, but you still must design a template flexible enough to provide protection but still allow access to those who need it.

- ✔ **Very little adoption of the RMS technology by vendors is currently available.** Other than Microsoft, very few software companies have bought into RMS; therefore, not many RMS enabled applications are available.

Chapter 6

Managing Accounts, Groups, and Shares

Although many other features are sexier, setting up user accounts, security groups, and data shares are three of the most common tasks performed by someone managing security on a Vista system. This is true regardless of which version of Vista you use and whether you're a home user or part of a larger corporate infrastructure. *Accounts* represent the people who use the system. *Groups* are how you set most permissions within the system to those accounts. And *sharing* is how most of those permissions provide value by securing data accessed from outside the system.

In this chapter, you see how to provide access to data through sharing as well as how to create and manage the underlying building blocks that allow you to control that access in a secure way.

The Vista Identity Model

The Vista identity model includes two major pieces: identification and authentication, which are actually very simple concepts:

  ✔ **Identification** is how the computer knows who you are. You achieve this through creating an account and assigning it a friendly username.

  ✔ **Authentication,** on the other hand, is how the computer ensures that you are who you say you are. You achieve this by assigning something to the user account to prove your identity to the computer. This can involve using something as simple as a password or something more complex, such as a fingerprint reader.

After you identify yourself to Vista and it accepts whatever you present to authenticate yourself, Vista can create your user session properly. Your user session includes such items as your preferences for the general appearance of the computer (your desktop and screen saver), which folder shows as Documents for you, and maybe even which programs start automatically.

The identity model, however, goes beyond your choices of whether your computer just dings at you when you do something wrong, or has Homer Simpson exclaiming, "D'oh!!!" Your identity also determines what Vista allows you to do on the computer — and possibly other computers — from a security perspective.

Your identity was established when you initially logged on to Vista, but the operating system (OS) itself has an identity named Local System that it uses to perform its internal tasks. In addition, other programs can be set to use different identities based on how they start. Understanding the identity under which an action takes place — *user context* — is very important when trying to manage security for your Vista machine.

You can change the user context for the programs you start. This concept is the basis for both Run as Administrator and User Account Control (UAC). (See Chapter 4 for a detailed explanation of the latter.) This choice enables you to use a different identity that allows you to perform actions that you normally wouldn't have the rights or permission to do.

Managing Accounts and Groups within Vista

You create accounts within Vista to establish an identity that you, or someone else, can use. However, performing actions within Vista is based on whether an account has the proper permissions. This is true whether you want to look at a picture, install software, or even log on.

When you create an account, Vista automatically adds it to the Users group. This provides the new identity with the ability to perform all actions that a normal user needs in his day-to-day use of Vista. When you choose to change the account type for the account to be an administrator, Vista removes the account from the Users group and adds it to the Administrators group, behind the scenes.

Built-in groups, known as *special identities,* include Authenticated Users and Everyone. Vista dynamically assigns these group memberships to an account when it first accesses the system based on parameters, such as if that account were authenticated or whether the account is accessing Vista locally or via the network. You can't add users to these special groups; however, you can use these groups to assign permissions to those types of accounts.

Although Vista has built-in groups that have rights and permissions assigned to them, you're not limited to using only the groups that come with Vista. For example, if you need to provide additional authority to an account but you don't want to provide all the privileges of an administrator, you can create a new group and then assign the advanced right or permission to that group. After this is completed, you provide the permissions to the account by adding it to the group.

Vista requires that you use an administrator-level account to add or modify user accounts or groups.

Vista Built-in Accounts and Groups

Vista comes with many user and group accounts that are predefined for its usage or yours. These built-in accounts, groups, and special identities generally preclude you from having to create anything other than your own account for Vista to work. Therefore, understanding each of these is extremely helpful for you when managing the security for your Vista computer. The following sections define some of the built-in accounts and groups and what they're designed for.

The following sections don't cover all the Vista built-in accounts, groups, and special identities. However, these that I cover are the ones that will be relevant to you when dealing with Vista security. For the complete list, open the Local Users and Groups MMC interface by choosing Start and then typing `lusmgr.msc` into the Search field. Information on the other accounts, groups, and special identities not listed here are available at the Microsoft Web site.

Administrator

Administrator is a built-in account that is part of the Administrators group. Using this account is unnecessary as long as you have at least one other account with Administrators group membership on the machine. Vista makes the first account you give it part of that group, so the built-in Administrator account is disabled by default.

The names Administrator and Administrators can get very confusing because they're so similar:

- **Administrators** is the name of the group that's provided all the rights necessary to manage your machine by Vista.
- **Administrator** is the default name of the built-in account that is part of the Administrators group.

To clear up this confusion, the name of the Administrator account can be changed without causing any issues. This is actually a security best practice.

Administrators

Administrators is a group with administrative rights to the machine. When you change a user from a standard to an administrator account, Vista adds that account to the Administrators group.

ANONYMOUS LOGON

ANONYMOUS LOGON is a special identity provided to anyone who has access to the system but doesn't authenticate in any way. This group is the only one that isn't included in the Everyone group. Therefore, you must explicitly assign permissions to this group for a resource (such as a file or a folder) if you need to allow this type of access to the resource.

Backup Operators

Backup Operators is a group with special permissions to Read/Write to files and folders even if they don't have those permissions assigned in the NT File System (NTFS) security of the file or folder. Use this group to assign all permissions necessary for any user or process that needs to perform backup or restore operations but that does not have Administrator privileges. For more information about Backup and Restore, see Chapter 8.

BATCH

BATCH is a special identity that includes any account that logs on through some batch process, such as the scheduled tasks. Use this group to assign permissions to resources for the group of accounts that run through some batch utility.

Event Log Readers

Event Log Readers is a group that provides permissions to view all event logs, including the security log. By default, Standard users can look at most of the logs through the Event Viewer. However, some logs are considered to have privileged data, so you need to be an Administrator to view them. However, you can use this group to assign the ability to view this data to non-Administrators.

Everyone

Everyone is a special identity provided to any account other than those who access the system through an anonymous logon. This group includes both the Authenticated Users group and the Guest account but not those users who log on anonymously.

I recommend that you use the Authenticated Users group rather than Everyone when you need to assign a permission to all users of the machine unless you specifically need to allow the Guest account to have access.

Guest

Guest is a built-in account used to provide someone without permissions on the machine the ability to log on and access resources. Microsoft specially crafted the Guest account to provide access that's more restricted than what a Standard user has. Enabling/disabling the account is controlled by the Password Protected Sharing setting within the Network and Sharing Center of Control Panel.

IIS_IUSRS

IIS_IUSRS is a group used to provide permissions to accounts used by Web pages within IIS. The IUSR built-in account is included in this group by default. However, you can choose to use accounts that you create to provide authority for IIS and add them to this group.

INTERACTIVE

INTERACTIVE is a special identity that includes any account that is logged on either directly to the machine or through a remote desktop connection. You can use this group to assign permissions to any user who has a desktop instead of any account that is allowed to access the resource through the network. This group is the opposite of the NETWORK special identity.

IUSR

IUSR is a built-in account that doesn't show when looking at the account interfaces, but Vista uses it to provide access when you choose to allow anonymous access to Web pages you publish through IIS. Some Microsoft documentation actually calls this account IIS_IUSR, but it shows as just IUSR within Vista.

LOCAL SERVICE

LOCAL SERVICE is a special identity that includes any service set to run as a Local Service. By default, this group provides the same access as the users group. You can use this group to assign permissions to the group of services that run as a Local Service. For more information about Local Service and when it's used, see Chapter 16.

NETWORK

NETWORK is a special identity that includes any account that accesses Vista resources over the network (other than via a remote desktop connection). You can use this group to assign permissions to any user who would access a resource (such as a file on a share) from another computer but not actually have a desktop session with yours. This group is the opposite of the INTERACTIVE special identity.

Network Configuration Operators

Network Configuration Operators is a group with special privileges in relation to networking within Vista. Use this group to manage the configuration of networking features to Standard User accounts.

NETWORK SERVICE

NETWORK SERVICE is a special identity that includes any service set to run as a Network Service. By default, this group provides the same access as the users group. Use this group to assign permissions to the group of services that run as a Network Service.

Performance Log Users

Performance Log Users is a group with special privileges in relation to the Vista Windows Reliability and Performance Monitor. Membership in this group specifically allows you to view real-time data in Performance Monitor, change the display properties while viewing real-time data, and create and modify Data Collector Sets. Use this group to assign these capabilities to Standard User accounts. However, you must add this group to the logon as a batch-job user right within security policy before any newly created Data Collector Sets will run. (See Chapter 16 for details on working with security policies.)

Performance Monitor Users

Performance Monitor Users is a group with special privileges in relation to the Vista Windows Reliability and Performance Monitor. Membership in this group specifically allows you to view real-time data in Performance Monitor as well as change the display properties while doing so. Use this group to assign these capabilities to Standard User accounts.

SERVICE

SERVICE is a special identity that includes any service set to run as a Service. By default, this group provides the same access as the Users group. Use this group to assign permissions to the group of services that run as a Service. For more information about Service and when it's used, see Chapter 16.

SYSTEM

SYSTEM is a special identity that is the Vista OS itself. By default, this group has all the permissions that the OS needs. However, if you lock down the system by removing permissions from other special identities or groups, you might need to add permissions directly to System.

Users

Users is a group for Standard User accounts. Vista places all new accounts in the users group and keeps them there unless you change the account type to Administrator.

Creating and Disabling User Accounts

A user account represents the identity portion of the Vista identity model and each person who uses a machine should have a separate user account. From a general perspective, this allows each person to have his own desktop and preferences. However, having each person assigned a user account is even more critical when it comes to the security of the system because Vista relies on the identity of the logged-in user to determine exactly what that person is allowed to do on the system.

Creating a user account and password

User accounts can be created through the User Accounts tool in Control Panel, the Local Users and Groups Microsoft Management Console (MMC), or even programmatically. The following are instructions for using the User Accounts tool available in all versions of Vista. (For more on MMC, see the sidebar, "User Management options: It all depends.")

1. **Open the User Accounts interface (as shown in Figure 6-1) by clicking the Add or Remove User Accounts link in the User Accounts and Family Safety area of Control Panel.**

2. **Click the Create a New Account link.**

3. **In the New Account Name text box (see Figure 6-2), type the username you wish to use and then choose the account type for the new account.**

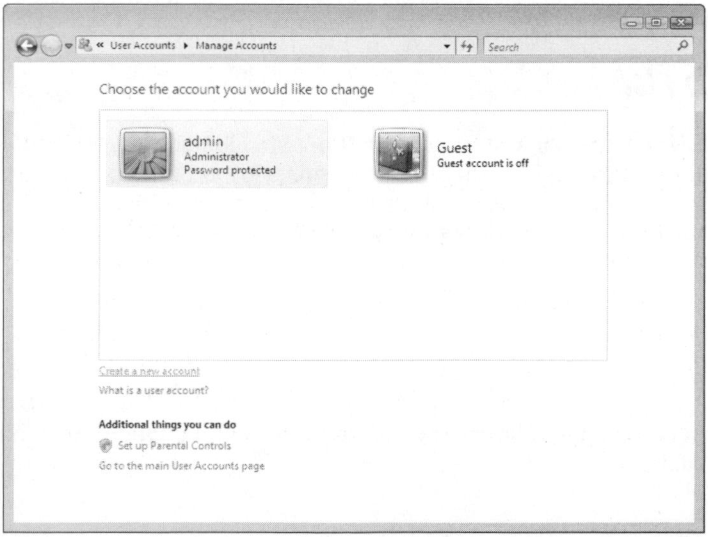

Figure 6-1:
The
Manage
Accounts
interface.

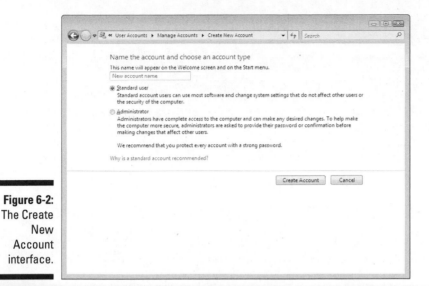

Figure 6-2:
The Create
New
Account
interface.

By default, the new account is a Standard user unless you select the Administrator radio button. See Chapter 4 for more information about Administrator and Standard User accounts.

4. Click the Create Account button.

Vista creates the account, but it creates it *without a password regardless of the security policy of the machine.* Continue these steps to add a password to the account.

5. Double-click the account that you just created.

This brings up the Change an Account screen (see Figure 6-3), which allows you to create a password for the account (along with many other things).

6. Click the Create a Password link.

7. In the New Password text box, type the password you want to create.

8. Retype the same password in the Confirm New Password text box.

9. (Optional) Create a password hint to help you remember the password you just created by using the Type a Password Hint text box.

If you do create a password hint, keep in mind that anyone can view this hint through the logon screen because (after all) it is there to help you remember your password. Therefore, having a hint might help someone else guess your account password — and hurt you.

10. Click the Create Password button.

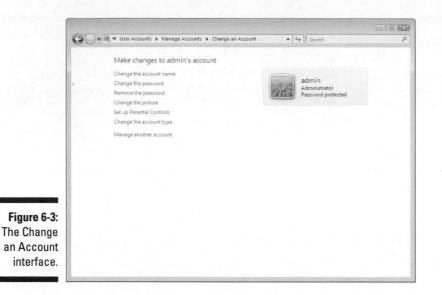

Figure 6-3:
The Change
an Account
interface.

Disabling/re-enabling a user account

One advanced option available only through the Local Users and Groups MMC snap-in is the ability to disable an account. This interface isn't available on the Starter, Home Basic, or Home Premium versions of Vista, however. Disabling an account means that although it can't be used for access, it still exists and can be re-enabled for use if you want. To disable an account, follow these steps:

1. **Open the Local Users and Groups Microsoft Management Console by typing** lusrmgr.msc **into the Search field.**

2. **Click the Users folder in the left pane of the interface.**

   This displays the list of users available for you to manage on the computer.

3. **Double-click the user that you want to disable.**

4. **Select the Account is Disabled check box.**

   The account is disabled.

When you want to re-enable the account, follow the same procedure but remove the check from the Account is Disabled check box.

Using the Select Objects Interface

The Select Objects interface is one that you will use over and over while managing Vista. Whenever you need to pick an account or a group as part of

User Management options: It all depends

The available User Management options all depend upon your Vista version. Some versions of Vista come with more features and functionality. This is especially true in managing the security in regards to users and groups. In the Starter, Home Basic, and Home Premium versions, the only interface you can use to create accounts is the User Accounts tool within Control Panel.

This tool allows you to create user accounts and change the account type from Standard user to Administrator (which adds the user account to the Administrators group in the background). In other versions of Vista, you can use the Local Users and Groups snap-in of the Microsoft Management Console (MMC) for all account- and group-related activities.

The MMC-based interface provides you with more options for managing both the user

accounts themselves and assigning access to resources for the users. This includes

✔ **Disabling an account**

✔ **Disabling the ability for the user of the account to change the password**

✔ **Setting a password to never expire**

  This overrides any security policy setting about password expiration.

✔ **Assigning a logon script, user profile, or home directory to a user account**

✔ **Creating new groups**

✔ **Assigning or deleting a user account to/from a group**

✔ **Assigning or deleting a group to/from another group**

performing an action (such as adding a user to a group), Vista directs you to this interface to perform the action.

The standard screen for this interface allows you to assign an object or objects if you know the exact names. However, if you don't know the exact name of an object, an advanced screen is available by clicking the Advanced button. This allows you to pick the object or objects from a list. Figure 6-4 shows the standard screen for selecting users, and Figure 6-5 shows the advanced.

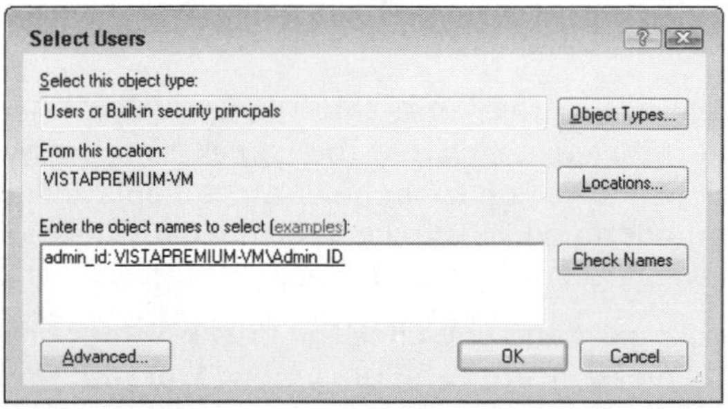

Figure 6-4: The standard Select Objects interface.

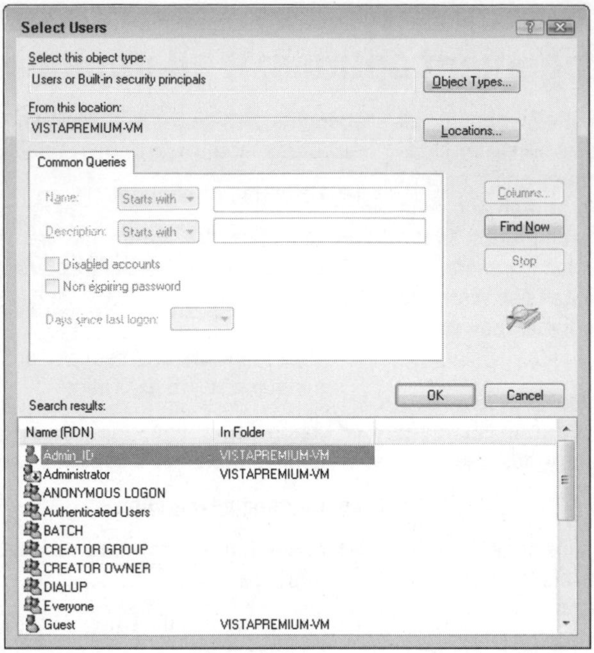

Figure 6-5:
The
Advanced
Select
Groups
interface.

Here are the elements in the standard window:

- **Select This Object Type:** This area shows the types of objects that the Select Users screen queries to confirm the name of the object you pick. In general, you don't need to use this in your work within Vista, but it could come in handy if you're trying to pick an object from a large domain.

- **From This Location:** This area shows the location where the object resides. By default, this shows the name of the computer that you're on.

- **Enter the Object Names to Select:** In this text field, type the name of the object that you want to pick. The entry for Admin_ID, as shown in this area in Figure 6-4, shows how the name of a user account can be entered.

  To pick multiple objects at the same time, separate each name with a semicolon (;).

- **Check Names:** After you enter names into the Enter the Object Names to Select text field, you can check that the names are valid by clicking this button. After Windows confirms the entry, it displays with the location context, underlined, as shown in Figure 6-4. (Look for the VISTAPREMIUM-VM\Admin_ID result there.)

  If the object doesn't exist and you click the Check Names button, a Name Not Found pop-up message appears, presenting you with the options of rechecking after changing the object type, location, or name you entered.

Here are the features available (as shown in Figure 6-5) after you click the Advanced button in the Select Objects window:

- ✔ **Select This Object Type:** This is as the same as the standard screen.

- ✔ **From This Location:** This is the same as the standard screen.

- ✔ **Find Now:** Clicking this button populates the Search Results section of the screen by starting the query of the Location for the information specified in the object types, common queries, and columns areas.

- ✔ **Search Results:** This area shows the results of the query for objects. Here, choose which objects you want to add to the Enter the Object Names to Select text field in the standard screen.

  - *To choose a single object,* simply double-click it. This takes you from the advanced screen and populates the standard screen with your choice.

  - *To choose multiple objects,* click the first object and then use the Ctrl or Shift keys in conjunction with the mouse to select others (the same as with most Windows interfaces).

In both windows, the OK and the Cancel buttons work pretty much like you expect:

- ✔ **OK:** Clicking this button applies the objects that you listed in the Enter the Object Names to Select text field. Windows checks to make sure that all objects are valid and then exits the interface.

  If the object doesn't exist when you check for it, a Name Not Found pop-up appears (see Figure 6-6) that presents you with the options of rechecking after changing the object type, location, or name you entered. You can also remove the object name from the list and move on.

- ✔ **Cancel:** Clicking this button exits the interface without applying the objects.

Figure 6-6: The Name Not Found dialog box.

Name Not Found

An object named "MissingUser" cannot be found. Check the selected object types and location for accuracy and ensure that you typed the object name correctly, or remove this object from the selection.

◉ Correct this object information and search again

Select this object type:
Users or Built-in security principals | Object Types...

From this location:
ADMIN-PC | Locations...

Enter the object name:
MissingUser

○ Remove "MissingUser" from selection

OK | Cancel

Creating Groups and Assigning Users

You can create groups through the Local Users and Groups MMC snap-in or programmatically. Unfortunately, this interface is not available on the Starter, Home Basic, or Home Premium versions of Vista. The following are instructions for using the MMC to create a group:

1. **Open the Local Users and Groups Microsoft Management Console by typing** lusrmgr.msc **into the Search field.**

2. **Click the Groups folder in the left pane of the interface.**

   After clicking the Groups folder, the interface should appear like the interface in Figure 6-7.

3. **Right-click the middle pane of the interface and then choose New Group from the contextual menu that appears.**

Figure 6-7:
The Local
Users and
Groups
MMC,
showing the
Groups
interface.

4. **In the Group Name text box of the New Group window that appears (see Figure 6-8), type the name you want to assign.**

5. **(Optional) Add an explanation of the purpose and composition of the group in the Description text field.**

Filling out the Description field isn't a requirement for creating a group. This option is intended only to provide you with a place to store details about the group that you create. However, I recommend that you take advantage of this text field whenever you create a new group so that you can always keep track of why you created this group in the first place and what it's used for.

New Group

Group name:

Description:

Members:

Add...   Remove

Help   Create   Close

Figure 6-8:
The New
Group
dialog box.

6. **Open the Select Users Interface to select the users or groups you want to add.**

   For more information on this interface, see the earlier section, "Using the Select Objects Interface."

   There is no practical limit to the number of accounts that can belong to a group or the number of groups that an account can be a part of. However, the more complicated your security structure is, the more difficult it is to manage.

7. **Click the Create button to create the group.**

   If you want to create more groups, repeat Steps 3–7 in the New Group interface. Otherwise, click Close.

Although the instructions I give here are only for the creation of a new group, you can use the Local Users and Groups MMC snap-in for all account and group management activities in the versions in which it's available. This includes, but is not limited to

   ✔ Adding or deleting groups or user accounts

   ✔ Managing group membership on existing groups or accounts

   ✔ Password management for any account on the machine

The Vista Access Control Model

Within Vista are two main components to the access control infrastructure. They are based on security settings that

- Apply to the entire computer
- Are directly applied to each individual object that you access

System and object-level security settings are the "locks" that Vista uses to keep your computer secure.

Each user carries a set of "keys" — a *token* — that tells Vista whether that user is allowed to perform whatever action he is attempting.

Vista compares the token of the user with the list of users/groups allowed to perform the action. If the user has the proper authority, Vista performs the action. If not, Vista either rejects the request or asks for a username and password that does. Which action Vista takes depends upon the settings for UAC. (For more information on User Account Control, see Chapter 4.)

System security settings

User rights control which groups of users that Vista allows to perform different functions with regard to the system security settings. You assign user rights to accounts or groups as part of the security policy that is applied to the computer. (For more information on security policy, including how to change settings, see Chapter 16.)

Changing the default user rights on the computer is something that you should generally avoid because the default assignment of user rights is one of the ways how Vista separates a user account type from the Administrator(s). However, assigning a user right to a group you create, or the general users, might be something that you want to change to solve a specific problem without having to provide administrative-level privileges to that group or user. Examples of when this may be useful would be to allow certain programs to run or to allow a Standard user to look at security logs.

Object-level security

An *object* is any item on the computer that you, a program, or Vista itself might try to access. These include (but are not be limited to) items such as files, folders, printers, shares, Registry keys, services, and processes. Object-level security is stored against the object within an area known as the *security descriptor*. Vista's security subsystem checks these settings to understand whether to allow a user access to the object. Object-level security usually can be managed through an access-control user interface although this isn't always the case, depending upon the object type.

Allowing Access to Data through Sharing

Vista allows you to share files (through either the Public folder or through sharing a specific folder that you choose) with people on other computers. Although these are great features if you need them, the most secure way to protect your computer (with regard to sharing) is to leave these features turned off. Using a wall — always more secure than a door — makes it much harder to get to what's on the other side.

Vista uses its Network and Sharing Center interface (see Figure 6-9) inside Control Panel to manage all the system settings related to its sharing features. You can find all the sharing controls in this screen within the Sharing and Discovery section. In line with each feature is an On/Off indicator (showing the status) as well as a button with a down arrow. To view or change the settings of a feature, click the corresponding down arrow to expand the section.

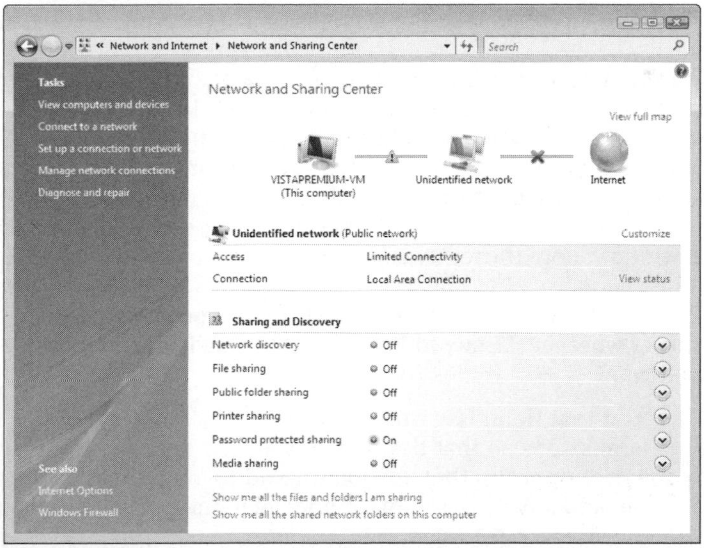

Figure 6-9:
The Network and Sharing Center default configuration.

File sharing

The file-sharing feature allows you to create share points at any folder within your file system so that users, on other computers, can access that folder and all the files underneath it from their computer. According to Microsoft documentation, this feature is available on all versions of Vista except Starter.

The setting for File Sharing within the Network and Sharing Center interface (refer to Figure 6-9) is a system-wide setting that controls whether you're allowed to "publish" these shares so that other systems can see them. However, the setting itself doesn't actually create a share. After you turn on file sharing for the computer through the Network and Sharing Center, you can share any folder as long as you have access to an administrative-level account.

Sharing is an Administrator function, even if you have full control of the folder.

Using a wizard to manage file sharing

The File Sharing Wizard actively manages the security of both the share and NTFS permissions on the folder. Therefore, changes made in this interface affect both sets of permissions rather than just the share permissions, even if you initially set the NTFS permissions through a different interface. For most people, the File Sharing Wizard provides everything necessary to manage sharing your data on the network. However, an advanced interface is available from which you can manage the permissions separately, if you want.

The following describes both how to create a share by using the wizard as well as the interface itself. First, right-click the folder you want to share and choose Share. Alternatively, you can choose Properties, click the Sharing tab, and then click the Share button. Either method brings up an interface similar to that shown in Figure 6-10.

In this window, note these items:

- ✔ **Password-protection statement:** This statement at the top of the screen shows whether Password-Protected Sharing is enabled or not for the machine.

- ✔ **The Add text field:** Use this text box to pick users or groups to add to the permissions so that they can access the share. If you know the name of the user or group that you want to add, you can type it into the field. You can add any user, group, or special identity through this method.

    For more information about the default users, groups, and special identities you can use, see the earlier section, "Vista Built-in Accounts and Groups."

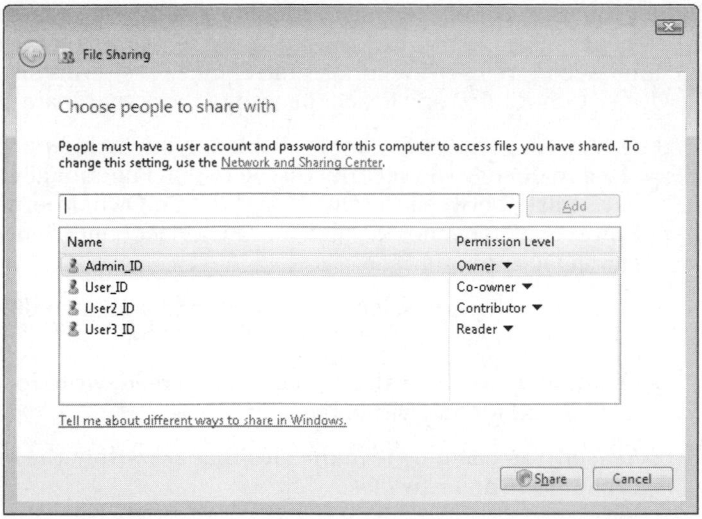

Figure 6-10:
The File
Sharing
Wizard.

✔ **The Add text field drop-down arrow:** Click the arrow next to the Add button to pull up the list of all the user accounts that you (or another Administrator-level person) created on the machine, along with the Everyone group and a choice to create a new user.

  • *Choosing any user account or the Everyone group* populates that choice into the text box.

  • *Choosing to create a new user* closes the interface and takes you to the account properties page for your own account.

✔ **The Add button:** Click this button to add whatever is in the text box to the security of the share. If the account/group doesn't exist, or if you mistype the name, a pop-up message appears to tell you that Vista cannot locate the user — in which case, you are returned to the screen where you can edit the text box again.

✔ **The name section:** When creating the share, Vista automatically populates this area with

  • *The name of the account* that you're using to create the share

  • *Any account that would show up* within the drop-down arrow box that already has NTFS permissions to the folder

For example, Figure 6-10 shows four accounts. Admin_ID is the account that I used to create the share; and User_ID, User2_ID, and User3_ID all had NTFS permissions on the folder prior to trying to create the share. The Users and Administrators groups also had NTFS permissions on the folder but were not pulled into the list because they're not user accounts that I (or another Administrator) created on the machine.

✔ **The Permission Level column:** This column shows and controls the types of permissions that are set for the share. Microsoft tried to make the interface more user friendly, so the choices are terms such as Owner, Co-Owner, Contributor, and Reader instead of the actual share permissions.

- *Owner:* All permissions are available to you, including the permissions to change the security on the folder. Functionally, no difference exists between the Owner and the Co-Owner permissions. However, you cannot manage the Owner account from within the sharing wizard interface.

- *Co-Owner:* All permissions are available to you, including the permissions to change the security on the folder.

- *Contributor:* You have the permissions to read, write to, and delete all files and folders within the share.

- *Reader:* You can only read the files that are within the share: You cannot save any new files.

Table 6-1 shows the four different terms, what they actually mean for a user, and how they translate to both Share and NTFS permissions.

You can change the permission level assigned to an account by clicking anywhere in line with the name or permission level. This highlights the user or group and also brings up a menu to the right of the column that shows the available permission levels with a check mark next to the current selection as well as the choice to remove.

✔ **The Share button:** This is the Save button for the interface.

✔ **The Cancel button:** Clicking this cancels the interface without creating the share or changing the permissions, depending upon which you were trying to do.

Table 6-1	Share Wizard Permission Levels	
Permission Level	*Share Permission*	*NTFS Permission*
Owner	Full Control	Full Control
Co-Owner	Full Control	Full Control
Contributor	Change	Modify
Reader	Read	Read & Execute

Next, assign the users or groups that you want to have access through the interface. After you make the assignments, click the Share button to have Vista create the share and assign both the Share and NTFS permissions that you specify.

If UAC is active on the machine, a pop-up message appears. Click Continue or enter a username and password with Administrator rights in the pop-up message. The file sharing window states that it is sharing items, which could take a few minutes. After the file is created, the file sharing window shows that that the folder is shared. Then you can copy or e-mail the path of the share so that you can provide it to others.

After you create the share, you might want to manage it at some point. Bring up the interface the same way, and it presents a screen that allows you to choose whether to change sharing permissions or stop sharing. If you choose to change sharing permissions, Vista presents you with the same interface that it did when you first created the share (refer to Figure 6-10). If you choose to stop sharing, Vista deletes the share.

Public folder sharing

The Vista Public folder is Microsoft's latest attempt to make sharing of files between users on a single computer, or across a network, as simple as possible for the nontechnical user. Unfortunately, Microsoft did a very poor job with this from a security perspective.

I recommend that you actively set up the share on the Public folder and define the security for yourself through file sharing rather than using this option (unless you are using the starter version of Vista, where this is your only option for sharing, according to Microsoft documentation).

Password-protected sharing

The Password Protected Sharing option within the Network and Sharing Center interface determines whether a user must authenticate to your machine to access resources across the network or whether he can access those resources by using permissions that you assign to Everyone or Guest. In the background, the basis for this decision is whether the Guest built-in account is enabled or disabled within your machine. Turning on the password-protected sharing option disables the Guest account, whereas turning it off enables it.

File or printer sharing and firewalls

When you enable file or printer sharing (including both file sharing and public folder sharing), Vista might pop up a message asking whether you want to enable file sharing for a public or for only a private network. Vista asks this question to correctly set the Firewall rules related to file and printer sharing. This is a relatively straightforward question if you're in a network at home or in a small office. In those cases, Vista wants to know whether you want people outside your home or office — such as people on the Internet — to be able to get files you choose to share. If not, you should choose to share only to the private network.

Unfortunately, some people have more complicated networks set up within their home or office environment. In those cases, the answer to this seemingly simple question is actually complicated. When you choose the private network from this pop-up message, Vista sets its Firewall rules related to file sharing to allow access only from the local subnet. Vista considers anything outside the local subnet as public, in terms of answering this question. Therefore, even if you're on a private network, if you have a router between yourself and the other computers that you want to share the files with, you need to choose to share it "publicly" from the pop-up message in order for Vista to establish Firewall rules properly.

If you need further explanation of Firewall rules and subnetting, see Chapter 11. However, if you're the person who set up your network and this last paragraph totally confused you, there is a 99.867 percent chance that none of what I just explained applies to your situation.

If you chose not to use Windows Firewall that comes with Vista, you need to manually change the settings within your firewall to allow the traffic to pass. (This is true even with other Microsoft products, such as Windows Live OneCare.) To emulate Windows Firewall settings, set your firewall to allow inbound Transmission Control Protocol (TCP) and User Datagram Protocol (UDP) connections on the following ports:

- UDP 137
- UDP 138
- TCP 139
- TCP 445

Finally, one piece of good news is that because Vista integrates the sharing settings with Windows Firewall, it automatically removes these rules from the firewall if you decide to stop sharing at some point in the future.

Chapter 7

Advanced Techniques for Managing Access

● ●

In This Chapter

▶ Understanding how Vista determines whether you have access to an object

▶ Managing NT File System (NTFS) permissions through standard and advanced interfaces

▶ Using the Regedit tool to secure your system

▶ Defining audit and event log policies

▶ Tips on defining object auditing for files, folders, Registry keys, and services

● ●

Microsoft has done its best to make Vista as secure as possible without compromising the ease of use that has made Windows so popular. One of the ways how Microsoft provides this ease of use is by not requiring you to understand all the complicated mechanisms for setting access control on your system. However, access control to different areas of Vista is a powerful tool that can help you secure your system — if you use it properly.

In this chapter, I discuss the fundamental concept of objects and their security mechanisms. Then, I show you how to protect your machine through NTFS permissions, the Registry, and auditing. A lot of information in this chapter is meant for those readers interested in the more advanced how-and-why of the Vista security system. This chapter goes into some advanced and complicated concepts that general readers might not be interested in.

Managing Object-Level Security

An *object* is any item on the computer that you, a program, or Vista itself might try to access. Objects include (but are not be limited to) items such as files, folders, printers, shares, Registry keys, services, and processes. Each object within the Vista operating system (OS) has a security structure attached to it. The settings in this structure tell Vista who the owner of the object is, which users and groups are allowed or denied access to the object, and whether Vista should create a record in the Security Event log based on the attempt to access the object. The storage structure for these settings is the *security descriptor*.

During object creation, the user performing the action is entered into the security descriptor as the *owner*. This is a special designation because it allows that user to manage permissions of an object even if he doesn't have any permissions specifically assigned to that object. You can change the owner of an object after creation if you have the Take Ownership permission on the file. This is usually only provided to you if you have Full Control permission over the object, however.

Another area of the security descriptor is a listing of the users or groups that have permissions on the file. This list is the *Discretionary Access Control List* (DACL), which functions as the lock in lock-and-key security system of Vista. Each DACL comprises a set of *Access Control Entries* (ACEs) that specify a set of permissions assigned to a single user or group.

You can view these individual ACEs by following these steps:

1. **Right-click the object for which you want to see the ACEs.**

2. **Choose Properties.**

3. **Click the Security tab.**

4. **Click the Advanced button.**

   This view shows the individual ACEs that make up the DACL for an object. Figure 7-1 is an example of the DACL for a folder named Example Folder.

Figure 7-1: The Advanced Security Settings for Example Folder.

Advanced Security Settings for Example Folder

Permissions

To view or edit details for a permission entry, select the entry and then click Edit.

Object name: C:\Example Folder

Permission entries:

Type	Name	Permission	Inherited From	Apply To
Allow	Marketing (ADMIN-PC\M...	Full control	<not inherited>	This folder, subfolders a...
Allow	Security Admins (ADMIN...	Take ownership	<not inherited>	This folder, subfolders a...
Allow	Administrators (admin-P...	Full control	C:\	This folder, subfolders a...
Allow	SYSTEM	Full control	C:\	This folder, subfolders a...
Allow	Users (admin-PC\Users)	Read & execute	C:\	This folder, subfolders a...
Allow	Authenticated Users	Modify	C:\	This folder, subfolders a...

Add...   Edit...   Remove

☑ Include inheritable permissions from this object's parent

☐ Replace all existing inheritable permissions on all descendants with inheritable permissions from this object

Managing permission entries

OK   Cancel   Apply

The last important area of the security descriptor is the listing of the settings for auditing the object. *Auditing* is the method that Vista uses to know when to create an entry in the Security Event log to show that a specific action occurred. For example, if you want to know whenever someone tries to write to a specific file, set the auditing for that file object to record Write attempts.

The list of security settings for auditing is stored in the *System Access Control List* (SACL). Like the DACL, the SACL contains a set of ACEs; however, the entries within the SACL don't determine whether access is allowed but whether the successful or failed access is recorded to the Security Event log. If you're an administrative user, you can view or change these entries from the Auditing tab. (For a detailed description of this, see the upcoming section, "Using Regedit to view and modify the Registry.") Whether Vista checks the SACL is based on whether the Audit Object Access setting is turned on within the security policy of the machine. (For more information on security policy, see Chapter 16.)

The security descriptor is a key concept in understanding object-level security; however, it's only one part of the puzzle. To understand the "key" portion of the lock-and-key analogy, you need to know how the combination of permissions assigned to the account as well as the groups it belongs to, build the effective permissions of the account. On the other hand, to fully understand the "lock" portion, you need to know how the DACL and SACL for an object are built through inherited and explicit permissions. The next two sections explain how Vista uses these concepts.

Effective permissions

When you attempt to access an object, your session presents your user token to the Vista security subsystem for authorization. (For more details on user tokens, see Chapter 6.) Vista then compares your account and group memberships (set of keys) to each ACE in the DACL (the lock) to see whether a match exists. If a match is found, you are either allowed or denied access, based on the setting. If no match is found, the access attempt is denied. If Audit Object Access is turned on, Vista then runs through the same matching process with each ACE in the SACL. If a match is found, Vista writes the information to the Security Event log.

Effective permissions refers to the totality of permissions that you have on an object, based on the combination of permissions assigned to your account and any groups to which you belong. For example, the security permissions stored in the security descriptor of an object are as follows in Table 7-1:

Table 7-1	Example Access Control List	
	Permissions	*Type*
Administrators	Full Control	Allow
SYSTEM	Full Control	Allow
Marketing	Full Control	Allow
Users	Read & Execute	Allow
Authenticated Users	Modify	Allow
Security Admins	Take Ownership	Allow

If you log on to the machine with an account that is a Standard User account, you're a part of both the Users and the Authenticated Users group. This means that you receive the Read & Execute permissions from the Users group as well as the Modify permissions (which includes all the permissions of Read & Execute plus others) from the Authenticated Users group. The combination of the permissions from these group memberships means that your effective permissions on the file are such that you can perform any action against it that Vista allows with Modify permissions.

What would the effective permissions be if your account were a part of the Security Admins group as well as a Standard User account? You still get the Read & Execute permissions from the Users group and the Modify permissions from the Authenticated Users group. However, the Take Ownership permission (which is not part of the Modify permissions) is added to the mix because of the Security Admins group membership. This means that your effective permissions on the file is Modify plus Take Ownership.

Finally, if your account were also a part of the Marketing group, your effective permissions for the file is Full Control. Full Control contains all the permissions available for the object. Therefore, the combination of the group memberships allows you to perform any action against the file.

Instead of always making you perform these calculations to determine the effective security of an account or group against an object, Vista provides you with an interface. However, this interface doesn't take into account all the different ways how you can receive permissions to an object, so the results might not be 100 percent accurate.

To use the effective security interface, follow these steps:

1. **Open the properties of the object.**

   Right-click the object and choose Properties.

2. **Click the Security tab, as shown in Figure 7-2.**

   If the Security tab isn't available, you (obviously) can't view the effective permissions interface. To read why the Security tab might not be available, see the sidebar, " File- and folder-level security aren't always available," elsewhere in this chapter.

3. **Click the Advanced button.**

4. **Click the Effective Permissions tab.**

5. **Click the Select button.**

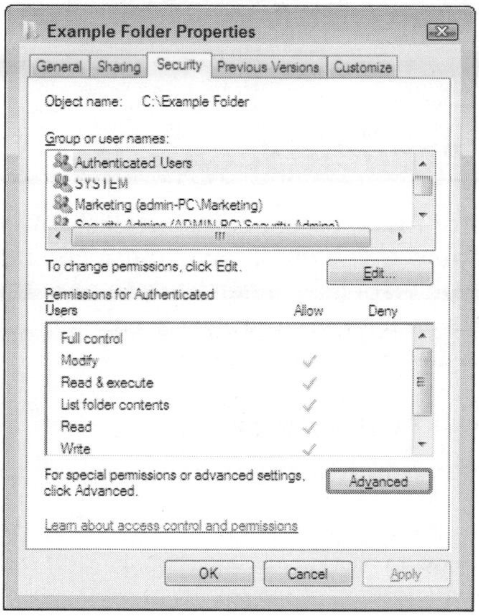

Figure 7-2:
The Security
tab for
Example
Folder.

6. **Select the user or group for which you want to determine the effective permissions.**

   For more information on this interface, see Chapter 6.

   The Effective Permissions area of the tab shows the granular permissions for that account or group, as shown in Figure 7-3.

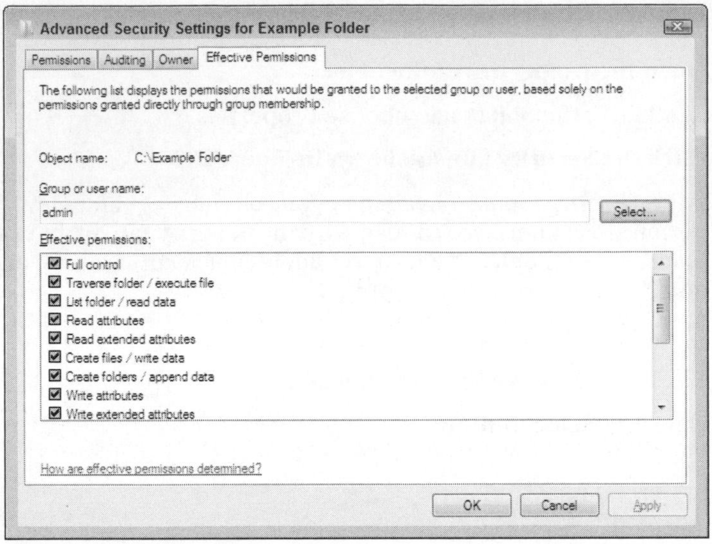

Figure 7-3:
Effective
permissions
for the
Admin
account.

Inherited versus explicit security

Although the security descriptor for an object contains all the information related to the security of that object, you don't have to directly manage all settings on every object. Instead, Vista uses *inheritance* to pass these settings from one level to all the objects underneath that level. This means that Vista builds the object-level security in one of two ways:

- ✔ **Explicit:** Vista sets the security on the object itself.
- ✔ **Implicit:** Vista applies settings from another object considered to be a parent of the child object.

Here's an example, with a file named C:\Data\fud.doc:

- ✔ fud.doc is the child of the Data folder.
- ✔ The Data folder is the parent of the fud.doc file.
- ✔ The C:\ drive is the parent of the Data folder as well as the grandparent of the fud.doc.

Therefore, fud.doc inherits settings from both the C:\ drive and the Data folder.

For the ease of management, use inheritance to set your object-level security whenever possible. Managing the security on a single object that cascades those settings is much easier than managing security in many different places. However, sometimes you'll likely want to secure objects even more, and you need to understand certain concepts before making those changes:

- **Application order is important.** Permissions that are explicitly set on an object are listed in the object's access control list (ACL) before ones that are inherited, and one inherited from a direct parent are checked before ones inherited from a grandparent. For example, because of how the ACL is set up, Vista checks the security explicitly set on the fud.doc file, and then the security inherited from the Data folder, and finally the security inherited from the root of the drive for the C:\Data\fud.doc file.

- **Inheritability of a permission can be set.** Permissions can be set to apply only to the object where it is explicitly set, to all child objects, or even to only specific types of child objects.

- **Child objects generally inherit permissions by default.** When a child object is created, it automatically inherits the permissions of the parent that are set to be inheritable.

  In the Microsoft world, specific object types exist for which the default security is set to block inheritance or to not inherit to other objects. These object types are generally found in Active Directory (AD) or deep within the OS, so you really won't be dealing with them in terms of Vista security. However, you should understand that not all objects inherit permissions by default if you're managing items outside the normal Vista interfaces.

- **Inheritance can be blocked.** Vista allows a child object to block the inheritance of settings from a parent object. You accomplish this in the following manner:

  a. *Open the properties of the object.*

     Right-click the object and choose Properties.

  b. *Click the Security tab.*

     This brings up the interface in Figure 7-2, as shown earlier in the chapter.

  c. *Click the Advanced button.*

  d. *Click the Edit button.*

     This brings up the interface shown in Figure 7-4.

  e. *Deselect the Include Inheritable Permissions from This Object's Parent check box, as shown in Figure 7-4.*

  f. *Choose whether to copy or remove the inherited permissions from the object in the pop-up shown in Figure 7-5; click the appropriate button.*

     If you choose to copy, all permissions that are being inherited will be explicitly set within the security descriptor. This means that no change will happen in the effective security of the object after blocking inheritance.

If you choose to remove, only permissions that are explicitly set against the object will remain intact after blocking inheritance.

Both options are equally valid. The right choice depends on what you're trying to achieve by blocking inheritance. In either case, you can change the permissions immediately afterward, so which option you choose isn't critical.

g. *Click either OK or Apply to make the new permissions effective.*

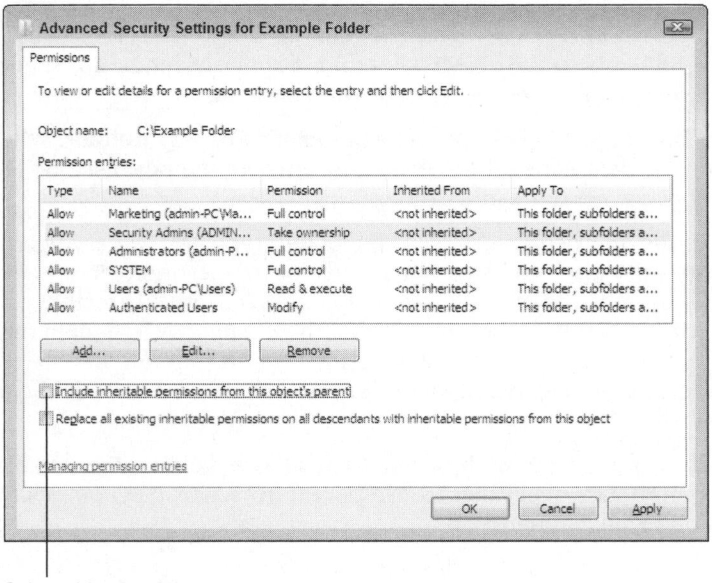

Figure 7-4:
Example
Folder with
blocked
inheritance.

Select this check box.

Figure 7-5:
Copy or
remove
inherited
permissions
here.

You can reinstate inheritance at any time by going back into the interface and selecting the check box indicated in Figure 7-4. If you do this, however, I recommend that you remove any explicit permission entries that are duplicates of the inherited ones. (This will be the situation if you chose to copy the inherited settings when you blocked inheritance.)

✔ **Permissions can be changed only where they are explicitly set.** Although you can view the permissions that are inherited by an object through the Advanced view of the Security tab, you can change only that permission at the level where it's actually set. Therefore, if the C:\Data folder gives read permission for all files and folders underneath, you can't remove that permission entry on the C:\Data\fud.doc file itself.

✔ **Permissions can't be changed from above.** You can't change explicit permissions on a child object from the parent. Therefore, if the C:\ Data\fud.doc provides explicit access to the marketing group, you can't remove that permission by a security setting at the C:\Data folder. The only exception to this rule is that you can remove all explicit permissions from all child objects of a folder via the Replace All Existing Inheritable Permissions on All Descendants with Inheritable Permissions from this Object check box, in the Advanced view of the Security tab, as shown in Figure 7-4.

Not all objects have parent/child relationships with other objects. Therefore, inheritance is a valid concept for file system and Registry objects, but not file share or service objects.

Protecting the File System through NTFS Permissions

NTFS permissions are object-level security settings that are set against file or folder objects. Microsoft intends that you use these permissions as a tool to ensure that only the proper users get access to the data stored on the machine. By default, the permissions are set on most files and folders in such a way that all users of the system have at least some level of access after they log on.

If all users of the system having at least some level of access isn't acceptable to you, you can set the security of certain files and folders so that only you, or a specific group of users that you specify, can access them. If this were the case, specify the security that you want via the Security tab of the Properties interface. Follow these steps:

1. **Open the properties of the file or folder that you want to manage.**

2. **Click the Security tab.**

    If the Security tab isn't visible, see the "File- and folder-level security aren't always available" sidebar to find out why. If this is the case, you can't manage the NTFS permissions on your machine through an interface.

3. **Click the Edit button.**

4. **Click the Add button.**

5. **Select the user(s) and/or group(s) for which you want to add the permissions.**

For more information on this interface, see Chapter 6.

File- and folder-level security aren't always available

The interface for managing file- and folder-level security is the Security tab within the Properties interface. Unfortunately, this interface isn't available to everyone using Vista — and for different reasons. Perhaps you're on a Vista Home Basic, Home Premium, or Starter version. According to Microsoft documentation, you can't manage permissions on specific files or folders through a Microsoft-provided interface in these versions. Another reason why security settings for files and folders might not be available is that the drive is formatted as FAT32

instead of NTFS. File and folder security settings are commonly known as *NTFS permissions* because they are actually a function of that type of file system. FAT32 doesn't have these options built into it, so security can't be set at the file or folder level.

To find out what file system your computer drives use, open Disk Management. (Click Start and then enter **diskmgmt.msc** into the Search field.) The formatting for each drive is shown under the File System column, as shown in the figure here.

The File System column

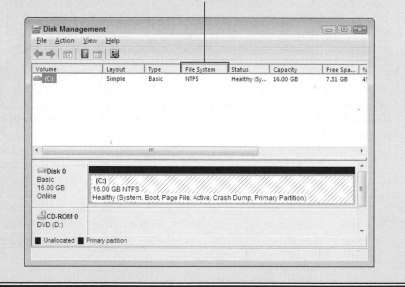

6. **Click OK in the Select Users or Groups interface to accept the user or group listed in the text box.**

   Adding the user or group in this way automatically provides them with both the Read and Read & Execute permissions for a file and the Read, Read & Execute, and List Folder Contents permissions for a folder. In addition, for a folder, this permission is inheritable by all subfolders and files contained within it. (For more information about inheritance, see the "Inherited versus explicit security" section, earlier in this chapter.)

   If this standard level of read permission is all you want to add, click OK.

   The permissions for the user or group appear in the Permissions window in the lower part of the screen, as shown in Figure 7-6. To change these permissions, select the appropriate check box under the Allow or Deny column.

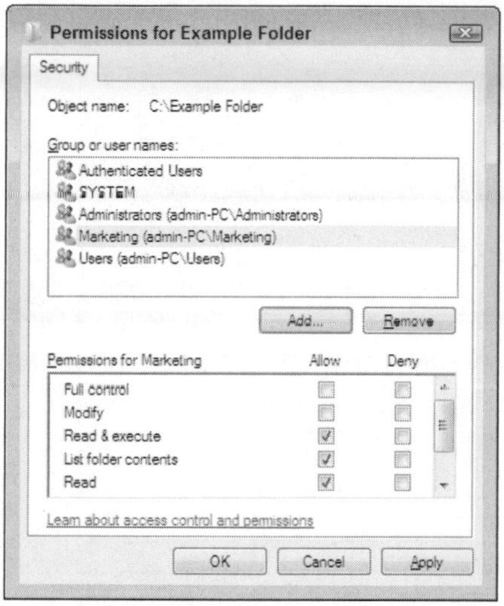

Figure 7-6:
The standard permissions editing interface.

7. **Click OK to accept the changes that you have made to the security of the object.**

   Permissions aren't set on the object until after you click either OK or Apply.

In addition to managing the specific permissions for a folder, you might need to change the inheritance values of a file or a folder. To manage these settings, use the Advanced interface of the Security tab, as follows:

1. **Open the properties of the file or folder that you want to manage.**

2. **Click the Security tab.**

If the Security tab isn't visible, see the sidebar, "File- and folder-level security aren't always available" to find out why.

3. **Click the Advanced button.**

4. **Click the Edit button.**

This brings up a window similar to the one shown in Figure 7-7. In this window, take note of several items:

- *Listing of permission entries:* Explicit ACEs are listed at the top of the permission entries before the inherited ACEs, and the direct parent folder's ACEs are listed before the grandparent folder's ACEs. This is an illustration of the ordering of the DACL discussed in the "Inherited versus explicit security" section, earlier in this chapter.

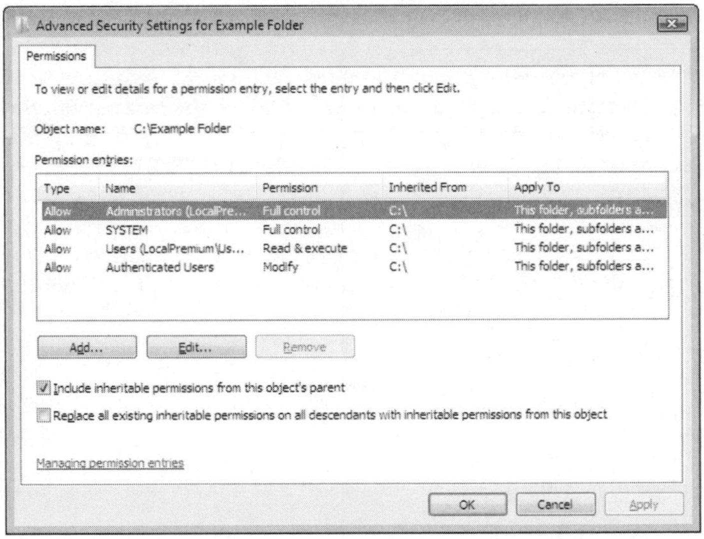

Figure 7-7:
The
Advanced
NTFS
Security
Settings
interface.

- *Inherited From column:* This column shows where the explicit security setting for that permission is located. This is important because although you can view all the applicable security settings for the file or folder through this interface, you can edit it only where it is explicitly set.

- *Apply To column:* This column shows what types of child objects will inherit the security from this one.

- *Add, Edit, and Remove buttons:* Use the Add button for creating explicit ACEs on the object. Use the Edit button to manage explicit permissions for that object. If the permission is inherited (rather than explicit), the Edit button allows you to only view the information. The Remove button is available only for explicit permissions; use it to delete the entry. Otherwise, it's grayed out.

- *Inheritable permissions check box:* The Include Inheritable Permissions from This Object's Parent check box determines whether permissions are allowed to be inherited. If you clear the check box, a pop-up dialog box immediately asks whether you want to copy the inheritable permissions into the explicit security of the object or to remove all the inherited permissions.

- *Replace permissions check box:* The Replace All Existing Inheritable Permissions on All Descendants with Inheritable Permissions from This Object check box allows you to overwrite the explicitly defined permissions on all child objects. This check box actually tells Vista to perform a one-time action, so it won't block the ability to set permissions on child objects in the future — and it won't be selected when you return to the interface.

The check boxes at the bottom of the Advanced Security Settings screen are affected by clicking anywhere in the area — not just on the check box itself. Many times, I've almost changed the security of an object while just trying to bring that window to the front. If the Inheritable Permissions check box is changed, it does present you an immediate pop-up that you can cancel. If the Replace permissions check box is selected by mistake, it gives you a warning pop-up when you click either OK or Apply, stating that you are about to replace the explicit permissions on all descendants and asking whether you want to continue. You can cancel this action by clicking No. Always pay very close attention to any pop-ups you receive while working in or exiting this screen.

5. **Double-click the permission entry that you want to edit or view.**

   Or, highlight an entry and then click the Edit button to bring up an interface similar to Figure 7-8. In this window, take note of several items:

   - *Change button:* Use this to reassign a permission entry to another user or group; just select a different user.

   - *Apply To drop-down menu:* Choose how this ACE is inherited to child objects in this menu.

   - *Permissions area:* This area contains the detailed permissions that you can allow or deny to the group or user to which the ACE applies. You assign these Allow or Deny permissions by checking the proper box in this area. By clearing any check box, you remove that permission assignment.

   - *Clear All button:* Click this button to clear all check boxes in the permissions area. That way, you can work from a clean slate.

   - *Container Only check box:* Selecting this check box sets the inheritance of the permissions set in this ACE as applicable only to the direct child objects of this folder.

6. **Use the check boxes and inheritance settings to change the permission as needed.**

7. **Click OK to accept the changes to the ACE or click Cancel to exit without saving your changes.**

8. **Click OK to accept the changes to the DACL.**

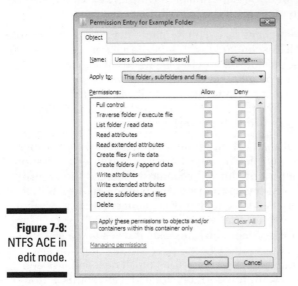

Figure 7-8:
NTFS ACE in
edit mode.

Understanding How to Lock Down the Registry

The *Registry* is a special part of Vista used to store information needed by both the OS and applications that you install. This information is usually things that the Microsoft or application developers want to make configurable in some way rather than hard-coding it into the software itself. For this reason, information stored in the Registry (also known as *settings*) can be very important to how your machine operates.

Microsoft emphasizes the importance of Registry data by constantly warning users of the dangers of editing the Registry. The danger is even worse in regard to changing the security within the Registry structure. Therefore, you should never make changes to the Registry structure, the information included in it, or the security surrounding it unless you specifically know the effects of the changes that you're making. This section is not intended to encourage you to change anything other than auditing settings within the Registry. Instead, read along here to gain an understanding of how to change the Registry if you ever need to.

Because the Registry contains many of the settings that control how Vista operates, much of what you do to control the security of your system actually changes Registry data. This includes managing the security of your system through policies, such as security options and administrative templates. (For more information on security policies, see Chapter 16.) In most cases, I recommend using the Microsoft-provided interface to change these settings rather than editing the Registry directly. However, some options are available only by editing the Registry directly.

The Registry structure comprises hives, keys, and values.

- ✔ **Hives:** *Hives* are special keys that Vista uses for specific purposes. Each hive represents the root of a Registry structure and contains the keys that actually hold values and data. Of the five hives in the Vista Registry structure, the two you are most likely to work with are

    - *HKEY_LOCAL_MACHINE* (abbreviated to HKLM)

      HKLM contains the data used by Vista for the machine itself.

    - *HKEY_CURRENT_USER* (abbreviated to HKCU)

      HKCU contains the data for the currently logged-on user. Registry edits that enhance your security generally will pertain to your machine or your own user environment. However, if you need to change settings for users other than the currently logged-on user, you have to find that specific user's settings within the HKEY_USERS hive instead of using HKCU.

- ✔ **Keys:** *Keys* are the actual Registry objects and are therefore the only items within the Registry that have a security descriptor attached to them. Key objects have child/parent relationships with the other keys in the structure the same way that NTFS objects do. However, unlike NTFS objects, keys can both contain other keys (a key stored within another key is a *sub-key*) and have information stored against them in the form of *values*. Each key has a default value associated with it. In most cases, information is stored against a value created within the key.

- ✔ **Values:** Values is information stored within the key and referenced by Vista and/or applications. There can be an unlimited number of values stored against a key. Each value comprises three components:

    - *Name:* The value name is referenced when you set or change data so that you know which data you want to access.

    - *Type:* Data stored in the value can be in many different formats. The type designation tells Vista the format of the data within that value.

    - *Data:* This is the actual setting for the value that is referenced by an application or Vista.

Using Regedit to view and modify the registry

The Registry Editor is the Microsoft-provided interface used to view and modify Registry keys, values, and security. To use this interface, you must have administrator rights within Vista. To start the Registry Editor, click Start and then type **regedit.exe** in the Search field. This brings up an interface similar to the one shown in Figure 7-9.

Navigating the Regedit interface is very similar to navigating the file system in Windows Explorer. Keys are displayed in a similar fashion as folders in that they have a white, side-pointing arrow when they are closed and a black down arrow when open. The main difference between the navigation in the two interfaces relates to the right-hand pane. In Windows Explorer, this pane shows the files and folders contained in the folder specified in the left. The right-hand pane in Regedit, however, shows the values stored against the key specified in the left and none of the sub-keys.

To create a new sub-key, or a value against a specific key, follow these steps:

1. **Choose the key in the left-hand pane and then right-click the right-side pane (or right-click the key in the left pane).**

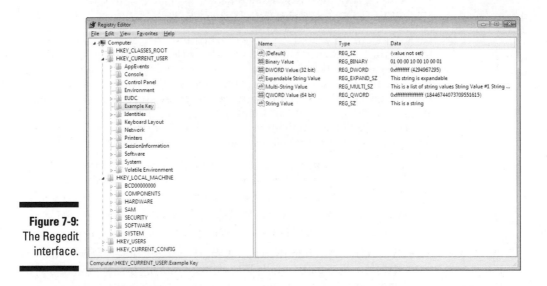

Figure 7-9:
The Regedit
interface.

2. **From the pop-up menu, choose New and then either a key or a type of value.**

Although all Registry data is actually stored in a binary format (which you can also view by choosing the Modify Binary Data option from the contextual menu on an already created value), the type of value used to display the data could be important based on what format Vista or the application that requires that value expects.

As soon as you choose the key or type of value to create from the pop-up, Vista automatically creates it with a default name and no data.

3. **Change the default name to what you want.**

As soon as the key or value is created, Vista automatically allows you to rename it. If you make a mistake and you can no longer just type it in, right-click the object and choose Rename from the contextual menu. This is the same method you use to change the name of an existing key or value within the Registry.

4. **Change the data to what you want.**

Either double-click the key/value or right-click and choose Modify from the contextual menu. This is the same method that you use to change the data in an existing key or value within the Registry.

As soon as you make a change to the Registry, it becomes effective, and the OS or software can begin to use it immediately. Also, any deletions of data from the Registry are immediate, so you can't dumpster-dive in the Recycle Bin to allow you to recover something you just deleted. Therefore, you must exercise extreme caution when editing the Registry.

To specify security on any key, follow these steps:

1. **Right-click the key in the left pane and choose Permissions.**

This brings up an interface that shows only the Security tab, as shown in Figure 7-10, instead of all the tabs that you would see in the Properties view of a file or folder.

2. **Click the Advanced button.**

This brings up a window similar to the one shown in Figure 7-11. For a detailed explanation of the options in this window, please refer to the explanation of Figure 7-7 earlier in this chapter.

3. **Double-click the permission entry you want to edit or view.**

Or, highlight an entry and then click the Edit button. Either action brings up a window similar to the one shown in Figure 7-12. For a detailed explanation of the options in this window, please refer to the explanation of Figure 7-8 earlier in this chapter.

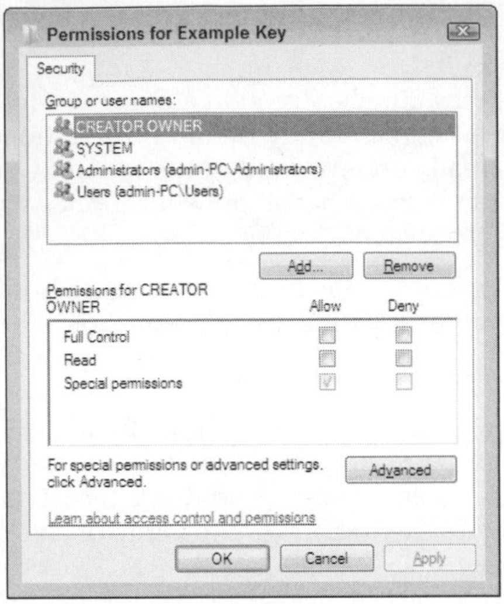

Figure 7-10:
The Registry editor standard permissions interface for the example key.

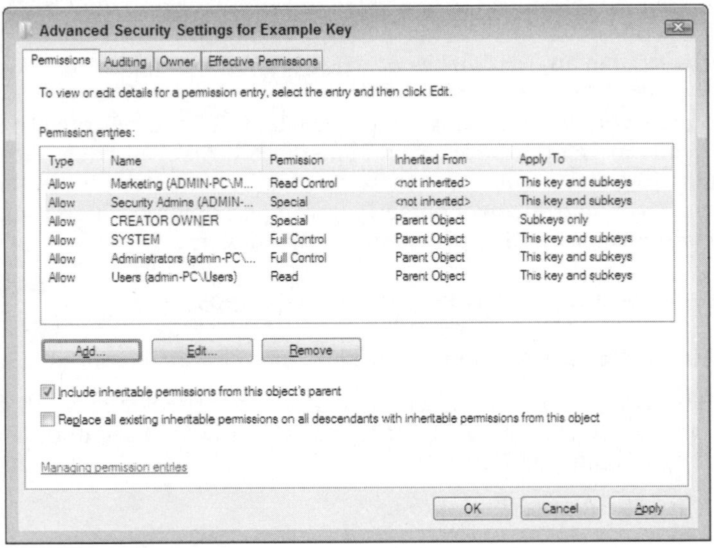

Figure 7-11:
The Advanced Registry permissions settings interface.

4. **Use the check boxes and inheritance settings to change the permission as needed.**

5. **Click OK to accept the changes to the ACE or click Cancel to exit without saving your changes.**

6. **Click OK to accept the changes to the DACL.**

Follow these steps to specify auditing on any key:

1. **Right-click the key in the left pane and choose Permissions.**
2. **Click the Advanced button and then click the Auditing tab.**

   This brings up a window similar to the one shown in Figure 7-13.

3. **To add a new ACE to the SACL, click Add.**

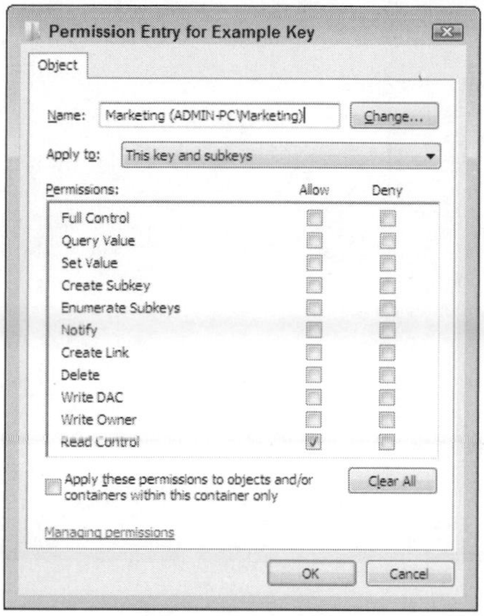

Figure 7-12:
The Registry ACE in Edit mode.

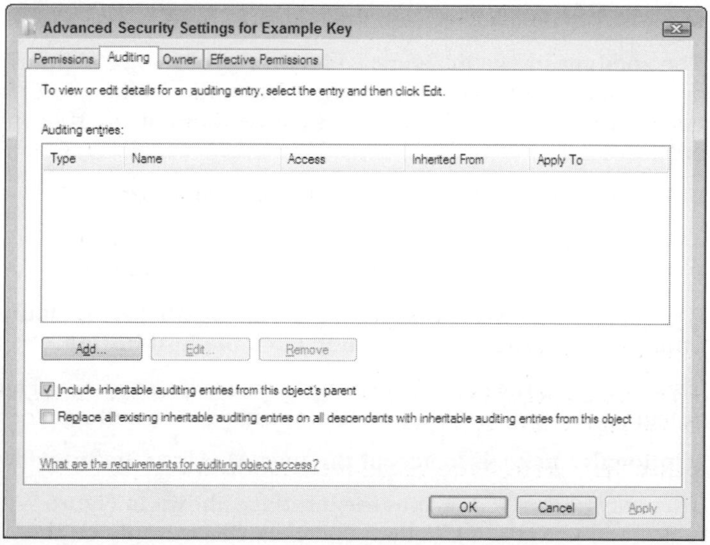

Figure 7-13:
The Registry auditing interface.

4. Select the user(s) and/or group(s) for which you want to add the permissions.

For more information on this interface, see Chapter 6.

5. Click OK.

This brings up the Auditing Entry Setting interface, as shown in Figure 7-14.

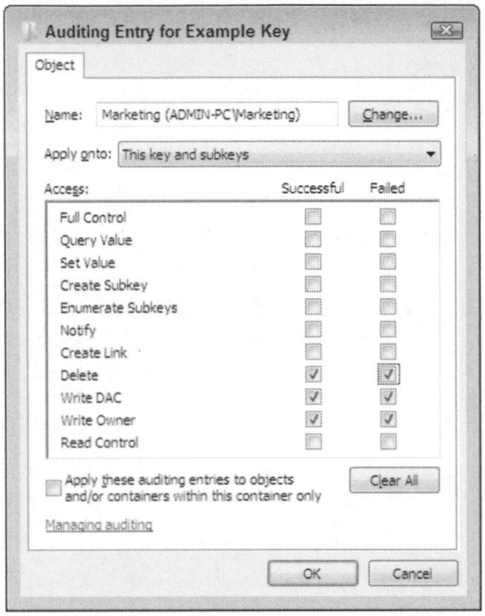

Figure 7-14:
The Auditing
Entry setting
interface.

6. Select the check boxes for the Successful and Failed accesses you want to audit for the user or group you pick in Step 4.

The auditing shown in Figure 7-14 tells Vista to write a security event if any member of the Marketing group attempts to change the DACL, change the owner, or delete the key, regardless of whether that attempt is successful.

7. Click OK to accept the new ACE into the interface.

This only adds the ACE into the interface shown in Figure 7-13. The ACE is not added to the SACL until you click OK or Apply on the Auditing tab.

8. (Optional) To change the settings for an existing ACE, double-click the entry, or click the entry and then click the Edit button.

This brings up the same interface shown in the upcoming Figure 7-15. Select or deselect the check boxes to change the settings for that ACE.

9. (Optional) Click OK to accept the new ACE into the interface.

This only adds the ACE into the interface shown in Figure 7-13. The ACE is not added to the SACL until you click OK or Apply on the Auditing tab.

10. **(Optional) To delete an existing ACE, click the entry and then click the Remove button.**

    Choosing immediately removes the entry from the interface without a pop-up; however, the ACE isn't removed from the SACL until you click OK or Apply on the Auditing tab.

11. **Click OK or Apply on the Auditing tab to apply the changed ACEs to the SACL in the security descriptor of the object.**

Registry keys to pay attention to

All Registry data is critical for one reason or another. However, some Registry keys are more crucial to the security of your system. Either these keys contain data that supports security functions within the system, or a malicious user (or piece of software) could utilize them to lower the defenses of Vista. I don't recommend changing the security for these keys, but I do recommend configuring auditing for Write operations to the keys that concern you. (For information on configuring auditing, see the section "Using Regedit to view and modify the Registry," earlier in this chapter.)

The following is a list of the most important keys to protect against modification and what the keys control:

✔ **Run and RunOnce keys:** The Run and RunOnce keys reside in both the HKLM and HKCU hives and perform the same functions. (For more about hives, see the section "Understanding How to Lock Down the Registry," earlier in this chapter.) Vista uses these keys to start applications when the machine boots. All values stored within the Run keys are started each time the machine boots, whereas the values in the RunOnce keys run only one time and are then deleted. Many viruses and spyware will, therefore, attempt to place data into the Run and/or RunOnce keys so that they execute the next time you start Vista. The different Run and RunOnce keys are

```
HKLM\Software\Microsoft\Windows\CurrentVersion\Run
HKLM\Software\Microsoft\Windows\CurrentVersion\RunOnce
HKCU\Software \Microsoft\Windows\CurrentVersion\Run
HKLM\Software\Microsoft\Windows\CurrentVersion\RunOnce
```

✔ **Local Security Authority key:** Vista uses values in the Local Security Authority key to configure some basic security behaviors of the system, including the settings surrounding anonymous access to the system. The Local Security Authority key is located at

```
HKLM\System\CurrentControlSet\Control\LSA\
```

✔ **Event Log key:** The values in this key can be used to set the parameters that Vista utilizes to manage the event logs, including the Security Event log. This includes the maximum size of the log and the retention of Event log data. The Event Log key is located at

```
HKLM\Software\Policies\Microsoft\Windows\EventLog\
```

✔ **Server Parameters key:** Vista uses values stored in the Server Parameters key to configure the operation of the server service. Although Vista is a client OS, the server service is a required service that enables Vista to operate. Some specific values within this key control whether certain data can be accessed without providing authentication. The Server Parameters key is located at

```
HKLM\System\CurrentControlSet\Services\LanManServer\
      Parameters
```

✔ **Windows Defender key:** Vista uses the `DisableAntiSpyware` value in this key to disable Defender. Windows Security Center might notify you of this change in status depending upon its settings; however, changing this value could be a target of malware in the future. The Windows Defender key is located at

```
HKLM\Software\Policies\Microsoft\Windows Defender
```

✔ **Security Center key:** For domain-based machines, you can turn off the Windows Security Center through this key. However, it will have no effect on standalone Vista devices. The Security Center key is located at

```
HKLM\Software\Policies\Microsoft\Windows NT\Security
      Center
```

✔ **Phishing Filter keys:** The Phishing Filter keys reside in both the HKLM and HKCU hives and perform the same function. Vista controls the use of the Phishing Filter through this key. A malicious user could use this value to specify that the filter be turned off, and the user won't be prompted to change it. The Phishing Filter keys are located at

```
HKLM\Software\Policies\Microsoft\Internet Explorer\
      PhishingFilter
HKCU\Software\Policies\Microsoft\Internet Explorer\
      PhishingFilter
```

Keeping an Eye on Your System

Preventing unauthorized access by properly setting the security on your system is your first line of defense for any computer system. However, as easily as you set the security, someone else with the same authority can change it. If this occurs without your knowledge, you might expect to be secure when you are not. Therefore, any good access management strategy has to be backed up with a way to capture what is occurring on the system. This is *auditing and logging*.

Auditing is specifying what events on the machine Vista should look for. *Logging* is writing a record of those events to a specified place for storage. Vista has an incredible amount of auditing and logging capabilities built into it. Logs can actually be as large as 2 terabytes (TB) — if you have the space to store that much data. However, for the purposes of this book, I focus only on security auditing and logging.

Auditing and logging policies

By default, Vista comes with no auditing defined for security events. This doesn't mean that no security auditing or logging occurs because Vista has built-in logging for what the developers felt were the most critical security events. However, you design exactly what other events you want to audit.

The Vista security auditing settings can be managed through any of the policy interfaces. (See Chapter 16 for more information on security policies and how to manage them.) One way to bring up an interface is as follows:

1. **Click Start and then type** secpol.msc **into the Search field that appears.**

   This brings up the local security policy interface, as shown in Figure 7-15. Here, you can edit any of the local security policies, including the audit policy. You can also choose to use gpedit.msc, but the steps for getting to the audit policy are not the same as listed here.

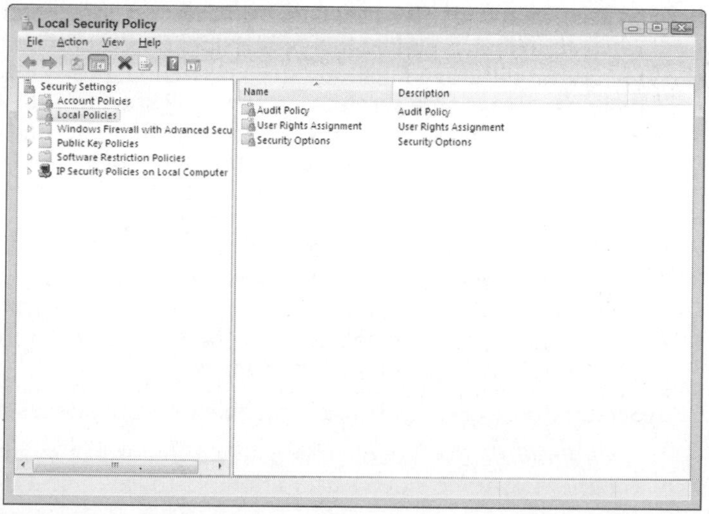

Figure 7-15: The Local Security Policy interface.

2. **Expand Local Policies (click the arrow in the left pane).**

3. **Click Audit Policy, in the left pane, to display the main audit policies in the right pane.**

There are 9 main audit policies, but Vista has the added ability to allow you to get even more detailed, if you want, by adding 50 different subcategories.

The following list explains the basic audit policies you can specify through the interface and provides the security best practice for each one.

- *Audit Account Logon Events:* Enable this policy to record an event in the Security Event log when the computer is used to authenticate or reject the logon attempt. This policy is really for use on a Domain Controller rather than a client machine. This policy can be set for both success and failure of logon events.

  Security best practice for Vista is to set this to No Auditing.

- *Audit Account Management:* Enable this policy to record an event in the Security Event log when an account is managed in some way. Changing or setting a password, renaming/disabling/enabling an account, adding an account to a group, and creating/deleting an account or a group would all generate an account management event. This policy can be set for both success and failure of logon attempts.

  Security best practice is to enable this for both success and failure.

- *Audit Logon Events:* Enable this policy to record an event in the Security Event log when a user logs on to this computer. This policy can be set for both success and failure of logon events.

  Security best practice is to enable this for both success and failure.

- *Audit Object Access:* Enable this policy to have the computer check an object's SACL when the object is accessed and record an event when specified. Enabling this policy doesn't generate any events on its own although Microsoft does predefine SACLs for some items (such as some services), so you will start to see new events when it is enabled. (For more information about setting object SACLs, see the upcoming section, "Defining object auditing.") This policy can be set for both success and failure of object accesses.

  Security best practice is to enable this for both success and failure.

- *Audit Policy Change:* Enable this policy to record an event in the Security Event log when there is a change to user rights policies, audit policies, or trust policies. This policy can be set for both success and failure of audit policy changes.

  Security best practice is to enable this for both success and failure.

- *Audit Privilege Use:* Enable this policy to record an event in the Security Event log when a user attempts to exercise a user right.

This policy can be set for both success and failure of privilege use. Enabling this policy generates a great number of events and therefore should be used only when you're troubleshooting an issue or have a specific plan for the data.

Security best practice is to enable this for failure only.

- *Audit Process Tracking:* Enable this policy to track some detailed process activity and record an event in the Security Event log. This policy can be set for both success and failure of process activities. Enabling this policy generates a great number of events and therefore should be turned on only when troubleshooting an issue or when trying to respond to a security incident.

  Security best practice for Vista is to set this to No Auditing.

- *Audit System Events:* Enable this policy to record an event in the Security Event log when a system event occurs. *System* events are events such as shutting down the computer. This policy can be set for both success and failure of system events.

  Security best practice is to enable this for both success and failure.

4. **Double-click whichever policy you want to manage (or right-click and choose Properties) to bring up the interface shown in Figure 7-16.**

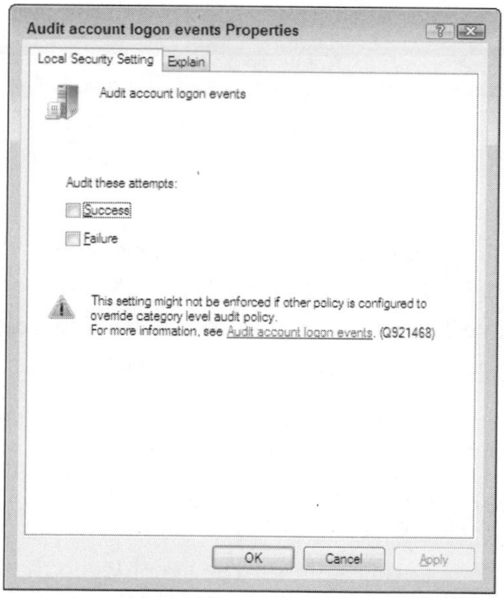

Figure 7-16:
The audit policy setting interface for audit account logon events.

5. **Select or deselect the Success or Failure check boxes to specify the correct amount of auditing.**

6. **Click OK to accept these settings.**

In addition to the audit policies, the policies listed in the following list tell Vista how to manage the Security Event log itself. Unlike the local policy settings, these can't be accessed through the local security policy Microsoft Management Console (MMC); instead, you must use the Group Policy Object Editor as follows:

1. **Click Start and then type** gpedit.msc **into the Search field.**

   This brings up the Group Policy Object Editor, as shown in Figure 7-17. Here, you can edit any of the local security policies, including audit policy, as well as the administrative templates.

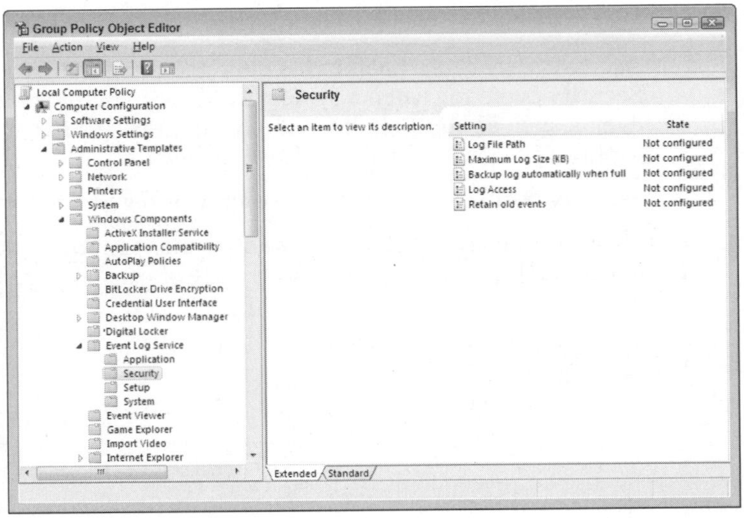

Figure 7-17:
The Group
Policy
Object
Editor
interface.

2. **Under Computer Configuration in the left pane, expand Administrative Templates by clicking the arrow next to it.**

3. **Under Administrative Templates, expand Windows Components.**

4. **Under Windows Components, expand Event Log Service.**

5. **Under Event Log Service, click Security to bring up the security log settings policy options in the right pane.**

   The following list explains the security log settings you can specify through the policy interface:

   • *Log File Path:* Vista normally stores the event log in the system32 or system64 directory (depending upon whether you're using the 32- or 64-bit version of Vista). However, this setting allows you to change the storage location. Typically, use this setting if you need to store the log files on a second partition or physical drive because of space limitations on the system drive.

- *Maximum Log Size (KB):* Vista allows the security log to grow to the size specified in this setting (a limit of 2TB). By default, this setting in Vista is 20,480K (translates to 20MB). When the security log hits the maximum size, Vista takes action based on what you told it to do through the other security log settings.

  The maximum size of the security log should be based on ensuring that you have the data to meet the auditing requirements of your own environment. For example, allocate enough room so that you never actually hit this limit — and if you do, it will occur only after you no longer need to keep them. However, the larger the size of the log, the more chance for memory fragmentation. which slows performance and could cause you to lose events.

- *Backup Log Automatically When Full:* When the log file reaches its maximum size and the Retain Old Events policy is enabled (see the upcoming bullet on this), enabling this policy tells Vista to create a new security log while renaming the old one so that all log file data is retained. If Retain Old Events is not configured or disabled, this setting has no effect. Using this setting should be based on ensuring that you have enough data to meet the auditing requirements of your environment. Enabling this can allow you to have a lower Maximum Log File Size setting and still retain all your data. However, removal of old log data is now your responsibility instead of Vista's — and you might have to look through multiple logs to find the data you need.

- *Log Access:* By default, only administrators are allowed to view and manage the security log. This setting allows you to specify additional access to the security log for nonadministrators. The setting itself requires the use of a Security Descriptor Definition Language (SDDL) string to set the security descriptor for the log. Defining the SDDL string is a complicated procedure that is beyond the scope of this book; however, you can find information about creating this setting at the Microsoft Web site. The best security practice is to not set this unless you have a user or group that needs this access but does not have administrative rights.

- *Retain Old Events:* When the log file reaches its maximum size, this policy determines Vista's behavior. If this setting is enabled, depending upon the setting for the Backup Log Automatically When Full policy (see the earlier bullet), either old events will be kept and all new security events will be lost, or the current event log will be saved under a different name and all new events will be written to a new log. If this policy is disabled, new events overwrite the old events in the current log.

6. **Double-click whichever policy you want to manage (or right-click and choose Properties) to bring up the editing interface.**

Defining object auditing

Enabling the Audit Object Access policy (in the preceding section) does nothing by itself. This policy only tells Vista to check an object's SACL as part of an access attempt. If a match is found, Vista writes an event to the Security Event log. Because most object SACLs are empty by default in Vista, you must define exactly what types of accesses for which you want to have a record.

Like most auditing decisions, you have to be aware of what you define. It is very easy to impair your ability to understand the events with real security implications by creating too much noise in the logs. Each object type has its own quirks in how best to define the auditing, and the following sections provide tips for the object types you are most likely to audit.

NTFS object auditing

NTFS objects are the files and folders stored within the NTFS. Because these objects are hierarchical, they allow for the inheritance of permissions from a parent (folder) to a child (subfolder or file). For more information about inheritance, see the "Inherited versus explicit security" section, earlier in this chapter. Auditing is defined on NTFS objects through the Auditing tab, which is available only in the Advanced Security interface. (For information about accessing this interface, see the "Protecting the File System through NTFS Permissions" section, earlier in this chapter.)

When defining auditing for NTFS objects, keep the following tips in mind:

- ✔ **Use audit settings for passive actions only where it is absolutely necessary.** *Passive actions* (such as reading, listing, and executing) generally occur more often and do not actively change the data. Therefore, you're more likely to fill up your event log with trivial data by auditing passive actions. Sometimes, you definitely want to do this kind of auditing (for example, to audit Read attempts for a file that contains all your passwords), but try to limit this as much as possible.

- ✔ **If you do need to set auditing on passive actions for all files within a folder, use the Files Only option.** You can manage auditing for NTFS the same way that you manage permissions, meaning that you can set the SACL at the highest container level and use inheritance to pass down the settings. However, this can mean that a Read attempt on a file within a folder will generate many event log entries because Vista may log the Read attempt against each folder in the path.

  To eliminate this problem, choose the Files Only option from the Apply Onto drop-down box on the Auditing tab. This limits the logging to only the Read attempt on the file itself while still allowing the manageability that using folders to set permissions gives you.

✔ **Don't use the Files Only option if you want to audit for the creation of a file.** Creating files and folders are actions taken against the folder that contains them. If you specify Files Only when auditing the Create Files/Write Data or the Create Folders/Append Data access, the setting won't apply to the folder. Thus, creating of a new file or folder won't generate a security event.

✔ **Set as many different entries in the SACL as you need but keep performance in mind.** If you decide that you need to set multiple entries in the SACL of an object to get the level of auditing you require, do so. However, keep in mind that Vista must look through and compare every entry in each object's SACL as part of the access attempt to that object. Therefore, avoid defining a series of the settings for different individual users instead of a single one for a group that they all belong to.

Registry object auditing

Keys are the only Registry objects within Vista, and are (therefore) where auditing must be set. (For more information about the Registry, see "Understanding How to Lock Down the Registry," earlier in this chapter.) Because these objects are hierarchical, they allow for the inheritance of permissions from a parent (key) to a child (subkey). For more information about inheritance, see the "Inherited versus explicit security" section, earlier in this chapter. Auditing is defined on keys through the Auditing tab that is available only in the Advanced Security interface. (This interface is extremely similar to the NTFS interface, as I describe in the "Protecting the File System through NTFS Permissions" section, earlier in this chapter.)

When defining auditing for Registry objects, keep the following in mind:

✔ **A particular Registry value can't be audited directly.** Because values stored against a key aren't objects, they don't have a security descriptor, which is how SACLs are defined. As an illustration of this concept, I will try to put it in another context. It should be plain to see that it is possible to have Vista audit access to a Word document but not to you writing a new sentence inside it. The Registry key is like the Word document because it is an object. However, the values stored within the key are like the data inside the document — and, therefore, aren't something that you can audit directly. So, if you want to audit the change to an existing value within a key (or the creation of a new value), specify the Set Value access setting on the key.

✔ **Set passive auditing for interactive users only.** Avoid auditing passive actions (such as querying and enumerating) on keys unless absolutely necessary. However, if this is the case, set the audits for only actual users of the machine rather than Vista itself. Vista constantly reads information from the Registry, and your event log will fill with useless data if you try to audit these actions by the background processes.

Service object auditing

Although Microsoft doesn't provide a Security tab for services, they are actually objects with security descriptors (just like files, folders, and Registry keys). Unlike NTFS and Registry objects, services are not hierarchical, so you must set the auditing on each individual service object. You can set this through a policy interface that shows the services (either a template or the Group Policy Object Editor in a domain environment; for more information on these interfaces, see Chapter 16) or the SC.exe command line utility (which is fairly complicated). Like the other objects, audits of services are effective only if Audit Object Access is enabled.

When defining auditing for service objects, keep the following in mind:

- ✔ **No default setting exists for service object auditing.** Audit settings (as well as permissions) for each individual service have been custom-crafted by Microsoft for Vista. The majority of the services are set to audit all failures, but there is not a default auditing level that you can assume for any service object.

- ✔ **The policy interfaces set auditing to Everyone-Full Control for failure by default.** Although the interface pulls the list of services from the local machine, it does not pull the SACLs. This can lead to a false sense that you're not changing the auditing level for that service when you accept this default.

  I advise that you accept the default but watch whether the log file begins to have an excessive amount of failure audit records for a particular service after you set this policy.

- ✔ **Only set success auditing for active actions.** Active actions within service objects are items, such as Change Template/Config, Start, Stop, Pause and Continue, Delete, Change Permissions, and Take Ownership.

Part III
Preserving and Protecting Data

The 5th Wave   By Rich Tennant

"Drive carefully, remember your lunch, and always make a backup of your directory tree before modifying your hard disk partition file."

In this part . . .

Preserving and protecting your data is such an integral part of a security plan, yet many users in home, small office, and even enterprise environments often don't do as good of a job as they could. As a result, their data — sometimes sensitive or irreplaceable — is put at risk of being lost or stolen.

In this part, discover how to identify exactly what data is important to you and then how to preserve it by using the Vista Backup and Recovery tool. You can also read how to protect your sensitive data by using Vista encryption tools, Encrypting File System (EFS), and BitLocker.

Chapter 8

Backing Up So You Can Always Restore

*B*acking up your system and data is a fundamental security component that's often overlooked and underused by even the most technically adept and business-savvy people. Unfortunately, such oversight can produce stomach-churning consequences when irreplaceable files or hundreds of hours of work are lost.

The good news is that Vista Backup is a capable and easy-to-use tool — and, when used correctly, it can provide you a great deal of mileage in your data protection journey. Although Vista Backup can do most of the heavy lifting itself and can run at scheduled intervals, properly preserving your data still requires a little research and planning. Specifically, you need to understand your data security requirements, find out about the available backup and recovery options, and then decide when and how to use those options.

In this chapter, I help you through this planning process. And to further ensure your success, I throw in a few tips on how to organize your data so that backing up and restoring is a breeze.

Why Should I Back Up My Data?

Backing up is not just for the security-obsessed. Even if you don't consider yourself all that security-conscious, I bet you easily recognize that some of the data lurking around on your hard drive, if lost, would be difficult — or even impossible — to replace.

Having an adequate backup-and-restore strategy is serious business that should not be taken lightly. Just ask those colleagues and friends who spent hours and hours after a crash rebuilding their systems and feeling that gut-wrenching agony you get when you realize you've lost — and unfortunately, never backed up — that precious picture of Aunt Betsy, that critical document you invested hundreds of hours in, or any of those other painfully irreplaceable files.

Here are some reasons why backing up must be part of your security plan:

- **Hardware failure:** Your system is made up of intricate mechanical components that eventually are destined to fail. When those components fail — especially your hard drive — your precious data will likely be lost with it. If your data is backed up, however, component failures are just a matter of inconvenience until you replace the component and restore any data.

- **User error:** Let's face it — we all make mistakes. Eventually, your spouse, junior, the dog, or perhaps even you will delete, overwrite, or lose that precious file that you have invested hours and hours of work in. Sometimes losing a particular file and having to rework the data that it holds will be only a minor inconvenience. Other times — such as when financial or medical documents go missing — the loss is much more serious. At that particular moment, if you don't have an appropriate backup and restore strategy, you will desperately wish that you had.

- **Downtime and loss of productivity:** If you use your system to perform essential tasks, having your system or data unavailable for several hours or even days would severely impair your personal or professional productivity. This often translates into the loss of cold, hard cash. Implementing an appropriate backup-and-restore strategy can reduce the amount of time that your system and data is unavailable, therefore also keeping any productivity and monetary losses to a minimum.

- **Malware:** As more computers stay connected to the Internet, so increases the risk that your system and data may become infected with viruses or Trojan horse programs. Although antivirus tools can go a long way toward protecting your data, your system will become infected from time to time, and the integrity of your data will be challenged. The proper backup-and-restore strategy can make an otherwise heart-palpitating event a minor inconvenience.

When it comes to your digital data, the cards are stacked against you. In all likelihood, something eventually will occur that causes your data to be lost. Minimizing (or dealing with) that loss requires more than just rolling the dice and getting lucky. It's a matter of having a backup-and-restore strategy that meets your needs and it's a matter of consistently executing on that strategy. You can either have a proper backup strategy so that you can always restore your data when it is lost, or you can wish that you did when you lose it!

Choosing Your Vista Backup Options

Choosing the right Vista backup and restore options isn't quite as easy as just reaching in a hat and picking one, but I am happy to say that choosing the right options is far from difficult. As you begin your journey to having a backup-and-recovery strategy that provides you the ability to protect and restore your data consistently, you first need to understand what backup options Vista provides.

The backup and restore options offered in Vista are more comprehensive and user-friendly than any of the options previously offered in any native Windows backup utility. These options provide you the full range of backup capabilities — from capturing the state of your system at a particular moment in time to backing up a single precious data file that you need an extra safe copy of, and most everything in between. In the coming sections, I look at the backup and recovery options offered by Vista.

Vista system restore point

Similar to Windows XP but more robust and improved, Vista provides the ability to create a snapshot of your system: essentially a picture that captures the state of your system at a particular moment in time, which enables you to revert to a previous state if a particular change starts causing you grief. For example, if you install a software program, add hardware, or make a configuration change, and then things start getting unstable, revert to a previous restore point. Your system is in the state that it was in prior to that change.

Vista System Restore automatically captures those snapshots for you by watching specific files and folders for changes. When changes occur to those files or folders, Vista records them. The tool also allows you to manually create a restore point. This is useful if you plan to make some changes to your system and you want to record the latest configuration immediately preceding that change. To use this feature, simply make a restore point (which I show you how to do in the upcoming section, "Creating a restore point"). Then, if the configuration change goes south, you can restore your system to the previous configuration.

You can configure System Restore to monitor and record the following:

- ✔ **Performance Options:** System Restore monitors visual effects, processor scheduling, and virtual memory settings.

- ✔ **User Profile Settings:** System Restore monitors any changes in your desktop settings and user account information.

- ✔ **Startup and Recovery:** System Restore monitors and records any changes in your system startup and failure options and dump file configuration.

- ✔ **Hardware:** Any changes in Device Manager and Windows Update Driver Settings are recorded and monitored.

A system restore point applies only to the files related to the operating system (OS) and doesn't allow you to revert to previous versions of most data files such as Word documents, PowerPoint presentations, or other application-related files. Of course, if your OS fails completely, you have a hardware failure, or a natural disaster occurs, a system restore might not help you. It is very important to understand exactly where a particular restore point will take you. I have seen many colleagues revert to a system restore point that was made weeks or months previously, only to find that they had lost particular configurations that they were expecting. If you revert to a restore point that was prior to a device driver or application being installed or some other configuration change that was made to your system, those changes will no longer be reflected in your configuration. If you find yourself in such a predicament, you can, however, revert to a newer restore point to regain those configurations.

Backing up files and folders

The Vista File and Folder Backup Wizard provides a quick and easy-to-use interface to back up specific file types and folders. You can choose what you want to back up yourself, or you can accept the default settings that the wizard provides. Before deciding to accept the default settings or make selections yourself, first understand what gets backed up — and what doesn't — by default:

- ✔ **Files types that are not backed up by default:** System files, encrypted files, program files, temporary files, and files that are in your Recycle Bin

- ✔ **File types that are backed up by default:** Pictures, music, e-mail, documents, TV shows, compressed files, and other files that are not included in the files that are not backed up

The Vista File and Folder Backup Wizard is likely one of those options that you will decide to use in your backup strategy. It can be used in concert with other Vista backup options and allows you the opportunity to get very granular in your backup strategy. Therefore, if you want to back up a particular file every day because it changes often but need to back up others only once per month (because they hardly ever change), you can easily accomplish those tasks with this option. The option allows you to do a manual backup or schedule for a more convenient time.

CompletePC Backup

Vista offers an excellent feature that lets you create an image of your system — *CompletePC Backup.* Essentially, this feature takes a snapshot of your system's settings, files (data), applications, boot volume, and system volume, as well as other volumes on your computer that you choose. You save that "image" of the system to restore later if needed. To make it even better, the CompletePC Backup utility tracks those changes to your hard drive so you can continue to update the backup image only with those changes. CompletePC Backup offers a far more comprehensive backup than the File and Folder Backup Wizard in that it essentially backs up your entire hard drive. Therefore, you can always have the latest copy of your hard drive to restore quickly and easily.

The CompletePC Backup option is very similar to third-party imaging tools that allow you the opportunity to take a complete hard drive image, without the additional cost of purchasing that third-party software. Although CompletePC Backup isn't available on the Vista Home Basic or Premium versions, it is available in the Business, Enterprise, and Ultimate versions.

The CompletePC Backup option serves a specific and extremely useful purpose. If you have a catastrophic hard drive failure, you simply replace the drive with a drive of the same type and size, and restore. An hour later, your system is up and running with the same applications, configurations, and data that you had prior to the failure. You don't have to reinstall your applications, configure your e-mail, or replace data. It's the same as it was when you last did a CompletePC Backup. If your system and data availability is important to you and you can't afford to take several hours (perhaps even days) to rebuild your OS, install and reconfigure your applications, and restore your data, this is an option that you should seriously consider.

Shadow Copy

Have you ever wished that you could do something over? Or perhaps revert to a previous version of a particular moment in your life? Well, in the digital world, Vista Business, Enterprise, and Ultimate versions allow you to do just that. The *Shadow Copy* feature not only allows open files to be backed up, but also allows users access to previous versions of their files. This feature creates a *point-in-time copy* of your files — better described as a *previous version* — so that you can retrieve different versions of a document. This is a very useful feature if you or someone you know tends to *overwrite* (save over) precious files. If you ever want to go back in time to a previous version of that file, now you can. (Now, if Microsoft can only come up with something that can do that for a few other things in life.)

Supported devices

The Vista Backup and Recovery utility provides some features that can meet the needs of most ambitious home and small office users. In previous versions of Windows, many users felt the need to go beyond the native Windows backup utility and purchase sometimes-costly, third-party backup and recovery utilities to accomplish what they now can accomplish with Vista's native utility.

Here are a few considerations worth mentioning that are not available in Vista but are available in third-party products:

- ✔ **Support for database backups:** The Vista Backup and Recovery utility will meet the needs of most home and small office users. Although the utility can back up Microsoft Access databases files, the utility does have some limitations with regard to backing up some databases, such as SQL, Oracle, and so on. If you use these types of databases, you likely need to use a third-party backup and restore product to preserve the information stored in them.

- ✔ **Off-site backups:** Although you can always take your backed-up data to an off-site location for storage, some backup services allow you to back up your data over the Internet. This is useful if you want to protect against natural disasters or if you travel a lot and need to recover your data while on the road.

- ✔ **Advanced backup methodologies:** Third-party backup software offers more options for incremental and differential backups and does a better job at backing up open files. Although Vista will make most home and small office users happy, if you have a need for these advanced methodologies, perhaps you should look at some third-party products. These products are more costly, however, so weigh the added functionality against the larger expense.

In Vista, you can back up to a secondary internal or external hard drive, a CD or DVD with writing capability, a network location, or a removable USB device.

Vista does not support tape drives.

Identifying Your Requirements

As essential as it is to understand the options that are available to you to backup and recover your system and data, that alone is not enough to get you where you need to be. To have a successful backup and recovery strategy, you need to understand the available options and also use those options that meet your requirements. Here are some considerations to take into account so that you can identify your backup and restore requirements:

- **What data you want to preserve:** All data is not created equal. You can break down data into three distinct areas: personal/business, application, and system configuration data. As important as identifying the *type* of data that you have on your computer is, it's just as important to understand its *value* to you. Only then can you select the right backup options that will preserve it appropriately. Is your goal to preserve your personal or business data and protect it from loss or to keep your system functioning and stable? For some, it may be both so that you have the ability to fully restore a copy of the entire system and data in the case of a crash. In addition, remember that some data requires more storage space. If you want to back up video or audio files, you will require more space and need to plan accordingly.

  - *Personal/business data:* This kind of data includes files such as your résumé, e-mail, financial information, or perhaps even medical information or proprietary business information.

  - *Application data:* This is data held in files that your applications use when tracking progress, when gathering input, or for configuration. For example, certain games have files that are continuously updated by the gaming application when the game is saved. In this way, all progress you made playing *The SIMS* is captured in a file that can be backed up (if you chose that it's important enough).

  - *System data:* For the most part, system data is used by the OS to function properly. Backing up this data is important if you're interested in preserving your system (which I will get into more later) so that you can quickly recover in the event of an OS failure or configuration issue.

- **Backup and recovery time:** More than ever, your time is precious, and you probably don't want to invest hour after hour preserving data that can easily be replaced. For that matter, the effort required to back up even the irreplaceable data might be too much time and effort for some people. A balance must be struck between the value of data and the time that you invest in backing up and restoring that data. Fortunately, Vista Backup and Recovery makes striking this balance easy and also makes backing up your data quick and painless. Still, backing up and recovering takes time. Keep in mind the time requirements, as follows:

  - *Backing up:* Although Vista makes backing up your data painless, some options require more time and effort than others. This is particularly true in the beginning when you first configure your backup job. For example, it takes more time to configure and run that first backup image than it does to back up a single file. After that, you simply put the backups on autopilot and schedule them to run at a convenient time.

- *Time to recover:* This is where the rubber hits the road for many of us: When recovering backed-up data, how long will your system or data be unavailable? Having an understanding of your tolerance for unavailability will guide you when selecting what media you back up to and what Vista backup option you select.

✔ **Storage media:** Each Vista backup option requires a certain amount of space to perform the backup, depending on a variety of things. Because some storage media is more expensive than others, understand what storage media you will most likely be using. Such an understanding can guide you when selecting the most appropriate backup option for you. Check out Table 8-1 for some options.

Table 8-1	Storage Device/Media Options	
Device/Media	*Storage Volume*	*Advantages*
CD burner	Up to 800MBon one CD	CDs can bestored off-site; CD-RW can be used for backup multiple times.
DVD burner	Up to 9.4GB on a double-sided DVD; up to 4.7GB on a single-sided DVD	DVDs can be stored off-site; DVD-RW can be used for backup multiple times.
External hard drive(USB/ network) or thumb drive	*External drives:* Typically range in size from 60GB to 500GB *Thumb drives:* Typically range from several MB to 2GB	Portable to use on multiple computers; provides easy-to-access offline storage.
Internal hard drive	Vary in sizes, typically from 60GB to 500GB	Content is always online and available.
Network share	Whatever size available from system sharing storage space	No need to purchase additional space; space can be shared with others; security is easy to enforce.
Online backup	Varies on the service	Protects data from fire or other local disaster; useful if you travel frequently and need to restore data while on the road.

Understanding and considering your requirements is an important part of your backup and recovery strategy. Your requirements are the foundation for which you will select the options and develop your plan for preserving your data.

Putting Your Requirements to Paper

Because everyone's backup and recovery needs are slightly different, I can't provide you a cookie-cutter worksheet that you can follow precisely that will meet all your needs. However, I do suggest that you pick up a piece of paper and sketch out something similar to Table 8-2 so that you can truly understand your requirements. Among the things you should list on this table are

- ✔ **Your requirements:** In the Requirements column in Table 8-2, I list some common requirements, but you should add any additional requirements that you might have or modify those listed if they don't apply to you. Your storage requirements should indicate the amount of storage space that you think that you will need. However, you won't likely be able to answer that question until you go through the following step where you inventory the data that you need to back up. Your storage constraints should indicate what storage space you have available to you. Understanding these will better help you select the backup and recovery options that are available to you.

- ✔ **Your data:** In the Data column of Table 8-2, list all the data elements that you want to protect and then align them with the corresponding requirements.

- ✔ **Your system:** Use the System column of Table 8-2 to list the requirements that are applicable to your system, not the data that resides on your system. For example, if it's important that your system be available as quickly as possible, capture those requirements. This will enable you to better understand which Vista backup options meet your requirements.

By completing the information in Table 8-2 and putting your requirements to paper, you build the foundation for your backup and recovery requirements and truly gain an understanding of what you need to accomplish when backing up and restoring your system or your personal, business, or application data. You use this information later as part of the upcoming "Planning Your Backup and Recovery Strategy" section of this chapter. Items in italics in Table 8-2 are only examples — you should modify them accordingly.

Table 8-2	Backup and Restore Requirements Worksheet	
Requirements	**Data (Specifically identify the data to protect)**	**System**
Time to restore: Need to restore quickly.		*It is important that I have the ability to restore my system quickly and not need to reload the complete OS and applications.*
Time to restore: Restoring quickly is not required.		
Files change frequently.	*Documents folder*	X
Files do not change often and can be archived.	*Music folder*	
Storage requirements (estimate)		*System restore requires minimum 300MB disk space. CompletePC Backup requires more depending on disk size.*
Storage constraints. (Specify what storage space you have available to you.)		
Protection requirements: Backup or archival of data/ system; protect against local disaster (fire, flood, and so on);retention period.		
Criticality of data: (understand how important certain pieces of data are so you can select the appropriate method and media to protect it).		

Planning Your Backup and Recovery Strategy

Developing a backup and recovery plan for a home or small office user is much different than planning for an enterprise environment. Unlike an enterprise environment, home users don't need to rally management support, have reams of documentation, or go through formal testing procedures. Your backup and recovery strategy is simply about taking your needs and requirements, selecting the Vista backup and recovery options that best meet your needs, and committing to implementing those options. Here are a couple steps that can help guide you:

1. **Decide what your needs and requirements are.**

   I discuss these needs and requirements in the earlier part of this chapter and specifically in Tables 8-1 and 8-2. If you've read the earlier part of this chapter, you should already have come to some conclusions about your needs and requirements. Although your backup requirements will likely change often — maybe a piece of data that's not so important to you today might suddenly become critical to you tomorrow — you should have a solid understanding of what it is that you need to back up. If you keep on top of what data you need to protect and modify your plan accordingly, you'll be able to breathe easy knowing that you are appropriately protected.

2. **Review Vista options.**

   I discuss these options in the section, "Choosing Your VistaBackup Options," earlier in this chapter. Review these options so that you're adequately familiar with each of them and can then select those that can help you when developing your plan. Additionally, your knowledge of these options will go a long way toward protecting your system or data in the future.

3. **Map your needs and requirements to the backup and recovery options.**

   This is the part of your plan where you select the options that you're going to use to meet your needs. Chances are that your plan will include multiple Vista backup and recovery options: Perhaps one option is good for one piece of data, but another might be required to protect another piece of data. Take the requirements you put to paper in Table 8-2 and match them against the various backup and recovery options available. For each requirement that you developed by using Table 8-2, select the appropriate backup and recovery option.

   Table 8-3 provides you with an overview of the options available in the various Vista versions.

4. Commit to implementing those options.

After you select the options to use to preserve your system or data, commit to implementing those options. This means that you need to understand when and how often you are going to use each option that you have chosen to use.

Table 8-3		Vista Backup and Recovery Options			
Backup and Recovery Options	**Vista Version**	**Use**	**Data Type Preserved**	**Backup/ Recovery Time**	**Storage Media**
System Restore Point	All	Protect OS from corruption	System configuration only	Fast backup and recovery	Back up within the OS itself, so the only option is the hard drive.
File and Folder Backup	All	Backup of specific data	Application and personal data	Dependent on how much data is backed up and how it is done	Media must be large enough to handle how much data is backed up, but it can be as small as you want.
System Image (Complete PC Backup)	Business, Enterprise, Ultimate	Capture of all data on machine for use in rebuilding	All	Slow backup but allows for fast recovery much data is compared with rebuilding the machine from scratch	Dependent upon how within the image Usually must be done on at least a DVD.
Shadow Copy	Business, Enterprise, Ultimate	Backup of open files and version control of files	Application and personal data	Fast backup and recovery	By default, reserves 15 percent of each hard drive volume, but both size and location can be configured.

You select your options and commit to executing those options to preserve your data. That sounds like a plan to me! After your backup and recovery plan is in place, you can start implementing the plan by configuring the Vista options you chose. See the section, "Organizing Your Data So It's Easy to Back Up," later in this chapter for the how-to information on performing backup and recoveries.

Most people who experience unrecoverable data loss aren't those who lack the knowledge to back up their data, but those who simply fail to execute their backup plan consistently. With the knowledge that you gain here and a commitment on your part to back up your system and data regularly, you never need to experience that gut-wrenching pain of losing your precious data.

Preserving Your System

Preserving your system is as important a part of your backup-and-restore strategy as preserving your data. Your system is the host of that precious data you hold so close to your heart, and when your system isn't available, neither is that data that you so desperately need to access. Vista provides two ways to preserve the state of your system — a system restore and CompletePC Backup — so that when something goes eerily wrong, you can restore and get back to working in no time.

Creating a restore point

A system restore is one of my favorite tools because it provides one of the few opportunities in the digital world where you can have a "do over" — that is, you can go back to a previous state where everything was okay. During a system restore, Vista automatically scans the system for changes and performs a restore when it detects that certain system settings have changed. You can also choose at any point to manually create a restore point. I suggest doing this immediately before making any significant system configuration changes so that you have an opportunity to back out of those changes in the event that something goes wrong.

To create a system restore, perform the following steps:

1. **From the Start menu, choose Control Panel.**

   In default Vista view, choose System and Maintenance and then click Backup and Restore Center. In classic view, choose Control Panel⇨Backup and Restore Center.

2. **From the Backup and Restore Center (as shown in Figure 8-1), select the Create a Restore Point or Change Settings task from the left Tasks pane.**

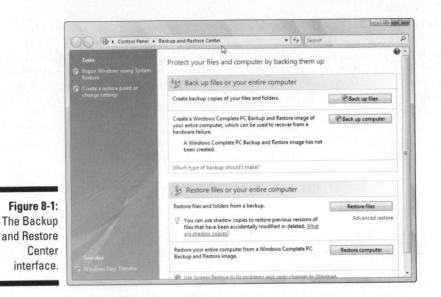

Figure 8-1:
The Backup
and Restore
Center
interface.

On the System Protection tab of the System Properties dialog box, as shown in Figure 8-2, you can create a system restore for any fixed disks on your system. (See Figure 8-2.)

Figure 8-2:
The System
Protection
tab of
the System
Properties
dialog box.

3. **In the Available Disks pane, place a check mark next to the disk on which you want to create a restore point.**

If you have multiple disks, you might see more than one disk displayed. Select the system disk, usually described as Local Disk (C:) (System).

4. **Click the Create button.**

5. **In the Create a Restore Point dialog box that appears (as shown in Figure 8-3), enter a name for your restore point and then click Create.**

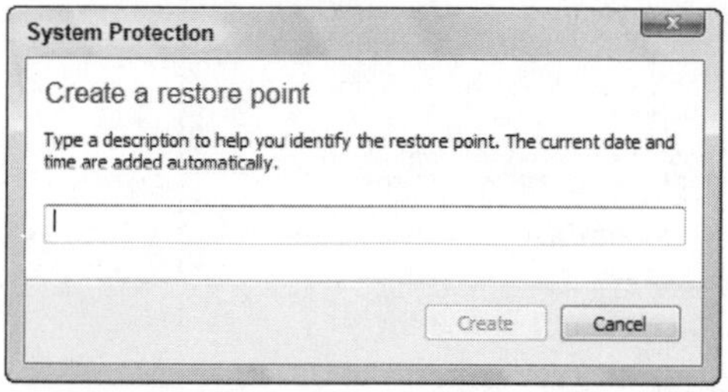

Figure 8-3:
Create a
restore
point here.

System Protection

Create a restore point

Type a description to help you identify the restore point. The current date and time are added automatically.

Create   Cancel

6. **Click OK when complete.**

A system restore point applies only to the files related to the OS and doesn't allow you to revert to previous versions of data files.

Restoring your system to a previous system state

Restoring your system to a previous restore point from the Backup and Restore Center is a very simple task. You can provide options to revert to the last restore point, or you can choose to browse the previous restore points that were created. As a rule, always use the latest restore point. However, say you have a problem for several days. In those situations, using the most recent restore point might not eliminate the problem. In those cases, you wouldn't want to use the latest restore point, but one that was taken prior to the first occurrence of the problem.

To restore, perform the following steps:

1. **From the Start menu, choose Control Panel.**

   In default view, choose System and Maintenance and then click Backup and Restore Center. In classic view, choose Control Panel⇨Backup and Restore Center.

2. **In the Backup and Restore Center window (refer to Figure 8-1), select the Repair Windows Using System Restore task from the left Tasks pane.**

3. **From the Restore System Files and Settings window (as shown in Figure 8-4), select the appropriate restore point.**

   You can select either the latest restore point or a previous one.

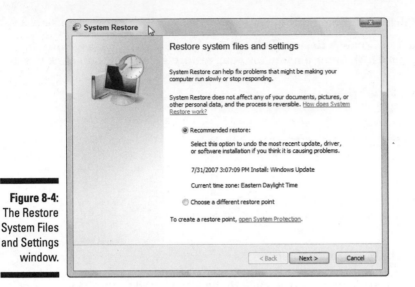

Figure 8-4:
The Restore
System Files
and Settings
window.

4. **Click Next.**

   Your selected restore point is displayed.

5. **Click Finish.**

   Your system is then restored to the selected restore point. It might take several minutes for the process to complete.

Organizing Your Data So It's Easy to Back Up

Vista provides a few options for backing up your data, depending (of course) on what it is that you want to achieve. No matter which options you choose, however, identifying and backing up your data is easier if you first know where it is. Before getting into how to use the various data backup and restore options, I first discuss how you can make finding that data and backing it up easier for you now and in the future.

If your backup strategy relies on doing backups of specific pieces of data, instead of using a CompletePC Backup image where both your system state and all the data on your system is backed up, organizing where you store your data can make the task much easier. This makes locating your data easier not only on a day-to-day basis, but also during the restore process.

A long time ago, Microsoft recognized users' need to organize their data and thus created the My Documents folder. Now, the Vista Documents folder is the default storage location for each user on a computer. Vista also provides a number of other folders — for Pictures, Video, and more — to allow for more detailed organization. Additionally, you can create your own folders within any of these to provide even further specificity to meet your own requirements.

You can change the location of Documents folder by right-clicking the Documents folder, choosing Properties, and then changing the path in the location tabs. This is something you might want to consider if you have a second partition or a hard drive with more room.

As you begin organizing your data, I suggest that you implement a strategy specific enough to allow you to organize your data with the following tips in mind:

- ✔ **Don't place individual files directly under Documents.** Folders are tools that help you organize your data. Having your files organized allows you to ensure that they get backed up, allowing you to restore them more easily.

- ✔ **Create an archive folder.** Create a folder under the Documents folder named Archive and shift older folders and documents that you haven't touched in a long time into this folder. Although Vista will back up based upon the type of file (and will ignore these folders), this still provides you value if there is something that you want to burn to CD or DVD for archiving instead of using the backup wizard.

- ✔ **Organize based on type of file.** If you organize your data based on the type of file (music files, videos, and so on), you can customize a backup job for a particular group of files or folders. For example, if you have a folder where you keep all your music files, you can create a backup job that uses a CD or DVD to archive those files.

Backing Up with Backup and Restore

Vista Backup and Restore Center allows you to use the Backup and Restore Files Wizard to back up and recover specific files, create and restore a CompletePC image (in the Business, Enterprise, and Ultimate versions of Vista), and create and revert to system restore points — all from one easy-to-use, central interface.

Backing up files with the Backup Files Wizard

With the Backup Files Wizard, you can perform a manual backup of particular types of files or let the wizard perform the backup automatically. Although the interface allows you to schedule a backup job to run automatically, it doesn't allow you to configure multiple jobs. Therefore, I recommend that you schedule a job that captures the types of files that you want to back up on a regular basis. For a more customized backup event, such as backing your music files to a CD or DVD, you need to run the job manually. To perform a backup with the wizard, follow these steps:

1. **From the Backup and Restore Center interface (refer to Figure 8-1), select Change Settings under the Back Up Files button.**

2. **Select the Change Backup Settings button.**

3. **When prompted with the Where Do You Want to Save Your Backup window (as shown in Figure 8-5), select a location.**

   Your choices are

   - *A hard disk:* The hard disk can be an internal or external disk, but it cannot be a flash drive device.

   - *CD:* Any writable CD-ROM.

   - *DVD:* Any writable DVD-ROM.

   - *On a network:* A network location can be a network resource or an Internet backup service.

4. **After you select the appropriate backup location, click Next.**

   You are prompted to select the file types to be backed up. Here, you don't specify specific folders. Instead, you're prompted to provide the *types* of files that you want to back up, such as pictures, music, videos, e-mail, documents, TV shows, compressed files, and additional files. Microsoft describes the *additional files* option as being any other files that do not fit in the other categories. However, system files, program files, and temporary files will never be backed up.

   If you move your cursor over each file category type, information about that particular category is displayed. I suggest that you become familiar with exactly what is included in each category type. Although the utility doesn't allow you to point to a specific folder, organizing your data at the folder level continues to be important during the restore process.

5. **After you select the file types that you want to back up, click Next.**

   You're prompted to configure how often you want to run this backup.

6. **Choose Daily, Weekly, Monthly, or specify what day of the week and what time you would like it to run.**

7. **Execute the backup by clicking the Save Settings and Start Up Backup button.**

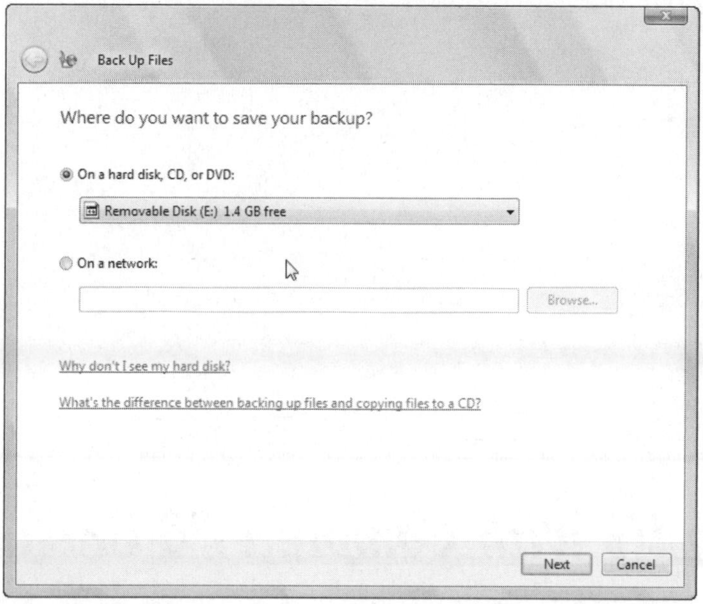

Back Up Files

Where do you want to save your backup?

⦿ On a hard disk, CD, or DVD:

Removable Disk (E:) 1.4 GB free ▾

○ On a network:

Browse...

Why don't I see my hard disk?

What's the difference between backing up files and copying files to a CD?

Next   Cancel

Figure 8-5:
Assigning
the location
of backup
files.

Restoring files and folders

The Backup and Restore Center interface provides an easy way to restore single files or entire folders that you backed up by using the Backup Files Wizard. Use the following steps to restore files and folders:

1. **From the Backup and Restore Center interface, click the Restore Files button within the Restore Files or Your Entire Computer section.**

   You are asked what you want to restore.

2. **In the Restore Files dialog box, shown in Figure 8-6, choose either Files from The Latest Backup or Files from an Older Backup. Then click Next.**

3. **Choose which files or folders that you want to restore by clicking the Add Files, Add Folders, or Search button.**

4. **After you add the files or folders that you want to restore, click Next.**

5. **Choose the location where you want to restore the files to (a folder on the system, a network share, or even another disk), and then click Next.**

6. **When the restore is complete, click Finish.**

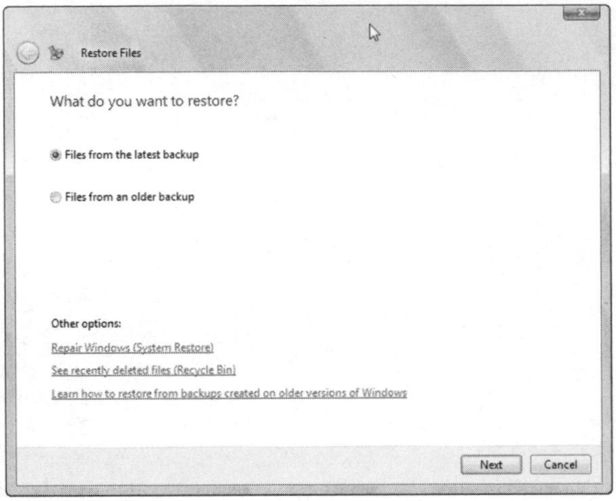

Figure 8-6:
Select
which files
to restore.

Backing Up with CompletePC Backup

This is one of my favorite features of Backup and Restore! Finally — a native OS utility that enables you to make an image of your system much the same way that expensive, third-party tools have enabled you to do for several years. CompletePC Backup allows you to back up your system state and all the data that lives on your system in just a few easy steps. This could save you hours of time if you were to run into a problem where you need to reinstall your OS and applications, configure your system settings, and restore your data. You simply restore your CompletePC backup, and you're ready to go! Use the following steps to back up your system and data with a CompletePC Backup:

1. **From the Backup and Restore Center interface, click the Back Up Computer button within the Back Up Files or Your Entire Computer section.**

    At the Windows CompletePC Backup window (shown in Figure 8-7), you are asked where you want to save the backup.

2. **Select the location where you want to save the backup and then click Next.**

A CompletePC Backup is a compressed bit image of your hard disk, so you need a considerable amount of space to perform this type of backup. The good news is that the wizard will indicate how much space you need to perform such a backup before you begin.

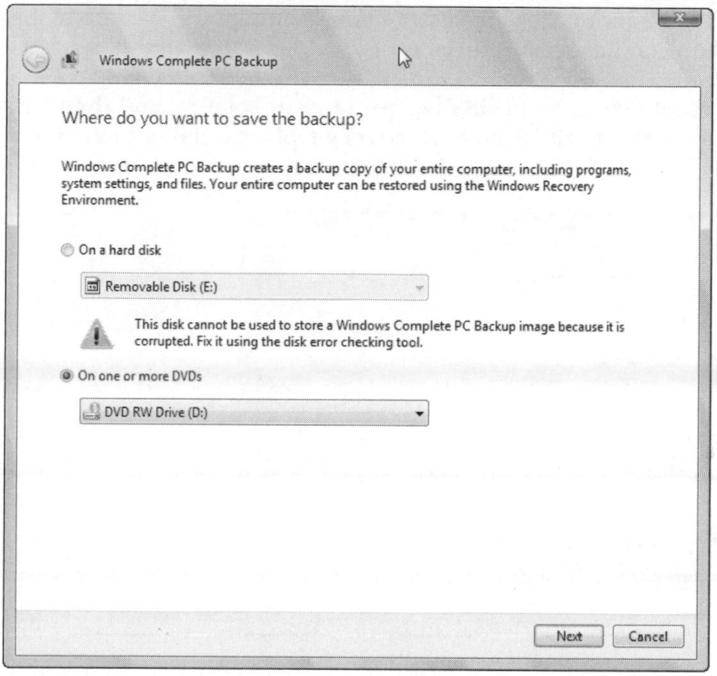

Figure 8-7:
Select
where to
save the
Windows
CompletePC
Backup.

> **Windows Complete PC Backup**
>
> **Where do you want to save the backup?**
>
> Windows Complete PC Backup creates a backup copy of your entire computer, including programs, system settings, and files. Your entire computer can be restored using the Windows Recovery Environment.
>
> ○ On a hard disk
>
> [ ] Removable Disk (E:)
>
> ⚠ This disk cannot be used to store a Windows Complete PC Backup image because it is corrupted. Fix it using the disk error checking tool.
>
> ● On one or more DVDs
>
> [ ] DVD RW Drive (D:)
>
> [Next] [Cancel]

3. **Verify that the settings are correct and that you have enough space to perform the backup. Then select Start Backup.**

   The CompletePC Backup runs. Depending on the size of the disk, this could take several minutes.

4. **When the backup is complete, click OK.**

Restoring a CompletePC Backup

If you're at the point where you need to restore your system with a CompletePC Backup, things probably have not been going very well. The good news, however, is that CompletePC Backup can be restored quite easily. The restoration process takes a little longer than the backup process, but you can breathe easy if you have a current CompletePC Backup to use as a restore. After you complete the restore process, you will have your system back just as it was when you made the backup — and in a lot less time that it would take to reinstall your OS and applications and restore your data.

You restore a CompletePC Backup from the System Recovery Options menu by booting from a Vista disc and pressing F8 at startup.

Use the following steps to restore your CompletePC Backup by using the Backup and Recovery interface:

1. **Boot from a Vista OS disc, press F8 at startup, and then follow the prompts to the System Recovery Options dialog box. (See Figure 8-8.)**

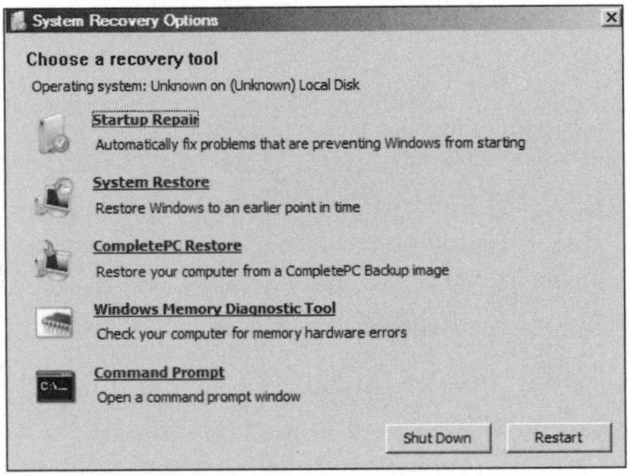

System Recovery Options

Choose a recovery tool
Operating system: Unknown on (Unknown) Local Disk

Startup Repair
Automatically fix problems that are preventing Windows from starting

System Restore
Restore Windows to an earlier point in time

CompletePC Restore
Restore your computer from a CompletePC Backup image

Windows Memory Diagnostic Tool
Check your computer for memory hardware errors

Command Prompt
Open a command prompt window

Shut Down   Restart

Figure 8-8:
The System
Recovery
Options
interface.

2. **From the menu in the System Recovery Options shown in Figure 8-8, choose CompletePC Restore.**

3. **From the wizard, select the CompletePC Backup with the appropriate date and timestamp that you want to restore. Then click Next.**

4. **Verify your selections, select any advance options, and then click Finish.**

   Your restore will take several minutes to run.

5. **Remove the Vista disc when your system restore is complete.**

   Your system is restored to the state it was in when you ran the backup.

A little about shadow copying

Although the Vista backup features allow you to revert to previous versions of a backup (if one exists), it offers yet another nice feature that allows you to revert to a previous file version that was captured as part of a system restore point. When performing system restore points, files that are updated are "shadow copied," providing a record of a previous version of the file.

I don't know about you, but I have mistakenly overwritten a file or two in my time and did not have an up-to-date copy of the file. With the Shadow Copy feature, you can now restore a file to a previous version — if one exists.

To restore a file that has an existing previous version, perform the following steps:

1. **Right-click the file and choose Properties.**

   The Properties dialog box appears.

2. **Go to the Previous Versions tab.**

   Any existing previous versions of the file are displayed for your selection. If no previous versions exist, the display window will be empty.

3. **To restore a previous version, highlight the appropriate version and then select Restore.**

   You are prompted with a Previous Versions dialog box asking whether you want to overwrite the newer version with the older version.

4. **Select Restore.**

5. **When the file has been restored, click OK.**

Chapter 9

Planning and Implementing Encrypting File System

In This Chapter

▶ Protecting sensitive data

▶ Recovering encrypted files

▶ Developing your file- and folder-encryption strategy

*P*rotecting sensitive data has never been more important. Just ask those organizations that had a data breach of customer data. Or ask those people who had their financial login and password information stolen from their computers, which were then used to access and drain their financial accounts.

Vista Encrypting File System (EFS) can help protect your sensitive information. Vista Encrypting File System helps protect your sensitive data if your computer is lost or stolen or from other unauthorized access.

In this chapter, you can discover the basics of encryption and under what circumstances EFS can help you and when you might need to turn to some other Vista or third-party tools for more complex protection. I show you the basic principles of encrypting your files and folders, backing up your encryption keys, and how to recover encrypted files. You can also read how and when to make EFS part of your security plan. Although this chapter won't make you an EFS expert, it will provide you with the foundation that you need to get started using EFS to protect your sensitive data.

Encryption 101

To use EFS, you need to understand a little about encryption. Encryption protects certain information from unauthorized disclosure, even if someone has the information. In other words, the intent of encryption is to make a piece of data unreadable to those unauthorized to read it.

The basic principle of making information unreadable by anyone but those for whom it was intended goes back even to the Egyptians, who used hieroglyphics to conceal writings.

Cryptographic techniques are used for a variety of purposes, such as

- Military intelligence
- Proprietary business information
- Personal information

Symmetric encryption

Symmetric encryption uses the same number, character, or word — or even a string of characters — in the text of a message to both encrypt and decrypt a message.

Because the message is changed, only those who understand how the original message was changed have the ability, or the "secret key," to translate the changed message into the real message. The sender of the message modified it with the secret key to encrypt the message so that others without the key could not read it. Message recipients have the same secret key, so upon retrieval of the message, they can decrypt the encrypted message and determine the message's intended meaning. In symmetric encryption, the same key is used to encrypt and to decrypt the message.

With symmetric encryption, anyone who has the key can both send and read messages.

Asymmetric encryption

Asymmetric encryption uses two different keys to encrypt and decrypt messages: These keys, although different, are related to one another.

- **Private key:** Used to *read* encrypted messages

  If information is encrypted by using the public key — for example. a document — the document can only be read (decrypted) by using the associated private key.

- **Public key:** Made freely available to *encrypt* messages

  Anyone who wants to send you a message can get the public key to do so. After the public key is applied, the data can't be decrypted and read without the private key, even if someone with the public key intercepts the encrypted message.

The public and private keys are a *key pair*.

Because you can't use just the public key to encrypt and decrypt the message, you can easily provide others with access to the public key.

Protecting Your Files and Folders with EFS

Encrypting File System is used to protect the files and folders on your system from unauthorized access. However, it really is the last layer of security. Many other controls are in place that control unauthorized access to your system and data. Encryption — EFS, in this case — is there to help protect your files from unauthorized access from those people who circumvent the other security controls.

What's new

The Microsoft Encrypting File System (EFS) made its debut long ago with Microsoft Windows NT. Encrypting File System in Windows NT was a bit clunky and hard to manage. Although many users were successful in encrypting their data, they ended up not being able to read the files themselves for one reason or another.

Not until the advent of Microsoft Windows XP did EFS really started catching some steam, and users started using it more often to protect their sensitive data. However, even in Windows XP, users lost readability of their own data.

Vista EFS is rather complex — and users, from time to time, will find themselves in a little bit of a mess. *Windows Vista Security For Dummies* guides you through the minefield.

Vista includes several new security, performance, and management enhancements to the EFS:

✔ **Smart card integration**

Now you can store your user keys and recovery keys on smart cards. This allows for data recovery without a dedicated recovery workstation.

✔ **Ability to encrypt paging file**

Vista EFS allows you to use EFS to encrypt the pagefile, allowing more security than in previous versions of EFS. The key is generated when the system starts up and is destroyed when the system shuts down, thus providing more security.

✔ **Offline Files cache encryption**

Vista EFS encrypts the Offline Files cache with the user's key, providing security so that only the user can access his associated Offline files cache.

✔ **Extended support of certificates and keys**

Vista EFS offers support for a variety of certificates and keys.

Use EFS in conjunction with other security controls as part of a defense-in-depth security strategy.

Table 9-1 illustrates whether EFS can help reduce some common security concerns.

Table 9-1	Protection Offered by EFS
Protection/Risk	*Does EFS Help Mitigate?*
Can protect data on laptop or desktop	Yes.
Protects your data from other users on shared computer	Yes, in protected files and folders.
Remote file and folder protection	Yes.
Protects data when sent in e-mail or across a network	No; data is decrypted before being sent.
Protects data on removable media	No.
Protects against booting the operating system with tools to gain administrative access to system	No; EFS does not protect system files.
Protects against loss of data from unauthorized deletion	No; users with the appropriate rights can delete an encrypted file.

In addition to the security concerns found in Table 9-1, you should be aware of the type of data that resides on your system and where it lives when considering whether to use EFS to encrypt the files and folders on your system:

- **Only files and folder on a NT File System (NTFS) volume can be encrypted.**

  Files encrypted with EFS are decrypted prior to being sent over a network or via e-mail or otherwise moved to a non-NTFS volume.

  However, you can use Web-distributed authoring and versioning (WebDAV) to transfer files in encrypted form.

- **Files and folders that are compressed cannot also be encrypted.**

  If you select to encrypt a file or folder and that file or folder is compressed, the system will uncompress and then encrypt.

- **Moving unencrypted files to an encrypted folder causes the files to be encrypted in the new folder.**

  If, however, you move the encrypted files from the encrypted folder to a folder that's not encrypted, the files won't be decrypted. A specific decryption operation needs to be performed to decrypt the files.

✔ **Certain files cannot be encrypted with EFS:**

- • Files with a system attribute

- • Files in the system root directory structure

✔ **Encryption doesn't protect other users on the system from seeing the file, nor does it protect them from deleting it.**

If a user has permission to delete the file, he can delete the file even if it's encrypted.

✔ **If a user gains access to your system by using your account or an account that has Data Recovery Agent authority to your encrypted files, he can decrypt and read your encrypted data.**

Only when accessing the files without the authority to view them is a user prevented from doing so.

How Encrypting File System works

Encrypting File System uses both asymmetric and symmetric encryption to provide

✔ **The performance benefits found in symmetric encryption**

Symmetric encryption has less overhead than asymmetric encryption.

✔ **Strengthened security, as found in asymmetric encryption**

Here's how EFS works:

1. When EFS encrypts a file, it follows these steps:

    a. *EFS locks the file and generates a File Encryption Key (FEK).*

    The FEK is a symmetric encryption key, so it can both encrypt and decrypt the file.

    b. *After the FEK is generated, the file is encrypted.*

    The FEK is used only for that file.

    c. *EFS uses the user's public key to encrypt the FEK.*

    The encrypted FEK is stored in a Data Decryption Field (DDF) in the header of an encrypted file.

2. When the file is decrypted, EFS follows these steps:

    a. *EFS retrieves the user's private key to decrypt the FEK.*

    b. *EFS subsequently decrypts the file with the FEK.*

Because the FEK isn't tied to a specific user, any user with FEK might be able to decrypt the file.

Encrypting folders

Encrypting File System lets you encrypt any folder that resides on your system. If you encrypt a folder, any files that you place in that folder are also encrypted.

This is beneficial if you need to organize your data so that you move only those files that might be sensitive to the encrypted folder to protect them.

To encrypt a specific folder, perform the following steps.

1. **Right-click the folder and choose Properties.**

2. **Select Advanced Properties.**

3. **In the Advanced Attributes window, select the Encrypt Contents to Secure Data check box, as shown in Figure 9-1.**

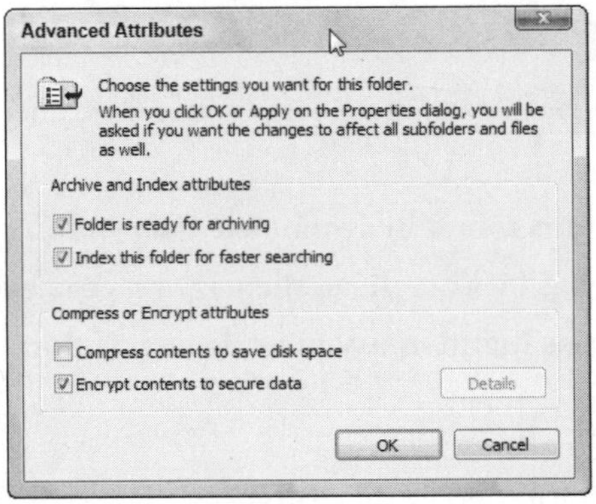

Figure 9-1:
A folder's
Advanced
Attributes
window.

Advanced Attributes

Choose the settings you want for this folder.
When you click OK or Apply on the Properties dialog, you will be asked if you want the changes to affect all subfolders and files as well.

Archive and Index attributes

☑ Folder is ready for archiving
☑ Index this folder for faster searching

Compress or Encrypt attributes

☐ Compress contents to save disk space
☑ Encrypt contents to secure data   Details

OK   Cancel

After you encrypt the specified folder, any files that you move into that folder are encrypted. However, any unencrypted files that were in the folder prior to encryption won't be encrypted. For those unencrypted files, you can either encrypt each file individually or move those files from the folder and then back into the folder. After they're moved back into the encrypted folder, they are then encrypted.

Your Vista computer's Local Security Policy provides functionality that you can use to enforce the encryption of the Documents folder for each user on the system. In this way, you can have some assurance that any files that a user stores in his Documents folder are protected by EFS. To do so, follow these steps:

1. **From the Start menu, choose Control Panel.**

2. **Depending on the view set in Control Panel, choose one of the following:**

   - *Default View:* Choose System and Maintenance⇨Administrative Tools⇨Local Security Policy.

   - *Classic View:* Choose Administrative Tools⇨Local Security Policy.

3. **In the left pane, select Public Key Policies.**

4. **Under Public Key Policies, right-click Encrypting File System and then choose Properties.**

5. **In the Encrypting File System Properties window, select the Encrypt the Contents of the User's Documents Folder check box, as shown in Figure 9-2.**

Figure 9-2 shows the EFS properties that allow you to enable encryption on each system user's Documents folder.

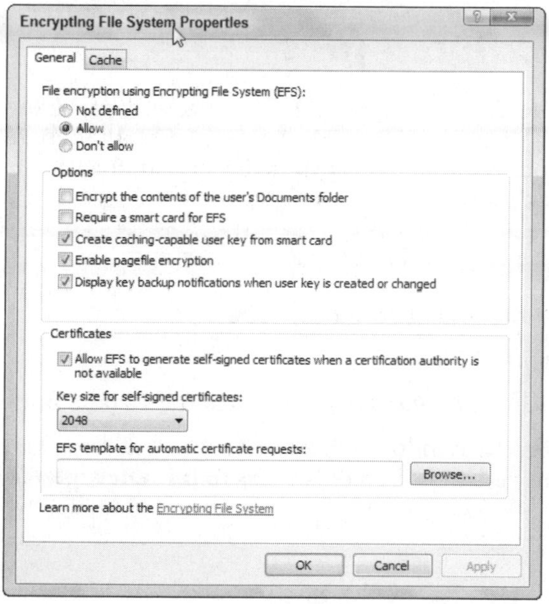

Figure 9-2:
EFS
Properties
window.

Don't use Local Security Policy to enforce encryption on each user's Documents directory without proper notification to and training of all users of the system:

If users aren't aware that such a level of protection is being provided, they won't know to place their sensitive files in that directory. Additionally, there is an increased risk of loss of data. If a user loses a private key stored within his profile, he also loses the ability to read his encrypted files. You can take steps to recover from such an event, but users must be aware whether EFS is in place so they can follow the proper procedures.

Encrypting a specific file

Encrypting File System allows you to encrypt an individual file without encrypting a folder or any other files in a particular directory. For those of us who might not have many files containing any type of sensitive information, this feature is very useful.

To encrypt an individual file, perform the following steps:

1. **Right-click the file and choose Properties.**

2. **On the General tab of the file's Properties window, click the Advanced button.**

3. **In the Advanced Attributes window (as shown previously in Figure 9-1), select the Encrypt Contents to Secure Data check box.**

Sharing encrypted files

From time to time, you'll probably want to share your digital files — maybe photos, documents, or even a PowerPoint presentation that contains some sensitive information. Wanting to encrypt a file so that unauthorized users can't access it doesn't mean that you'll never want to share that files.

To share an encrypted file, perform the following steps:

1. **Right-click the file and choose Properties.**

2. **Click the Advanced button.**

3. **On the Advanced Attributes window, click the Details button.**

4. **On the User Access Window, click the Add button and then select the user whom you want to have access to this encrypted file. (See Figure 9-3.)**

5. **Click OK.**

6. **Click OK at the User Access window.**

   The user has access to your encrypted file.

To give specific permission to the user, you can use NTFS permission at the file level. For example, if you want to allow a user to access an encrypted file but you want to grant Read permission — not Modify — provide Read permission at the NTFS level.

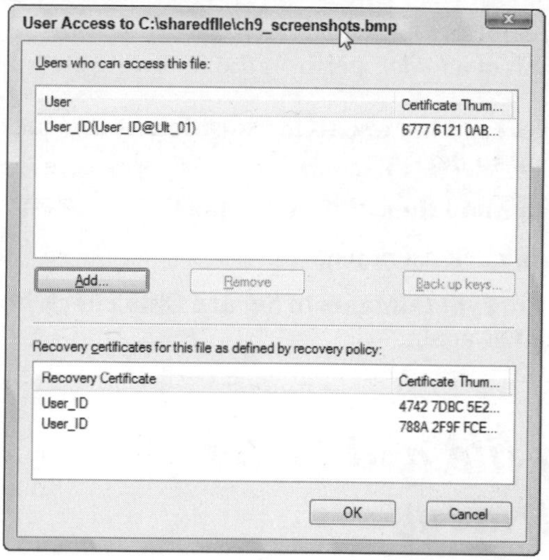

User Access to C:\sharedflle\ch9_screenshots.bmp

Users who can access this file:

User	Certificate Thum...
User_ID(User_ID@Ult_01)	6777 6121 0AB...

Add...   Remove   Back up keys...

Recovery certificates for this file as defined by recovery policy:

Recovery Certificate	Certificate Thum...
User_ID	4742 7DBC 5E2...
User_ID	788A 2F9F FCE...

OK   Cancel

Figure 9-3: The User Access window.

Data recovery

When I talk about data recovery, I mean the decryption of data encrypted by using EFS. Perhaps a user's attempt to protect certain files on his computer by encrypting them with EFS goes awfully wrong, and the user find that he can't read the data. Perhaps, too, a security-conscious employee left your organization and left encrypted data on his computer. Now you find yourself in a situation where you need to access that data for legitimate business purposes. What do you do?

The good news is that EFS can recover that data — under certain conditions.

If you're a designated recovery agent attempting to recover encrypted data, you must move the user's encrypted file to a computer where the recovery certificate and key are located.

Recovering files

To remove encryption from a *file,* perform the following steps:

1. **Browse to the location of the encrypted file that you want to decrypt.**

2. **Right-click the encrypted file and then choose Properties.**

3. **On the General tab, click Advanced.**

4. **Click to clear the Encrypt Contents to Secure Data check box, click OK, and then click OK again.**

Recovering folders

To remove the encryption of a *folder,* perform the following steps:

1. **Use Windows Explorer to browse to the location of the encrypted folder that you want to decrypt.**

2. **Right-click the folder and then choose Properties.**

3. **On the General tab, click Advanced.**

4. **Click to clear the Encrypt Contents to Secure Data check box, click OK, and then click OK again.**

Developing a file and folder encryption strategy

Using EFS can help you protect the files and folders on your system from being accessed and read by unauthorized people. However, to get the most from this tool, you need a file- and folder-encryption strategy that addresses the following essential planning steps.

User education

Although Vista makes EFS friendlier to the end user, EFS is a very complex tool. With the use of Group Policy in a larger environment or by manipulating the local security policy of a particular system in your home or small office, you can enforce EFS upon every user of the system (perhaps without users even knowing that you're doing so). Using EFS might provide some security benefit, but it also introduces some risk that users will lose a private key and not be able to read their encrypted data.

With some user education, you can limit that risk and get the most value from EFS. The information covered in this chapter won't make you an expert in deploying EFS in a large enterprise environment, but it will give you the information that you need to implement in your home or small office.

If you require users of your system to use EFS, share the information in this chapter with them so that they can use it appropriately.

Understanding what files to encrypt

It doesn't do any good to use EFS if you don't understand what type of data you should encrypt. And because EFS can't automatically hunt down sensitive files on your system and automatically encrypt them for you, it's your responsibility. There you have it — this is your mission if you choose to accept it!

Unfortunately, this decision isn't that easy. After all, when is a file sensitive enough that you should encrypt it? The answer is likely different for each user. Here are some guidelines as to the type of information that you might want to protect with EFS:

✔ **Does the file contain your or anyone else's Personally Identifiable Information (PII)?**

Consider sensitive information, such as name, address, Social Security number, and financial information that someone could use to perpetrate identity theft or other crimes of fraud.

Several states have laws that require that this type of data be encrypted: namely, data that is either

• Covered under *regulatory mandates,* such as the Health Insurance Portability and Accountability Act (HIPAA) or Sarbanes-Oxley

• Protected under *contractual obligations,* such as the Payment Card Industry (PCI) Data Standard

✔ **Does the file contain otherwise sensitive information?**

Maybe the data isn't considered Personally Identifiable Information (PII), but is such that you want to make sure that others cannot read it. This might be your résumé, your little black book, a letter to your girlfriend — who knows? Still, it's likely data that's private enough to you that you don't want it read by others without the authority.

Organizing your data

Because EFS isn't a full-disk encryption technology, you should organize your data in a way makes it easier to ensure that your sensitive data is encrypted. You can encrypt your Documents folder, or you can designate a different folder that you flag for encryption. You then put all your sensitive files in that folder to be encrypted. As you might imagine, organizing your data in an ad hoc fashion makes it virtually impossible to ensure that your data is properly protected. Therefore, you need to identify a way to organize your data.

Because your Documents folder can have a lot of files that don't need to be encrypted, I suggest using a folder within the Documents folder where you keep whatever data rises to the level of EFS protection. I suggest, however, that you not label this folder something as obvious as Sensitive Data, but use a name that's a little less intuitive to an intruder. You can then encrypt the folder with EFS and move any files that need that level of protection to that folder.

However you choose to organize your data, keep it as simple as possible. Keeping all your data in a central location — such as your Documents folder — makes it easier for you to locate and identify the data that needs to be protected. You can then organize your data in subfolders of the Documents folder to easily identify what it is and how it should be protected.

Backing up your encryption keys

Backing up or exporting your encryption keys is very important. That way, if you lose the private key stored in your user profile, you can recover your encrypted data.

To back up your private key, perform the following:

1. **Open the Certificate Manager by typing** certmgr.msc **at the Start menu Search prompt.**

2. **When the Certificate Manager console window opens, expand the Personal container (in the left pane) and then click the Certificates container.**

   You see a list of all the certificates installed on the system.

3. **Locate the proper EFS certificate that you want to back up, right-click, and then choose All Tasks⇨Export.**

4. **When the Certificate Export Wizard becomes active, click Next.**

5. **At the Export Private Key window, select Yes for the Export Private Key option and then click Next.**

6. **Choose the Personal Information Exchange option and then click Next.**

   You are prompted for a password.

7. **Select a strong password (and confirm it) to protect the private key that you're exporting.**

8. **Select the location where you want to export the encrypted key and then click Finish.**

When you password-protect a key, remember to place the key in a secure place. Not doing so circumvents the security that you're putting in place to protect your data. Anyone who gains access to this key can decrypt and read the information that you worked so hard to protect.

A word about roaming profiles

If you're one of the few using roaming profiles in your home or small office, you need to understand that the user's private key is stored in the user's profile.

When a roaming profile is accessed, the data is downloaded across the network. Because EFS doesn't protect data in transit, in this circumstance, the user's private key will traverse the network in an unencrypted form and *will not be protected.*

Technologies such as Internet Protocol security (IPsec) can help you mitigate that risk; however, this is beyond the scope of this book.

Chapter 10

Avoiding Data Theft with BitLocker

You've probably heard about situations in which a mobile computer is lost or stolen, with the Personally Identifiable Information (PII) of thousands, perhaps millions, of people just like you and me. In the wrong hands, names, addresses, Social Security numbers, and other sensitive information can leave people in a financial quagmire for years to come. This isn't some far-fetched fantasy, but (unfortunately) an event that occurs all too frequently. Finally, organizations are beginning to realize that they must to do something about breaches like this. Perhaps they feel some sense of moral obligation to protect sensitive data entrusted to them. However, for many more organizations, their recent willingness to spend a bunch of time and money to protect this data has far less to do with any sense of moral obligation and more to do with legislation.

Currently, more than three-dozen states have some sort of data breach legislation that requires notification if certain types of data are compromised. The standard for such protection at this point is that the data must be encrypted. After several high-profile data breaches left millions scrambling to protect themselves from identity theft and other crimes of fraud, more states are certain to follow through with their own data breach legislation, and the federal government is gearing up to take a swing at legislation to address this problem as well.

Make no mistake: This is not a new problem. Our sensitive information has been compromised in these incidents for years, but only recently has legislation existed that requires organizations to notify us when such a compromise occurs.

Whether you believe that such legislation ultimately helps protect our sensitive information or you believe that regulation will lead to the financial demise of many small companies, one thing is for sure: It has played a large role in getting everyone from CEOs to regular Joes like you and me to take more of an interest in protecting sensitive information.

In this chapter, you find out how you can use the Vista BitLocker encryption tool to help you protect your, and perhaps others', sensitive digital information.

Keeping Data Safe with BitLocker

For most of us, our computing systems have become an integral part of our lives. We use them to manage our finances, process medical reimbursement claims, file our taxes, and do online banking. Without a doubt, having our systems hold or process such information represents a certain level of risk. If the computer system in question is a laptop or other mobile device, even more risk occurs. Such a system is often the target of crooks who steal them to sell on eBay for pennies on the dollar. Perhaps a crook will even attempt to harvest sensitive information, which they (or others) can use to perpetuate identity theft or other crimes of fraud. Vista provides two useful tools to help you keep the data that resides on your systems safe:

 ✔ **Encrypting File System (EFS):** I discuss this in Chapter 9.

 ✔ **BitLocker:** I cover BitLocker in this chapter.

Independently or in concert, use these tools to bring an extra layer of protection to your sensitive information that lives on your computer in your home or small office. Use EFS to encrypt files and folders, and use BitLocker to encrypt files on a Windows operating system (OS) volume. Therefore, to protect the data on your OS volume and those files tucked away in other volumes of your system, use both products for optimal protection.

BitLocker is a drive-encryption tool offered on the Enterprise and Ultimate versions of Vista. Using BitLocker provides an additional level of security for your sensitive data against compromise and unauthorized access. It provides the following protections:

 ✔ **Boot protection:** If BitLocker is enabled on a system that has a Trusted Platform Module (TPM) of version 1.2 or higher, you can intentionally interfere with the normal boot process. No one can boot into the OS without supplying a password (personal identification number; PIN) or a BitLocker startup key (if this feature is enabled). This provides you an additional level of protection against offline attacks. The TPM features monitor BIOS, hard disk configuration, and other startup changes. Monitoring this is valuable because changes in these areas might indicate a security risk or system problem, such as your hard drive being removed and started in another system, disk errors, and so on. You can determine whether a TPM is present in your system or enable it within the BIOS. Because many different BIOS versions exist, check your system documentation for instructions on how to get into the BIOS of your specific system.

✔ **Encrypting user and system files:** BitLocker encrypts the user and system files on your Windows OS volume by using Advanced Encryption Standard (AES) level encryption. By default, AES 128-bit is enabled, but your configuration options include AES 256 and use Diffuser. If your system is lost or stolen, crooks can use a variety of tools to steal your precious data if the data isn't encrypted. BitLocker can reduce the risk associated with that security threat by encrypting any files that reside on the encrypted volume.

BitLocker Requirements

To take advantage of protecting your data with BitLocker, your system must meet the following requirements:

✔ **Windows Vista OS:** Although BitLocker is also supported on a Windows server OS, for the purpose of this discussion, I focus on the Windows Vista client OS. BitLocker is available only with Vista's Enterprise and Ultimate versions.

✔ **A TPM microchip:** Although TPM is listed as a requirement for BitLocker, you can actually enable BitLocker if your system doesn't have a TPM module. However, this requires that you boot from a USB device. Each time you start your computer, a startup key that is stored on the USB device is used as part of the boot process.

To boot from a USB device, your system must have a BIOS that supports booting from a USB device. Also remember that if you receive a TPM Not Found error, do not assume that your system does not have a TPM chip. Very often, it might need to be enabled in the BIOS. If you go into the BIOS during startup, you can enable it — provided that your system has the TPM chip.

✔ **A compliant BIOS:** Although typically not a problem, your BIOS needs to support the various features in BitLocker, such as TPM and booting from a USB device, depending on what options you choose to implement. To determine whether your system BIOS supports such functionality, read your system documentation or go into the BIOS during startup. Although BIOS menus vary, depending on the vendor, the menu is typically intuitive. You can check your boot options to determine whether USB is supported and TPM options are available.

✔ **Two NTFS drive partitions:** To take advantage of the Vista BitLocker encryption technology, you must have your hard drive partitioned with a system partition that contains the boot information in an unencrypted space. A second partition is needed that contains the OS and user data. This partition is what BitLocker Drive Encryption protects.

In the next section, I walk you through all the chores you need to do to get your system ready for BitLocker.

Preparing Your System for BitLocker

Encrypting your OS volume with BitLocker is a breeze; however, doing the up-front work to meet the requirements and preparing your system requires a fair amount of effort. In this section, I guide you through preparing your system to use BitLocker.

To take advantage of BitLocker Drive Encryption, you must have your hard disk partitioned to meet specific requirements. You need two NT File System (NTFS) partitions:

✔ **System volume**

The system volume must be a minimum of 1.5 gigabyte (GB) in size and set as the active partition.

✔ **OS volume**

As you might imagine, the significance of setting up these partitions depends on the current state of your system. Setting up these partitions is easier if you have a system that's being refreshed with Vista or set up for the first time. If however, you have a system that you've been using for a while and want to activate BitLocker, you'll have to put in a bit more effort. If you're lucky, you can use the BitLocker drive-preparation tool, which makes the task relatively painless. If the BitLocker drive-preparation tool doesn't work for you, you need to repartition your hard disk and reinstall the OS and any associated data.

Preparing a disk with no installed OS

Be sure to back up any data prior to following the steps in this section! Repartitioning your disk, as I outline in the following steps, makes that data inaccessible to you. *You must back up any data on this disk prior to performing these steps.*

To partition a disk that has no OS installed on it, follow these steps:

1. **Insert the Windows Vista CD/DVD and boot your system.**

   On some systems, you might need to invoke the boot options to boot from the CD/DVD.

2. **Select Installation language, time, currency format, and keyboard layout, and then click Next.**

3. **From the Install Windows Screen that appears, select Repair Your Computer.**

4. **In the System Recovery Options dialog box, make sure that no OS is selected.**

   If an OS is selected, click any empty area in the operating system list to deselect it and then click Next.

5. **Select Command Prompt from the System Recovery Options dialog box.**

6. **Type** diskpart **and then press Enter.**

7. **Type** Select Disk 0.

8. **Type** clean.

   This erases the existing partitions.

9. **Type** create partition primary size=1500.

   This selects the partition size of the primary partition, which must be at least 1.5GB.

10. **Type** assign letter=S **to designate this partition as the S: partition.**

11. **Type** active **to set this partition as the active partition.**

12. **Type** create partition primary **to create another primary partition.**

    This becomes the partition in which you install Vista.

13. **Type** assign letter=C.

14. **Type** list volume.

    This allows you to view the listings of each volume on the disk.

15. **Verify that you see two volumes that you created.**

16. **Type** exit.

    This closes the disport application.

17. **Type** format c: /y /q /fs:NTFS.

    This formats the C: volume.

18. **Type** format s: /y /q /fs:NTFS.

    This formats the S: volume. If you chose a designator other than the letter S for that volume, replace it in the command line.

19. **Type** exit.

20. **In the System Recovery Options dialog box, use the window icon on the screen or press ALT+F4 to close the window and return to the main installation window.**

21. Select Install Now to proceed with installing Vista.

You will install Vista in the C: volume, which will be your OS volume.

Preparing a disk with an operating system installed on it

For those of you with Vista already installed, you might be able to use the BitLocker drive-preparation tool to more easily prepare and partition your drive. Perform the following steps to use the BitLocker drive-preparation tool.

TIP

If you're using Vista Enterprise, you need to contact the Microsoft customer support services to obtain the drive-preparation tool. You can visit the Microsoft Support Web site at

```
http://support.microsoft.com/contactus/?ws=support
```

1. Choose Start button and type Windows Update **in the Search field at the bottom of the Start menu that appears. Click Windows Update in the results pane to open it.**

2. In the right pane of the Windows Update window, click the View Available Extras Link.

3. Select BitLocker and EFS Enhancements and then click the Install button, as shown in Figure 10-1.

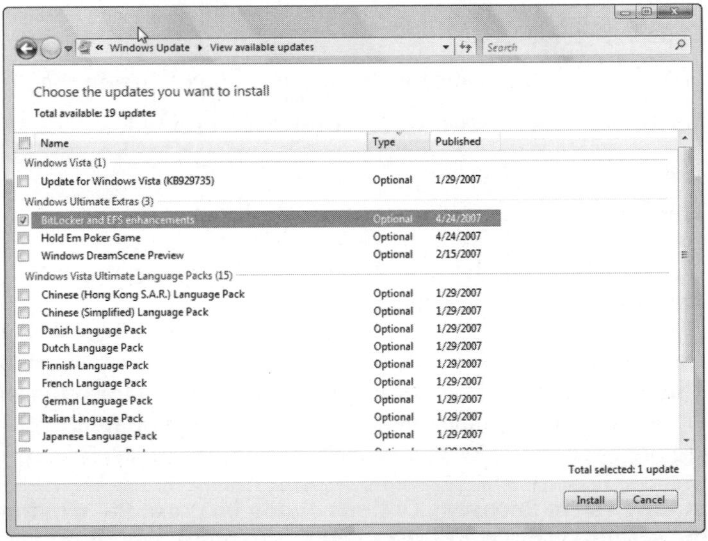

Figure 10-1: The BitLocker and EFS Enhancements Installation window.

4. **After installation is complete, choose Start⇨All Programs⇨ Accessories⇨System Tools and then choose BitLocker Drive Preparation Tool.**

5. **At the Welcome screen that appears, click I Agree.**

6. **Click Continue at the next Preparing Drive for BitLocker screen (as shown in Figure 10-2).**

    This screen is informational only and lets you know that you should back up files prior to continuing, that the process might take up to a few hours, and that you shouldn't store important files on the new active drive.

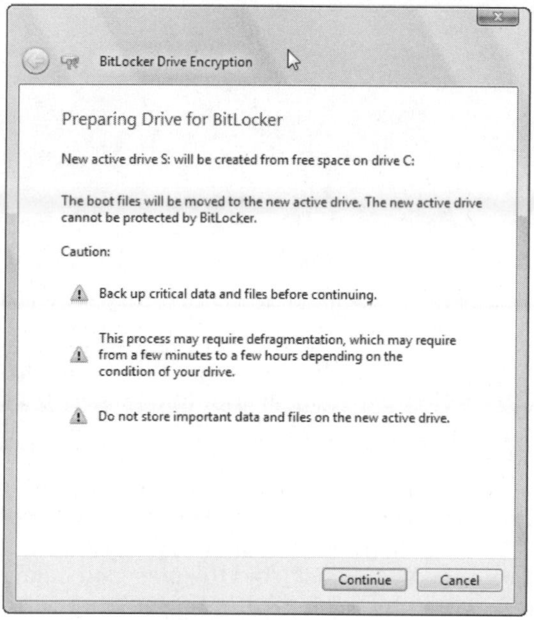

Figure 10-2: BitLocker reminds you to back up critical data before proceeding.

The BitLocker drive-preparation tool repartitions your drive. You see a progress dialog box, as shown in Figure 10-3.

7. **When the drive-preparation tool is done, click Finish.**

8. **Restart your system to let configuration changes take effect.**

    After your system reboots, BitLocker is enabled, provided that the additional requirements (such as your system having a TPM chip) are met.

The BitLocker drive-preparation tool might pop up an error under certain common conditions. The error might read

The BitLocker Drive Preparation Tool Could Not Find a Target System Drive. You may need to manually prepare your drive for BitLocker.

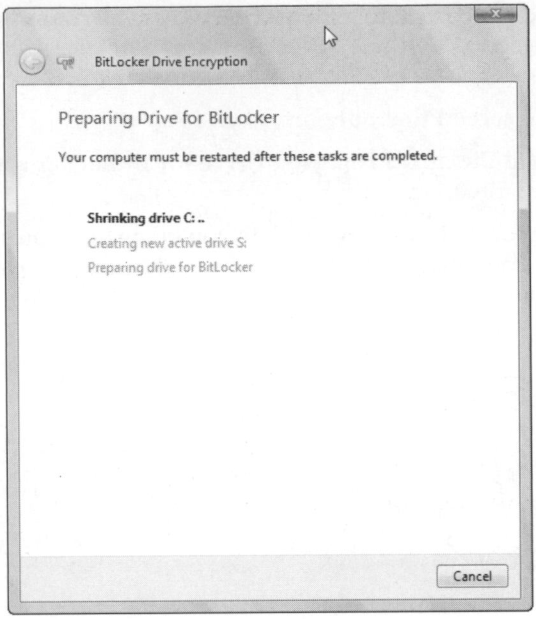

Figure 10-3:
The
repartition is
in progress.

This error might be caused by lack of free space. Approximately 10 percent of the active partition must remain free. If you receive this error, move files on the system partition to another partition. In addition, this error might be generated when the tool can't resize the partition because some files might not be able to be moved. (These files might be page files, hibernation files, and so on.) You might be able to fix this problem by disabling hibernation and disk paging. You can use Windows Pre-installation Environment (WinPE) to delete the `hiberfil.sys` file (Hibernation) and the `pagefile.sys` file. You boot the system with the WinPE disk, find the files, and delete them. You then restart the system, without the WinPE disk in, and boot with Vista. You can then rerun the BitLocker Drive Preparation Tool.

Setting Up BitLocker

After you make the necessary preparations, setting up BitLocker is easier than you might think. You can choose a variety of configuration options to set up BitLocker so that it makes sense for you in the home or small office. The local Group Policy Object Editor provides you an interface to configure various options in BitLocker. To edit the Local Computer Policy on your system so that you can configure these settings, use the Group Policy Object Editor interface, as shown in Figure 10-4.

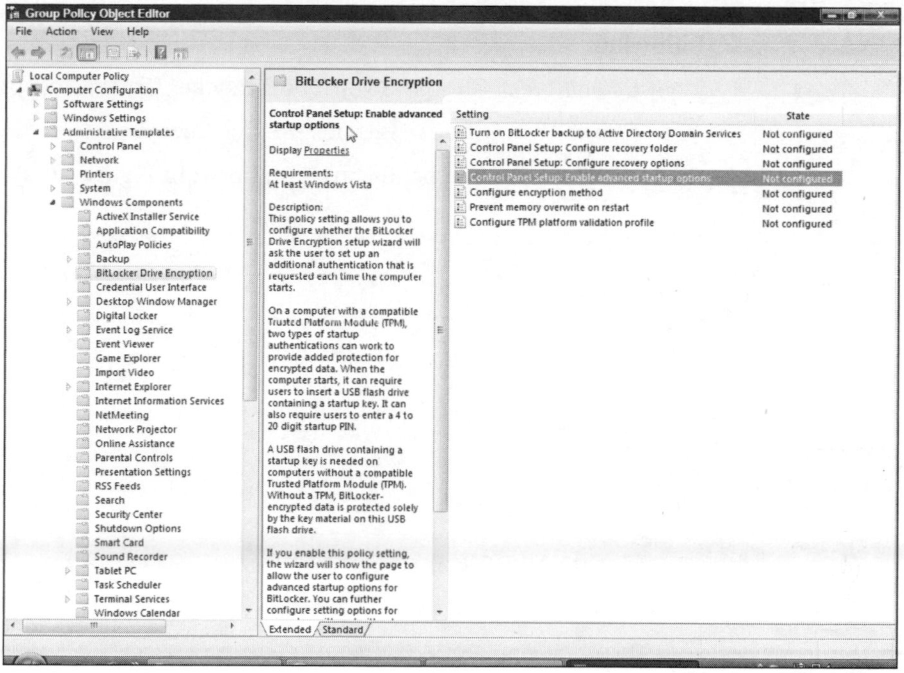

Figure 10-4:
The Group
Policy
Object
Editor.

REMEMBER

The changes that you're making are local to the system and don't need to be replicated through the domain. These changes take effect immediately.

Enabling BitLocker with basic options

Vista has a very easy-to-use interface to enable BitLocker drive encryption through Control Panel. You will likely use this interface often because it's the same interface that you use to temporarily disable BitLocker to install updates, or to decrypt your drive and remove BitLocker drive encryption altogether.

WARNING!

If you want to use the advanced options of BitLocker, namely TPM with PIN or TPM with startup, skip this section. You need to follow the directions in the upcoming section, "Enabling BitLocker with advanced options" because you can only configure your system to use TPM plus PIN the first time you turn on BitLocker. If you choose to enable BitLocker without a TPM PIN or startup key, you can't select it later without decrypting your drive and then re-enabling BitLocker with PIN or startup key.

   1. **Choose Start➪Control Panel.**

2. **Depending on the view that's set in Control Panel, choose one of the following:**
   - *Default View:* Choose Security⇨BitLocker Drive Encryption.
   - *Classic View:* Choose BitLocker Drive Encryption.
3. **Click the Turn On BitLocker link (as shown in Figure 10-5).**

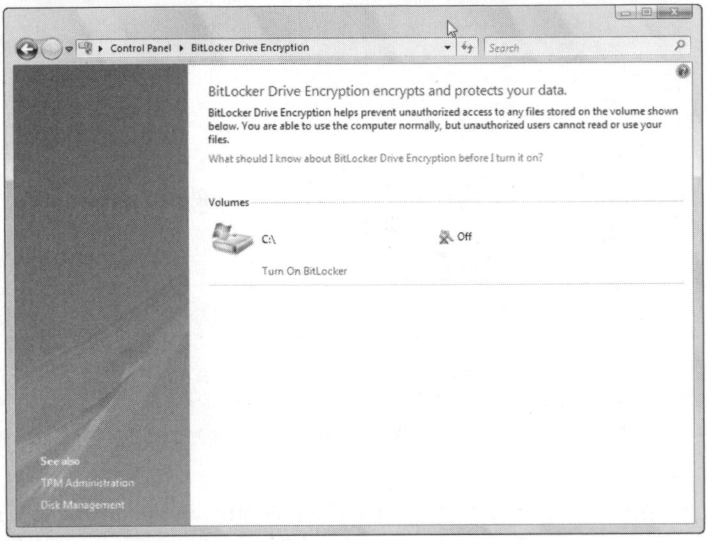

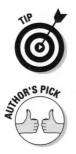

Control Panel ▸ BitLocker Drive Encryption
Search
BitLocker Drive Encryption encrypts and protects your data.
BitLocker Drive Encryption helps prevent unauthorized access to any files stored on the volume shown below. You are able to use the computer normally, but unauthorized users cannot read or use your files.
What should I know about BitLocker Drive Encryption before I turn it on?
Volumes
C:\
Off
Turn On BitLocker
See also
TPM Administration
Disk Management

Figure 10-5: Turning on BitLocker.

In the Save the Recovery Password dialog box (as shown in Figure 10-6), you are prompted to save a recovery password.

4. **Choose a location to save the password.**
   - On a USB device
   - To a folder
   - To print it

You need this password if BitLocker blocks your system from starting up. This sometimes occurs if your TPM detects certain conditions, such as disk errors and changes to the BIOS or other startup components. Saving this password is, therefore, essential to recover from such an event.

I suggest saving the file to a USB device so that you can store it apart from your system. If you store it on your system and your system doesn't boot, you won't be able to access it for reference. If you store it on a USB device, you can reference it from another system and enter the password to get the system to boot.

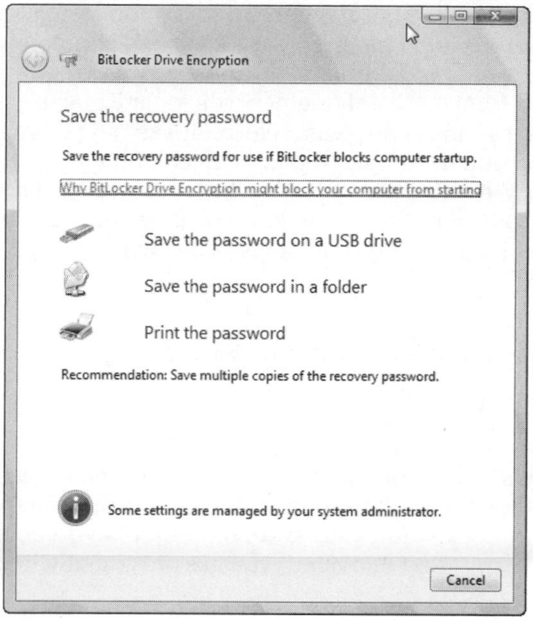

Figure 10-6:
Save the
recovery
password.

5. **After you save the password to the location of your choosing, click Next.**

   At the Encrypt the Volume dialog box, you're prompted to start using BitLocker to encrypt your OS volume.

6. **Select the Run BitLocker System Check check box and then select Encrypt.**

7. **Restart your system and insert the USB device with the password (assuming that is the option you selected from the Save the Recovery Password screen in Step 4).**

8. **After your system reboots, BitLocker device encryption loads. You need to remove the USB device when prompted.**

   Your system will boot to the OS. BitLocker encrypts your drive in the background. On the taskbar, an icon reports the status of the encryption while it occurs.

Enabling BitLocker with advanced options

BitLocker advanced options allow you to make additional configurations, such as using a TPM plus PIN or a TPM with a startup key. In addition, if you have a system without a TPM microchip, the advanced options provide you the configuration option to still enable BitLocker if you choose.

In addition to the standard TPM protection, such as monitoring for BIOS changes, hard disk errors, and changes in other startup components, these advanced options allow for an additional layer of security by allowing you to add a PIN that can be from 4–20 alphanumeric digits or a startup key. In the security world, these two items are often referred to as "something you know" (PIN) and "something you have" (startup key). Each of these options allow for additional security. If you choose to use a PIN, you need to enter the PIN at startup. If you choose to use a startup key, you store the key on a USB device, and you can't boot your system unless you have the key.

Enabling BitLocker on a system without a TPM chip

Not all systems have a TPM chip. BitLocker will let you know that you can't enable it if your system doesn't have one or if it's not turned on. When you attempt to activate BitLocker and your system doesn't have a compatible TPM chip or the TPM chip isn't activated, you are presented with an error.

Figure 10-7 illustrates an error on a system that doesn't have the TPM feature enabled. This same error would also display if the system didn't have a TPM chip. However, don't assume that because you receive this error, that your system doesn't have a compatible TPM chip. It might have a compatible TPM chip that's not enabled. You can check whether TPM is enabled by checking into the system's BIOS during bootup.

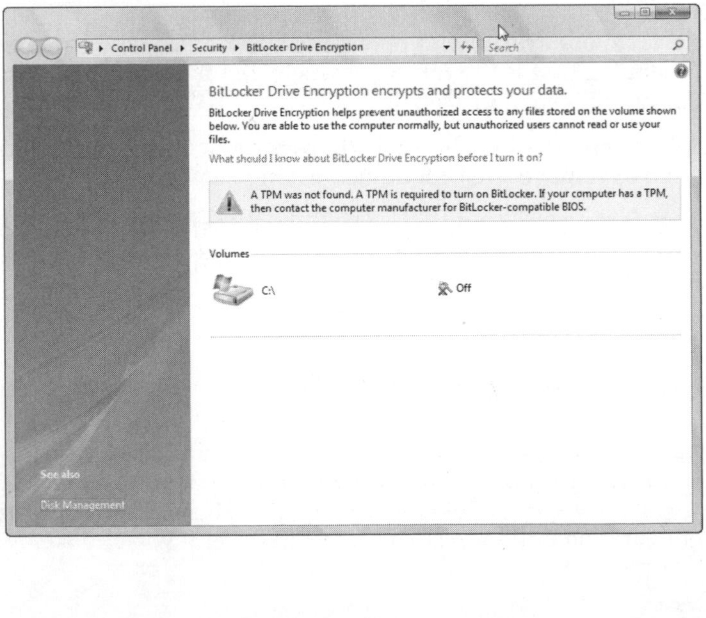

Figure 10-7: A BitLocker TPM not-found error.

If you want to enable BitLocker and you don't have a TPM chip in your system, perform the following steps:

1. **Choose Start, type** gpedit.msc **in the Search field, and then press Enter.**

   The Group Policy Object Editor opens.

2. **In the left pane of the Group Policy Object Editor, select Local Computer Policy to expand the container.**

3. **In the left pane, click Administrative Templates to expand, and then click Windows Components.**

4. **In the left pane of the Group Policy Editor Tool, click BitLocker Drive Encryption to expand.**

5. **Select Control Panel Setup: Enable Advanced Startup Options from the right pane of the Group Policy Object Editor.**

   The Control Panel Setup: Enable Advanced Startup Options dialog box opens.

6. **Select the Enabled option.**

7. **Select the Allow BitLocker without a Compatible TPM check box and then click OK.**

8. **Exit the Group Policy Object Editor.**

   To enable BitLocker Drive Encryption, see the earlier section, "Enabling BitLocker with basic options."

Adding additional authentication with TPM plus a PIN or a TPM startup key

The advanced options of TPM allow you to add an additional layer of security where a user must supply a password (PIN) or a startup key placed on a USB device before booting into the OS. Either method provides you with an additional layer of security if your system is stolen. With the TPM plus PIN, you need to supply a password at boot. With TPM and a startup key, you are required to supply a key on a USB device at boot.

Configuring TPM plus PIN

If you want to add the additional layer of security and use TPM with PIN, select a password that you won't easily forget but that's not intuitive to others. I recommend using a strong password consisting of alphanumeric characters. The PIN must be 4–20 digits long.

You can configure your system to use TPM plus PIN only the first time you turn on BitLocker. If you choose to enable BitLocker without a TPM PIN or startup key, you can't select it later without decrypting your drive and then re-enabling BitLocker with a PIN or startup key.

Perform the following steps to configure the TPM plus PIN:

1. **Choose Start, type** gpedit.msc **in the Search field, and then press Enter.**

   The Group Policy Object Editor opens.

2. **In the left pane of the Group Policy Object Editor, select Local Computer Policy.**

3. **In the left pane, select Administrative Templates, and then select Windows Components to expand the containers.**

4. **In the left pane of the Group Policy Object Editor, select BitLocker Drive Encryption.**

5. **In the right pane of the Group Policy Object Editor, select Control Panel Setup: Enable Advanced Startup Options.**

   The dialog box shown in Figure 10-8 opens.

6. **In the Control Panel Setup Enable Advanced Startup Options dialog box, select the Enabled radio button.**

7. **Under the Configure TPM Startup PIN Option heading, choose the appropriate option from the drop-down menu.**

   You can choose to allow, require, or disallow the startup with PIN with TPM option. Select Require from the drop-down menu.

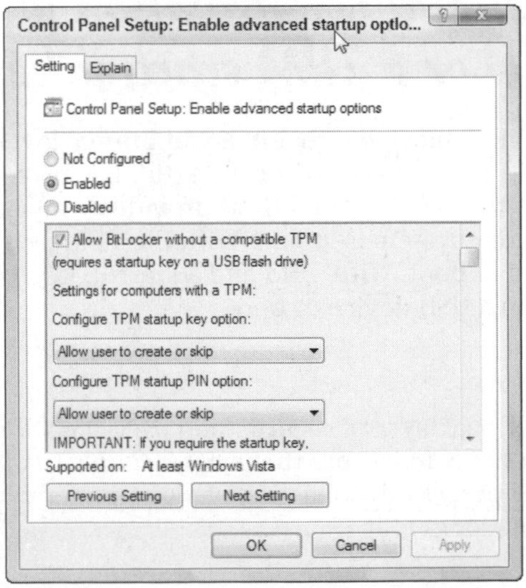

Figure 10-8:
Control
Panel
Setup:
Enable
Advanced
Startup
Options.

Control Panel Setup: Enable advanced startup optio...

Setting | Explain

Control Panel Setup: Enable advanced startup options

○ Not Configured
● Enabled
○ Disabled

☑ Allow BitLocker without a compatible TPM
(requires a startup key on a USB flash drive)

Settings for computers with a TPM:

Configure TPM startup key option:

Allow user to create or skip

Configure TPM startup PIN option:

Allow user to create or skip

IMPORTANT: If you require the startup key,

Supported on: At least Windows Vista

Previous Setting   Next Setting

OK   Cancel   Apply

8. **Click OK, and then exit the Group Policy Object Editor.**

9. **After the changes are in place, if you are in the default view, choose Start⇨Control Panel⇨Security⇨BitLocker Drive Encryption.**

   If you're using Classic view, choose Start⇨Control Panel⇨BitLocker Drive Encryption.

10. **Select Turn On BitLocker.**

11. **On the Set BitLocker Startup Preferences page (as shown in Figure 10-9), select Require PIN at Every Startup.**

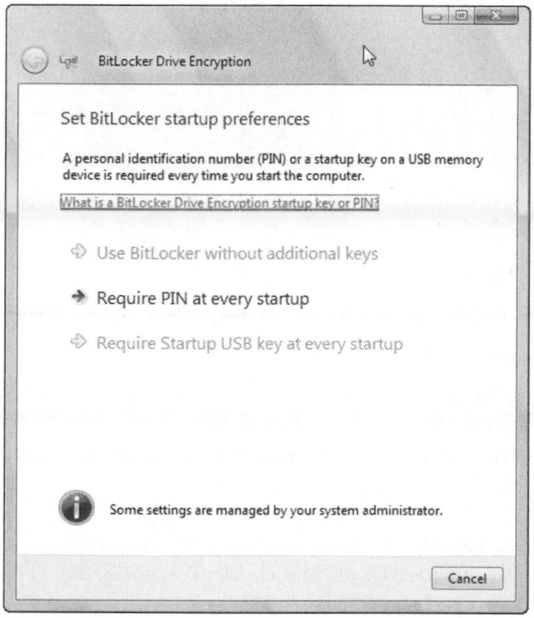

Figure 10-9:
The BitLocker Startup Preferences screen.

BitLocker Drive Encryption

Set BitLocker startup preferences

A personal identification number (PIN) or a startup key on a USB memory device is required every time you start the computer.

What is a BitLocker Drive Encryption startup key or PIN?

⇨ Use BitLocker without additional keys

➔ Require PIN at every startup

⇨ Require Startup USB key at every startup

ⓘ Some settings are managed by your system administrator.

Cancel

If you require the TPM plus PIN on startup, you must disallow the TPM with startup key. Likewise, if you require the TPM plus startup key option, you must disallow the TPM with PIN. If you don't, a policy error will occur, and the configuration won't be activated.

12. **Enter and confirm your PIN, as shown in Figure 10-10.**

    You are prompted to save your password on a USB drive or in a folder, or to print the password. The options that you have available depend on how you have the recovery options configured. See the section "Configuring recovery options," later in this chapter.

    To enable BitLocker Drive Encryption, see the section "Enabling BitLocker with basic options," earlier in this chapter.

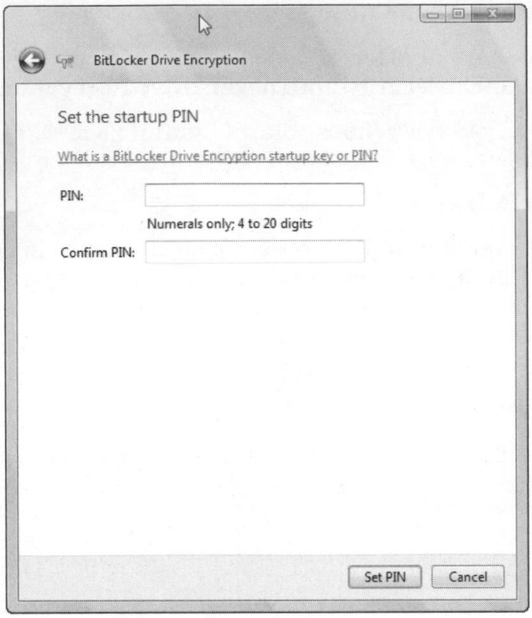

Set the startup PIN

What is a BitLocker Drive Encryption startup key or PIN?

PIN:

Numerals only; 4 to 20 digits

Confirm PIN:

Set PIN   Cancel

Figure 10-10:
Enter and
confirm the
PIN.

Configuring TPM with startup key

Selecting to configure your system for TPM with a startup key adds an additional layer of security. You need to provide that startup key at boot. This adds an additional layer of authentication. If you can't provide the startup key, the system won't be able to boot into the OS.

You can configure your system to use TPM plus PIN only the first time you turn on BitLocker. If you choose to enable BitLocker without a TPM PIN or startup key, you can't select it later without decrypting your drive and then re-enabling BitLocker with PIN or startup key.

Perform the following steps to configure the TPM with a startup key:

1. **Choose Start, type** gpedit.msc **in the Search field, and then press Enter.**

   The Group Policy Object Editor opens.

2. **In the left pane of the Group Policy Object Editor, select Local Computer Policy.**

3. **In the left pane, select Administrative Templates, and then select Windows Components to expand the containers.**

4. **In the left pane of the Group Policy Object Editor, select BitLocker Drive Encryption.**

5. **Select Control Panel Setup: Enable Advanced Startup Options (refer to Figure 10-8).**

6. **In the Control Panel Setup Enable Advanced Startup Options dialog box, select the Enabled option.**

7. **Under the Configure TPM Startup Key option, select Required from the drop-down menu.**

   Your choices are to allow, require, or disallow the TPM with startup key.

   If you require the TPM plus startup key option, you must disallow the TPM with PIN. Likewise, if you require the TPM plus PIN on startup, you must disallow the TPM with startup key. If you don't, a policy error will occur, and the configuration won't be activated.

8. **Click OK and exit the Group Policy Object Editor.**

9. **After the changes are in place, open Control Panel from the Start menu. Depending on the view set in Control Panel, choose one of the following:**

   • *Default View:* Choose Security⇨BitLocker Drive Encryption.

   • *Classic View:* Choose BitLocker Drive Encryption.

10. **Select Turn On BitLocker.**

11. **On the Set BitLocker Startup Preferences page (refer to Figure 10-9), select Require Startup USB Key at Every Startup.**

12. **At the Save the Recovery Password dialog box, select the location where you want to save the recovery password.**

   The options that you have available to save your startup key are dependent upon how you have the recovery options configured. See the upcoming section, "Configuring recovery options."

13. **When selected, Save to your location.**

Configuring Additional Security

BitLocker provides a few configuration options that allow you to configure additional security. Through the local security policy on the system, you can configure recovery options, advanced startup options, the encryption method that you would like to use, how your system handles memory rewrites to protect BitLocker secrets, and certain TPM configuration options. Of particular interest here are the encryption methods and memory-overwrite configuration options.

Encryption methods

You have a couple choices of encryption methods with BitLocker: Advanced Encryption Standard, better known as AES 128 or AES 256-bit, both with or without Diffuser. By default, BitLocker will use AES 128-bit with Diffuser as the method of encryption.

AES is arguably the most popular algorithm, symmetric key used today. It has been widely adopted by the U.S. government and has been tested extensively all over the world. Currently, it is considered to provide an extensive level of security. Diffuser provides additional security against attacks aimed at manipulating the encrypted data.

Diffusion happens when a cryptographic algorithm ensures that a modification of only a few bits will lead to many changes of the output bits of an algorithm. In this way, additional security is added to prevent attacks against encrypted data.

In the upcoming Figure 10-11, you can see the choices that you have to configure this setting. You can choose from the following:

- **AES 128-bit encryption:** This selection offers the standard AES 128-bit encryption method without Diffuser for protection against manipulation attacks.

- **AES 128 bit with Diffuser:** This is the default setting within BitLocker and includes both the standard 128-bit AES encryption algorithm with Diffuser for additional protection against manipulation attacks.

- **AES 256-bit encryption:** This selection offers standard AES 256-bit encryption without the Diffuser.

- **AES 256 with Diffuser:** This selection includes both the AES 256-bit encryption algorithm with Diffuser for additional protection against manipulation attacks.

AES encryption is a widely used standard that provides a great deal of protection. If you're using BitLocker, I assume that you're trying to protect some rather sensitive data, so I suggest using AES 256 bit with Diffuser.

To configure the encryption method, perform the following steps:

1. **Choose Start, type** gpedit.msc **in the Search field, and then press Enter.**

   The Group Policy Object Editor opens.

2. **In the left pane of the Group Policy Object Editor, select Local Computer Policy.**

3. **In the left pane, select Administrative Templates and then select Windows Components to expand the containers.**

4. **In the left pane of the Group Policy Object Editor, select BitLocker Drive Encryption.**

5. **Select Encryption Methods.**

   The Configure Encryption Method Properties dialog box opens (as shown in Figure 10-11).

6. **Select the Enabled radio button.**

7. **Select the encryption method of your choice from the drop-down list.**

   Your options are AES 128 bit, AES 128 bit with Diffuser, AES 256 bit, and AES 256 bit with Diffuser.

   Each option offers an excellent level of security and will more than likely suffice to protect your data. With that said, I recommend that you select AES 256 bit with Diffuser for (arguably) optimal protection.

8. **Click OK and then exit the Group Policy Object Editor.**

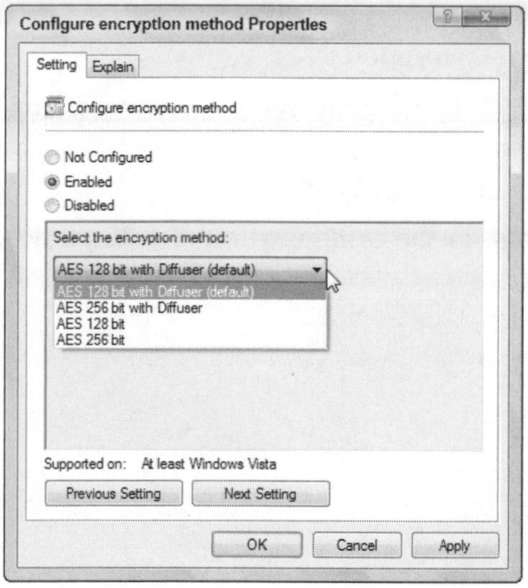

Figure 10-11:
Configure
Encryption
Method
Properties
dialog box.

Prevent memory overwrite

The Prevent Memory Overwrite setting allows you to control whether the memory of your system is cleared during a system restart. The options that you have available are as follows:

✔ **Not Configured:** This is the default setting. If this setting isn't configured, the system won't prevent memory overwrite during restart. That means the memory of your system will be dumped during a restart.

✔ **Enabled:** This setting prevents the memory on your system from being cleared during a restart. Although choosing this might improve the performance of your system during restart, it does allows for the potential exposure of BitLocker key information held in memory.

✔ **Disabled:** This setting has the same effect as if it were not configured. The memory is cleared during system restart, ensuring that any BitLocker key information is not at risk of compromise.

To configure the Prevent Memory Overwrite property, perform the following steps:

1. **Choose Start, type** gpedit.msc **in the Search field, and then press Enter.**

   The Group Policy Object Editor opens.

2. **In the left pane of the Group Policy Object Editor, select Local Computer Policy.**

3. **In the left pane, select Administrative Templates and then select Windows Components to expand the objects.**

4. **Select BitLocker Drive Encryption.**

5. **In the right pane, select the Prevent Memory Overwrite on Restart Properties policy.**

   The dialog box shown in Figure 10-12 opens.

6. **Select the radio button for the configuration of your choice.**

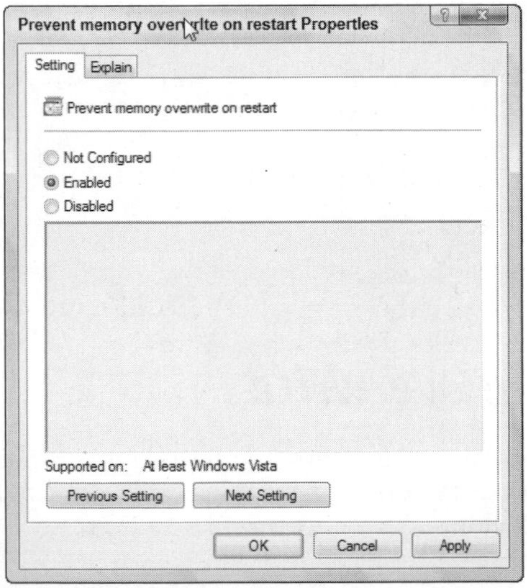

Figure 10-12:
This setting prevents memory overwrite on restart properties.

Although a relatively low risk for the home or small office user, I still recommend that you leave this setting not configured or disabled. This will dump your memory when your system is restarted, thereby limiting any exposure for your data to be extracted from the physical memory of your system.

7. **Click Apply, click OK, and then exit the Group Policy Object Editor.**

Recovering BitLocker-protected data

The ability to encrypt your data with BitLocker provides you significant security value. However, if something should go amiss, you must be able to recover your data encrypted with BitLocker Drive Encryption. Recovery provides a way for you to access this data; otherwise, you will essentially experience data loss. Although your data might still exist, you won't be able to access it.

Recovery folder options

BitLocker allows you to configure the default path that is displayed to the user when asked to enter a location of a folder to save the recovery password. By default, this setting isn't configured and will display the system's top-level folder view. This setting sets only the default location but doesn't limit the user from selecting another location. If you configure this option, the user can still navigate to a location of his choosing to store the recovery password/key. To configure this setting, perform the following steps:

1. **Choose Start, type** gpedit.msc **in the Search field, and then press Enter.**

   The Group Policy Object Editor opens.

2. **In the left pane of the Group Policy Object Editor, select Local Computer Policy.**

   The container expands.

3. **In the left pane, select Administrative Templates and then select Windows Components to expand the containers**

4. **In the right pane, click BitLocker Drive Encryption.**

   You see the different polices that can be set for BitLocker Drive Encryption.

5. **In the right pane, select the Control Panel Setup: Configure Recovery Folder Properties Policy to bring up the dialog box shown in Figure 10-13.**

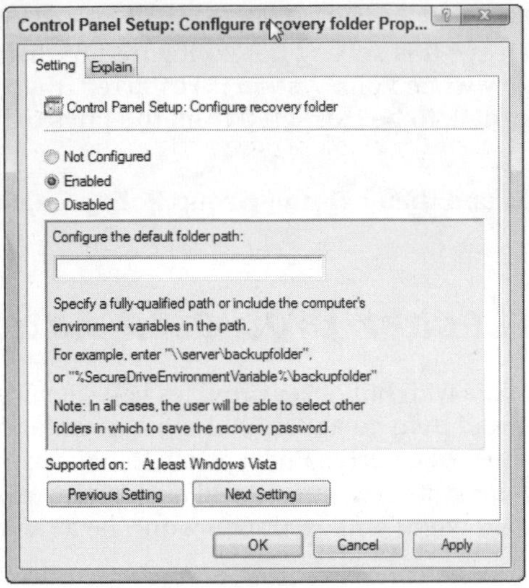

Figure 10-13:
Configure a
default path
for a
recovery
folder.

6. **Select the configuration that you want to choose.**

   The default settings will likely meet your needs. However, you can customize this folder if you prefer a different default recovery location. To read about the settings in greater detail, click the Explain tab.

7. **Click Apply and then click OK.**

Configuring recovery options

This setting allows you to configure whether BitLocker asks the user to save BitLocker recovery options, which provides the user a way to recover BitLocker. Without a way to recover, the user could end up losing data because the data is encrypted and unreadable. Safely saving the recovery password is essential.

This property provides two options to the user to unlock BitLocker-encrypted data. These options are as follows:

- ✔ **48-bit recovery option:** The user can type a random recovery password 48 digits in length. If this setting remains Not Configured or Disabled, the user is presented with a variety of options, such as printing the password, saving it to an external device, or even saving it as a text file.

- ✔ **256-bit recovery option:** The user can store a 256-bit recovery key on a USB device or as a hidden file in a folder, or print the password.

As shown in Figure 10-14, you have three options for both the 48-digit recovery password option and the 256-bit recovery key option. They are as follows:

- ✔ **Not Configured:** Selecting this option allows the user a variety of ways to save this recovery option, such as printing or saving it as a text file.

  These ways are not secure and should be avoided.

- ✔ **Enabled:** Selecting this option allows you to choose between the 48-digit and 256-bit options. *Note:* If you disallow the recovery password and require the recovery key, users can't enable BitLocker without saving to a USB device.

- ✔ **Disabled:** Selecting this option has the same effect as selecting Not Configured.

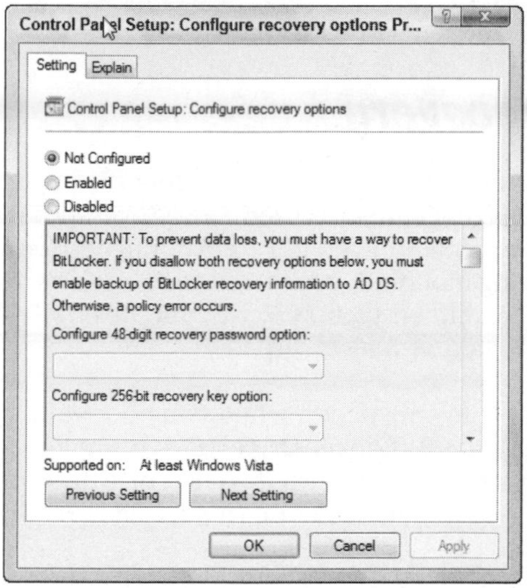

Figure 10-14:
The Configure Recovery Options Properties dialog box.

To configure the recovery options, perform the following steps:

1. **Choose Start, type** gpedit.msc **in the Search field, and then press Enter.**

   The Group Policy Object Editor opens.

2. **In the left pane of the Group Policy Object Editor, select Local Computer Policy.**

3. **In the left pane, select Administrative Templates and then select Windows Components to expand the containers.**

4. **In the left pane of the Group Policy Object Editor, select BitLocker Drive Encryption.**

5. **In the right pane of the Group Policy Object Editor, select Control Panel Setup: Configure Recovery Options (refer to Figure 10-14).**

   The Recovery Options Properties dialog box opens.

6. **Select the Enabled radio button.**

   Your options at this point are to select either a 48-digit recovery password option or a 256-bit option that can be used with a USB device. Either option will meet the needs of the home or small office user. Because security is a balance between protection and productivity, this decision is yours.

7. **From either the 48-digit recovery option or the 256-bit option (if you use a USB device to hold your key), select Require Password.**

8. **After you make this selection, click OK and then exit the Group Policy Object Editor.**

Performing a recovery

In many ways, how you configure recovery options sets the stage for how you perform a recovery of BitLocker-encrypted data. Several events can necessitate a recovery, such as your system's TPM configuration being altered, early boot files being modified, your need to replace hardware (such as the motherboard or TPM chip on your system), updates to the BIOS, a forgotten PIN, or a lost USB device with a startup key.

In the event that one of these events occur, when you boot your system, you find yourself presented with the BitLocker Drive Encryption Recovery Console instead of your system booting into the OS. The BitLocker Drive Encryption Recovery console will instruct you to perform a recovery. To do so, perform the following steps:

1. **Locate the recovery password that you saved when enabling BitLocker Drive Encryption.**

2. **At the BitLocker Drive Encryption Recovery Console screen, enter the password.**

   If you have the password stored on a USB device, select ESC. The system will reboot, and you need to insert the USB device that the recovery password is stored on.

3. **After entering the password or using the USB device with the stored password, press Enter.**

   The system will boot into the OS.

Turning Off BitLocker

BitLocker provides an easy-to-use interface to both temporarily disable Bit Locker or to decrypt your drive and get rid of it. If, for example, you want to install updates to your OS and other applications, you might need to temporarily disable BitLocker so that the application can use other files on the drive in an unencrypted format. This is a handy feature to keep you from going through the time-consuming procedure of decrypting, updating the system, and then encrypting the drive again.

There might also be an occasion where you no longer need to have the drive encrypted with BitLocker: say, if you no longer use that system to store or process sensitive data. Here, too, there is an easy-to-use interface to decrypt the BitLocker encryption on your drive.

To temporarily disable BitLocker or decrypt your drive, perform the following steps:

1. **Choose Start⇨Control Panel.**

2. **In regular view, choose Security⇨BitLocker Drive Encryption. In Classic view, choose BitLocker Drive Encryption.**

3. **Click the Turn Off BitLocker link.**

   After you select Turn Off BitLocker, you will are be prompted to either disable BitLocker Drive Encryption or decrypt the volume, as shown in Figure 10-15.

   Disabling BitLocker Drive Encryption is a temporary measure that can be used to temporarily turn off BitLocker, allowing you to install updates or to allow programs to gain access to unencrypted data. Decrypting the volume, on the other hand, might take a considerable amount of time (depending on the size of the hard disk) and essentially "uninstalls" BitLocker.

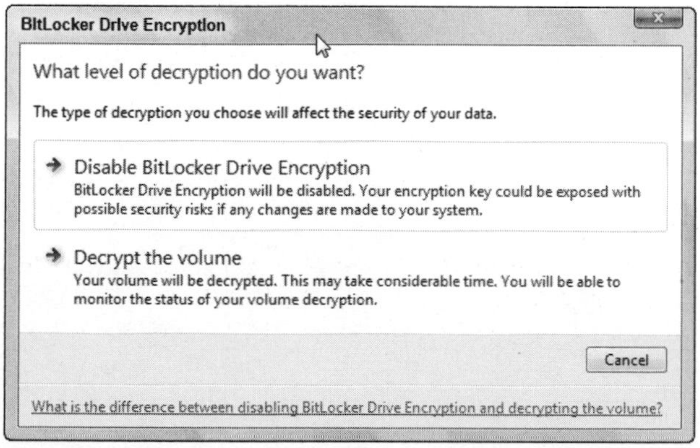

Figure 10-15:
Decrypting
or disabling
the drive.

BitLocker Drive Encryption

What level of decryption do you want?

The type of decryption you choose will affect the security of your data.

→ Disable BitLocker Drive Encryption
BitLocker Drive Encryption will be disabled. Your encryption key could be exposed with possible security risks if any changes are made to your system.

→ Decrypt the volume
Your volume will be decrypted. This may take considerable time. You will be able to monitor the status of your volume decryption.

Cancel

What is the difference between disabling BitLocker Drive Encryption and decrypting the volume?

4. **Make your selection and then click OK.**

Decrypting your drive will take longer than disabling BitLocker. You can continue to work in the background, but the amount of time it takes to decrypt your drive largely depends on the size of the drive.

On the taskbar, an icon reports the status of the decryption process while it occurs.

Knowing What BitLocker Can't Protect

Although BitLocker provides you the ability to protect your sensitive data, it does have a few shortcomings. However, if you know about those shortcomings, you can be better prepared to reduce any effect they might have on you:

- **Your password is only as secure as you make it.** If you let someone know your password, that person can access your data. BitLocker does not have any tricks up its sleeve that can tell you apart from anyone else if he provides the credentials necessary to log into your system. If another user provides those credentials, he has access to your sensitive data.

- **Data stored on your computer in an unprotected partition isn't secure.** BitLocker doesn't provide some of the protection offered by some other vendors that offer full-disk encryption products, where essentially all the data on the disk is encrypted. BitLocker encrypts the OS volume and any associated data on that volume. If you partition your disk and have an OS volume and a data volume, BitLocker won't protect all your data. In such a scenario, you need to use EFS to protect that data.

- **Data on the move isn't protected.** Data on the move is a serious problem, not just for corporations, but also for people just like you and me. Bit Locker doesn't provide protection for data that you put on an external drive, a USB device, or other removable media.

Part IV
Guarding against Threats to Network Security

"We take network security here very seriously."

In this part . . .

Network threats are likely the most common and most serious security problems that you face today. From viruses to spyware to phishing (and more), you're likely introduced to a variety of security risks that target you from across a network or the Internet.

In this part, see how to use those Vista tools that can help you protect yourself from these threats. However, I don't stop there. In addition to showing you how to use the Vista Firewall, Vista wireless networking tools; and Internet Explorer 7, I present a variety of tacks you can take to provide optimal protection against network-related threats.

Chapter 11

Configuring Your Firewall

*T*he firewall built into Vista is officially known as *Windows Firewall*. This firewall is a software application that surrounds your computer from the networks to which you connect so you can protect your system and data from the other computers and users on the network. The firewall either allows or blocks incoming and outgoing communication to or from other networks based on the information that you set within the configuration of the firewall. You can configure the Firewall in Vista to be very specific (with lots of complex options), or you can allow Vista to manage the settings for you.

In this chapter, I discuss the various interfaces that you can use to manage Windows Firewall as well as the different ways in which you can set firewall rules to better secure your system. Two interfaces allow you to access and manage your settings for the Vista Windows Firewall: the Windows Firewall applet, and the Windows Firewall with Advanced Security applet. In this chapter, I take a look at what each offers.

Using the Windows Firewall Applet

You access the Windows Firewall applet through Windows Control Panel. Although this applet doesn't provide all the options available from the Windows Firewall with Advanced Security applet, it does provide a simple and quick interface to change your Windows Firewall settings. At one point or another, most users will use the Windows Firewall applet to manage their firewall settings.

The Windows Firewall applet, as shown in Figure 11-1, provides you a simple and intuitive interface to manage your Firewall settings. From this interface, you can turn Firewall on and off, decide which programs and ports you will allow communication with, or even block communication altogether. In the same way that you can view the status of Firewall in Windows Security Center (WSC), you can view the status of Firewall on your system along with the basic settings that it is using.

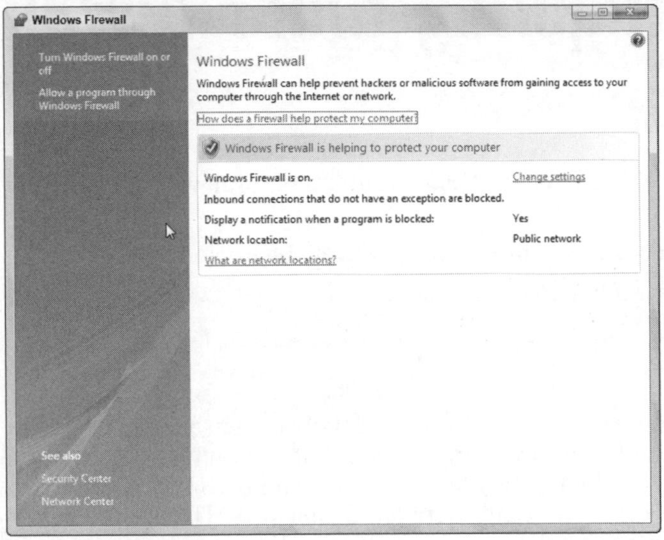

Figure 11-1:
The
Windows
Firewall
applet.

To open the Windows Firewall applet and view or manage the settings of Windows Firewall, perform the following steps:

1. **Navigate to Start⇨Control Panel.**

   The Control Panel dialog box opens.

2. **Depending on the view set in Control Panel, choose one of the following:**

   • *Default view:* Choose Network and Internet⇨Windows Firewall.

   • *Classic view:* Double-click the Windows Firewall applet.

   You can also access this applet by clicking the Windows Firewall link in the left pane of the WSC window. Chapter 3 provides more details on how to initiate Windows Firewall from the WSC interface.

3. **In the right pane of the Windows Firewall window, click the Change Settings link.**

   The Windows Firewall Settings window opens. (See Figure 11-2.)

   You use the three tabs in this interface — General, Exceptions, and Advanced — to configure the options that best meet your needs. I discuss these tabs in the next few sections.

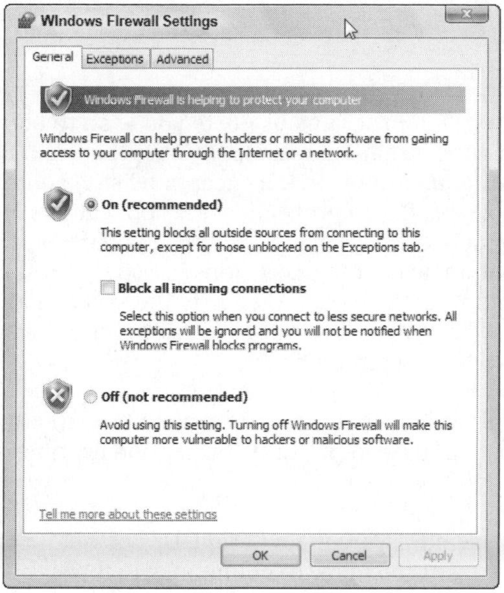

Windows Firewall Settings

General | Exceptions | Advanced

Windows Firewall is helping to protect your computer

Windows Firewall can help prevent hackers or malicious software from gaining access to your computer through the Internet or a network.

● On (recommended)

This setting blocks all outside sources from connecting to this computer, except for those unblocked on the Exceptions tab.

☐ Block all incoming connections

Select this option when you connect to less secure networks. All exceptions will be ignored and you will not be notified when Windows Firewall blocks programs.

○ Off (not recommended)

Avoid using this setting. Turning off Windows Firewall will make this computer more vulnerable to hackers or malicious software.

Tell me more about these settings

OK | Cancel | Apply

Figure 11-2:
The General tab of the Windows Firewall Settings.

General tab

From the General tab of the Windows Firewall Settings window, you can perform some basic configuration options for your Windows Firewall, as shown in Figure 11-2. These options include the following settings:

- **On (Recommended):** By default, this setting is enabled and is configured to block all outside sources from connecting to your system, except for those unblocked via the Exceptions tab.

  Some applications will configure themselves during installation to be on the Exceptions list. Don't assume that everything is blocked.

- **Block All Incoming Connections:** If this setting is enabled, all connections are blocked from connecting to your system, regardless of how the other settings are configured.

- **Off (Not Recommended):** If this is selected, you disable Windows Firewall.

You should always have Windows Firewall enabled unless you have a firewall loaded from another company onto your machine. Not having a firewall leaves you unprotected at a network level and provides both viruses and hackers the opportunity to take advantage of any vulnerabilities on your machine.

Exceptions tab

On the Exceptions tab of the Windows Firewall Settings window (see Figure 11-3), you can configure which programs or ports you wish to allow to communicate with your system. You can be reasonably sure that from time to time, you will need to add a program or port to the exception list. As much protection as Windows Firewall provides, it also prevents some applications from working. If you use an instant messenger program, for example, you need to include that application or ports that it uses in the exceptions list so that it you can communicate with the outside world. Because security is a balance between protection and productivity, you also need to exercise caution when adding an application or port to the exception list.

Opening a port might increase the risk to your system that an attacker can exploit. Do not add applications or ports to the exception list unless you really need to do so.

The Exceptions tab is straightforward in its design. By default, it provides a list of installed programs that you can allow to communicate through the firewall and a check box next to each one. Any program with a check in the check box is allowed; all others are denied.

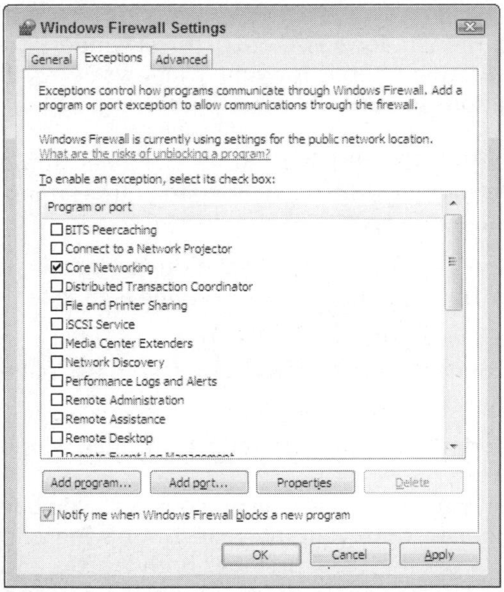

Figure 11-3:
The
Exceptions
tab of the
Windows
Firewall
Settings
dialog box.

> **Windows Firewall Settings**
>
> General | Exceptions | Advanced
>
> Exceptions control how programs communicate through Windows Firewall. Add a program or port exception to allow communications through the firewall.
>
> Windows Firewall is currently using settings for the public network location.
> What are the risks of unblocking a program?
>
> To enable an exception, select its check box:
>
> Program or port
> ☐ BITS Peercaching
> ☐ Connect to a Network Projector
> ☑ Core Networking
> ☐ Distributed Transaction Coordinator
> ☐ File and Printer Sharing
> ☐ iSCSI Service
> ☐ Media Center Extenders
> ☐ Network Discovery
> ☐ Performance Logs and Alerts
> ☐ Remote Administration
> ☐ Remote Assistance
> ☐ Remote Desktop
> ☐ Remote Event Log Management
>
> Add program... | Add port... | Properties | Delete
>
> ☑ Notify me when Windows Firewall blocks a new program
>
> OK | Cancel | Apply

To add a program to the list, perform the following steps:

1. Click the Add Program button.

The Add a Program window opens. (See Figure 11-4.)

2. **Click the Browse button.**

3. **Navigate to the program that you want to add to the list and select Open.**

   The application is added to the list.

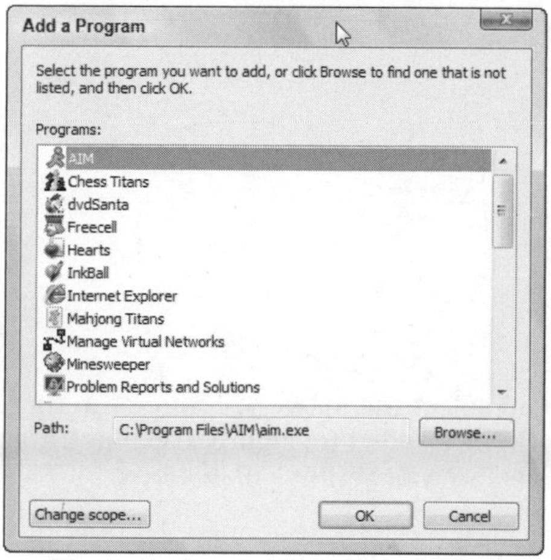

Figure 11-4:
The Add a
Program
window.

Click the Change Scope button from the Add a Program window to specify the set of computers for which this port or program is unblocked. However, for most home or small office users, the default scope is sufficient.

You can also allow communication through the firewall based on a specific port number. *Ports* are interfaces through which devices communicate at a network level. A *port number* is a number assigned to a program so that other computers know how to contact that program on your machine. Adding a port allows you to create your own specialized exception by telling Windows to allow communication through the firewall via a specific port number. To add a port, perform the following steps:

1. **From the Exceptions tab (refer to Figure 11-3), click the Add Port button.**

   The Add a Port window opens. (See Figure 11-5.)

2. **Select a name for the port, enter the port number, and then specify the protocol (TCP or UDP).**

Finally, selecting the Notify Me When Windows Firewall Blocks a New Program check box on the Exceptions tab (refer to Figure 11-3) tells Windows to pop up a message the first time a new program tries to communicate through the firewall and is denied access. This notification lets you (the user) know which programs are trying to gain access. If necessary, then you can add that program to the exception list.

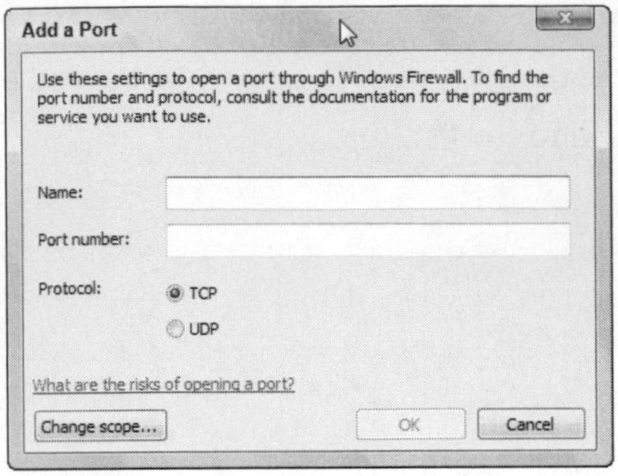

Figure 11-5:
The Add a
Port
window.

Advanced tab

On the Advanced tab, you can select the network connection that your
Windows Firewall settings will be applied to. Figure 11-6 illustrates the
Advanced tab of the Windows Firewall Settings dialog box.

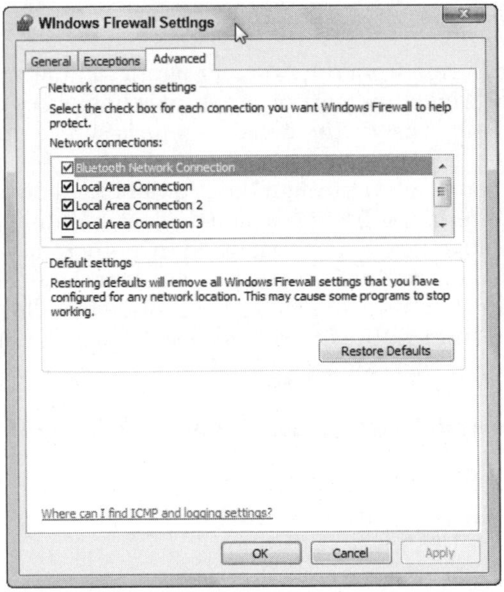

Figure 11-6:
The
Advanced
tab of the
Windows
Firewall
Settings
dialog box.

This tab offers the following settings:

✔ **Network connection selected:** If the check box for any connection is
  selected, Windows Firewall settings will be applied to that connection.
  Your system might have multiple network connections, such as a wireless

connection or hard-wired network connection. This allows you to apply certain settings to a specific connection.

- ✔ **Network connection not selected:** If the check box for any connection is not selected, Windows Firewall settings won't be applied to that connection.

- ✔ **Restore Defaults:** Clicking this button restores the defaults to *all* the network connections and deletes all settings of Windows Firewall that you made since Windows was installed.

Using Windows Firewall with Advanced Security Applet

Advanced security management of Windows Firewall is achieved by using the Windows Firewall with Advanced Settings applet, which (like many Windows applications) can be accessed in a variety of ways. You can access this application by performing either of the following steps:

Activating the application through the Local Security Policy:

1. **Choose Start.**
2. **In the Search field that appears, type** local security policy.
3. **Press Enter.**

Activating the application through the Microsoft Management Console (MMC):

1. **Choose Start.**
2. **In the Search field that appears, type** wf.msc.
3. **Press Enter.**

Activating the application through the program menu:

1. **Choose Start⇨Control Panel⇨Classic View⇨Administrative Tools.**
2. **Select Windows Firewall with Advanced Security.**

When you first open the Windows Firewall with Advanced Security interface (see Figure 11-7), notice how busy it is. Five different panes are immediately shown because all views are active. You can arrange the display to appear in a simpler, more appealing way. For the purpose of this chapter, I keep all the views active. However, if you'd like to customize your view of the Windows Firewall with Advanced Security applet, perform the following steps:

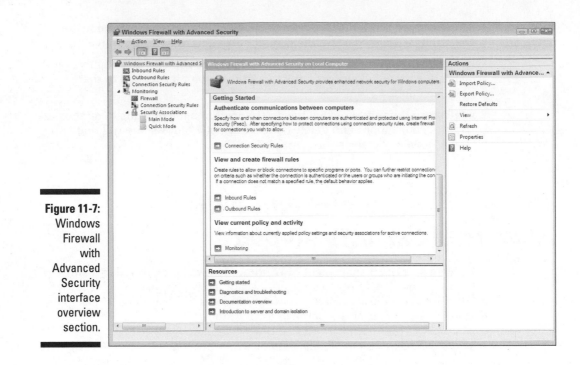

Figure 11-7:
Windows
Firewall
with
Advanced
Security
interface
overview
section.

1. **With the Windows Firewall application open, choose View⇨Customize.**

   The Customize View window opens.

2. **Select the items that you wish to be viewed.**

By default, three different panes are used within the interface in all contexts.

- ✔ **Console tree:** The interface displays a navigation pane as a console tree in the left pane. This pane defines the context of the other two panes. Figure 11-7 shows the highest level (Windows Firewall with Advanced Security) highlighted. Therefore, the middle pane (the working pane) is split in two, and the action items in the right pane are shown in that context.

- ✔ **Working pane:** The middle pane is the working area of the interface. This area shows the settings or data related to the context that you set in the console tree. This area also has navigation links to pull up other interfaces or switch context within the data displayed.

- ✔ **Action pane:** The right pane contains the actions that you can perform related to the context of the interface. Usually the actions can also be accessed by right-clicking in the working pane or by clicking the Action menu item.

The Windows Firewall with Advanced Security on Local Computer context is the default view when you open the interface and is the top-most view within the interface navigation. The working pane for this context is broken into

Overview and Getting Started sections as well as an additional Resources pane at the bottom of the middle section of the interface. These portions of the working pane are described in the next few sections.

The Overview section of the interface publishes the information for each network profile that's set in the Windows Firewall Properties interface. One of the best features of Windows Firewall is the use of rules that apply, depending upon the network context of your connection. That means that the rules you have set regarding what can connect to your computer (or what your computer can connect to) from your home network can be different than the rules you set as to what can connect from the Internet. These profiles are dynamic, so your machine will automatically determine which profile you should be using at any given time based on your available network connections.

The three different network profiles available to Windows for you to configure are as follows:

- **Domain Profile:** Windows uses this profile when your computer is part of an Active Directory (AD) domain and authentication can be achieved through all active network interfaces.

- **Private Profile:** Windows uses this profile when your computer is connected to a subnet that has been designated as private by someone with administrative privileges on the machine. This can be a home network behind a router or a local area network (LAN) at a trusted location.

- **Public Profile:** Windows uses this profile when at least one network interface is connected to a public or an unidentified network. The settings in this profile should be the most restrictive because you should assume that a public network is not a trustworthy environment.

Under each profile is a statement as to whether Windows Firewall is enabled. This is followed by the general rules of behavior for each profile. These general rules set the default behavior that the firewall uses when a matching rule is not available for that particular communication. The types of connections available are Inbound and Outbound, as follows:

- **Inbound connections:** This rule affects communication in which another machine is trying to connect to your machine. If you haven't set a rule that applies to the specific type of communication, Windows Firewall will block this type of connection by default in Vista.

- **Outbound connections:** This rule affects communication where your machine is trying to connect to another machine. If you haven't set a rule that applies to the specific type of communication that your machine is attempting, Windows Firewall allows this type of connection by default in Vista. Most of the complaints surrounding the security of Windows Firewall is based on this default behavior; however, it can easily be changed if you desire.

To open Windows Firewall properties, click the Windows Firewall link at the bottom of the Overview section.

The dialog box shown in Figure 11-8 appears, with a tab for each of the network profiles as well as the basic IPsec Settings. Each of the three profile tabs contains information about the Firewall state, settings, and logging for that particular profile. By default, all these items are the same, but the interface allows you to customize any item for a particular profile.

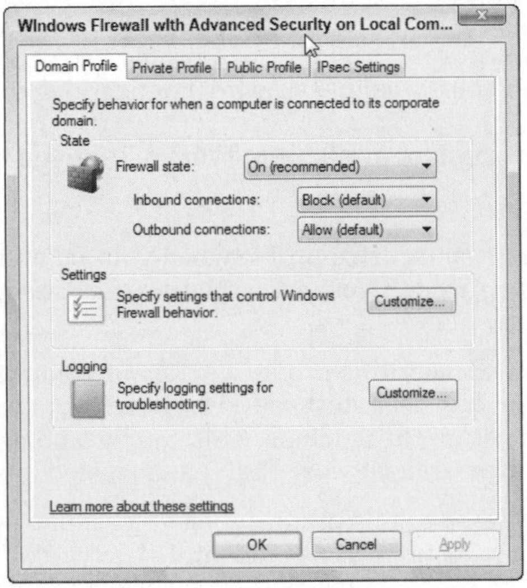

Figure 11-8:
The
Windows
Firewall
Properties
interface.

For the purposes of this exercise, look at the configuration of only one profile — the Domain profile. *Note:* Any of these profiles can be configured independently in much the same way. Here's a look at what you can configure.

✔ **Firewall State:** From this option, you can turn off Firewall for a particular type of connection but leave it on for another.

Unless you have a very good reason to use this for a limited amount of time, you should not turn off Firewall on any particular interface.

✔ **Inbound Connections:** This setting determines Firewall default behavior with regard to other computers trying to connect to yours. Here are the three options that you can choose:

- *Block (Default):* This is the default setting for inbound connections and tells Firewall to check all its rules for a match related to that type of traffic. If no match is found, Firewall will not allow the connection to occur. Choosing this option means that Firewall will deny any connection unless a specific rule allows it.

- *Block All Connections:* Firewall will deny all connections without even checking the rules that have been set up. This is useful when you want to protect your computer completely from all network threats without having to delete Vista default rules. Although this sounds great from a security perspective, you should be very careful before trying to use this setting because lots of background communication will no longer be able to operate.

- *Allow (Default):* Firewall will check through all its rules for a match related to that type of traffic. If no match is found, Firewall will then allow the connection to occur. Choosing this option means that Firewall will allow any connection unless a specific rule denies it.

✔ **Outbound Connections:** This setting determines the Firewall's default behavior with regard to your machine attempting to connect to another. Unlike inbound connections, only the Block and Allow options are valid for outbound connections, but they operate as described earlier.

The next area in the interface is the Settings area, which is accessed by clicking the Customize button in the Settings area. This brings up the interface shown in Figure 11-9.

Figure 11-9:
Windows
Firewall
Profile
Settings
interface.

✔ **Firewall Settings section:** You can choose how the application displays notifications to the user when a program is blocked from receiving inbound connections. If you choose Yes, the user will be notified. If you select No, the user will not be notified.

I suggest that you keep the default setting of Yes.

✔ **Allow Unicast Response:** This setting determines whether unicast response to multicast or broadcast network traffic is allowed. By default, Yes is selected. Setting this to No can interfere with the correct operation of protocols that use broadcasts; however, it will not affect DHCP unicast responses.

✔ **Rule Merging:** These settings apply to those machines that receive rules distributed by group policy, which typically are not home or small office users.

The final area in the interface is the Logging area. You access this by clicking the Customize button in the Logging area (refer to Figure 11-8), which brings up an interface like the one shown in Figure 11-10.

Figure 11-10:
The
Windows
Firewall
Logging
interface.

Customize Logging Settings for the Domain Profile	
Name:	:\system32\LogFiles\Firewall\pfirewall.log Browse...
Size limit (KB):	4,096
Log dropped packets:	No (default)
Log successful connections:	No (default)

Note: If you are configuring the log file name on Group Policy object, ensure that the Windows Firewall service account has write permissions to the folder containing the log file.

Default path for the log file is %windir%\system32\logfiles\firewall\pfirewall.log.

Learn more about logging

OK   Cancel

By default, Vista combines all the records for all types of connections into a single log file. This file is located at

```
C:\Windows\system32\logfiles\firewall\pfirewall.log
```

and is controlled by the path in the Name: textbox at the top of this interface. You can change this default behavior by choosing different logging paths for each of the different profiles, which will create a log file specific to each type of connection. This is an unnecessary action in most cases because it's easier to open the single log in Excel (or other spreadsheet program) and sort than it is to try to correlate data across the different logs. However, it is a nice tidbit of knowledge that could come in handy if you're trying to solve a specific problem.

The other settings in this interface control how large the log file can grow to before it starts to overwrite itself, as well as what type of data to log. By default, Vista doesn't log either dropped or successful connections to the firewall because this information is considered to be unnecessary unless you are going to be actively doing something with it.

Using the Getting Started Section to configure Firewall

The Getting Started section of the Windows Firewall with Advanced Security applet provides you a quick and easy way to authenticate communications between computers, view and create Firewall rules, as well as view current policy and activity. Read on to see how you can do this.

The Authenticate Communications between Computers section

The Authenticate Communications between Computers area of the Getting Started section allows you to specify how and when computers are authenticated by using *Internet Protocol security (IPsec)*. Although this is an interesting topic that I could easily write a few chapters on, the home and small office user will not likely use these settings. For those who are interested, however, Figure 11-11 illustrates the type of settings that you can configure here. For more information on implementing these configurations, I suggest that you spend some time at the Microsoft Windows Vista TechCenter on Microsoft TechNet.

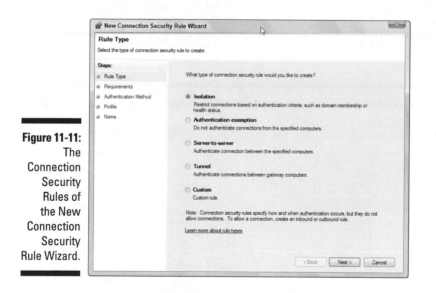

Figure 11-11: The Connection Security Rules of the New Connection Security Rule Wizard.

The View and Create Firewall Rules section

Click the View and Create Firewall Rules link in the Getting Started section to view your current Firewall rules and create new rules for both inbound and outbound connections.

Figure 11-12 illustrates the inbound rules set on my test system. Notice that in the middle working pane, you can see those inbound connections and a variety of information about them, such as the name, group, profile, whether the connection is enabled or disabled, and what action the system is taking.

In the right (Actions) pane, you can see that you can perform a variety of tasks, such as create a new rule, filter by profile, state, group, and so on. To create a new rule, perform the following steps:

1. **Double-click the New Rule link in the Actions pane.**

   The New Inbound Rule wizard opens. (See Figure 11-13.)

2. **Select what type of rule you want to set up.**

Although I don't walk you through the steps to make a rule, this interface allows you to create a rule for a program, port, predefined connection, or a custom rule. The wizard asks whether you want to apply the rule to a specific program or to all programs. After you set that, you can configure for the following:

- **Allow the Connection:** This allows both secure or unsecure connections to the particular program or port that you selected.

- **Allow Connection if it is Secure:** This allows only connections that have been authenticated and integrity protected through the use of IPsec.

- **Block Connection:** This blocks any inbound connection from that program or port.

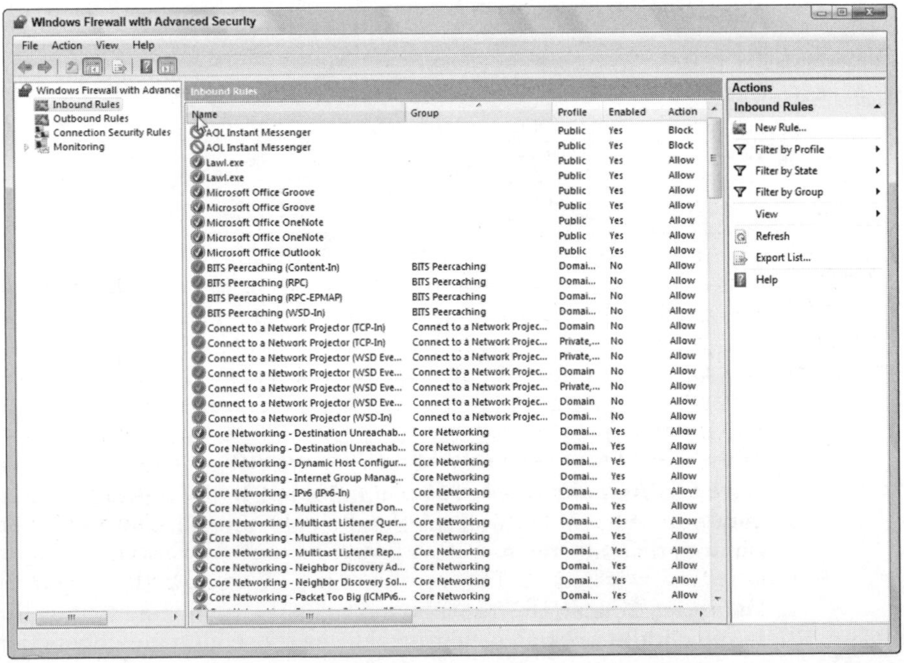

Figure 11-12:
View and create Firewall rules.

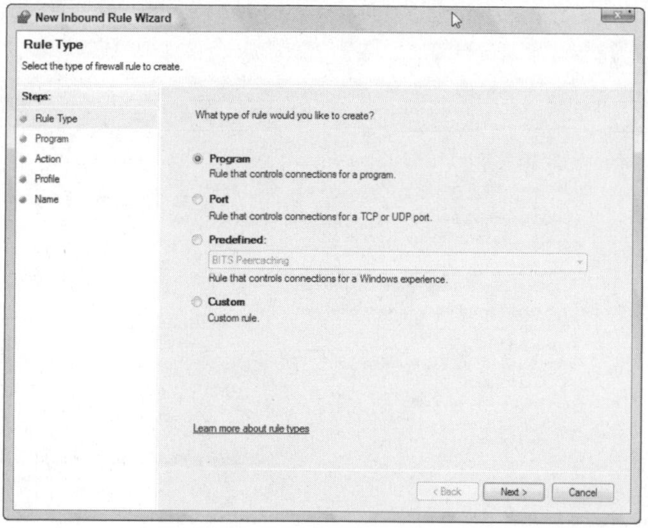

Figure 11-13:
Inbound
Rule Wizard
window.

Most home or small office users won't set up these rules for each program via this interface. However, I did want to point out that you have a great deal of specificity with both the inbound and outbound connections. If you were worried about a particular program making a connection to your system, you could set up an inbound rule to deny that connection from happening.

The Monitoring section

Finally, the Monitoring link in the Getting Started section provides you excellent interface to view information about your currently applied policy settings. See Figure 11-14.

Using the Resources pane

Windows Firewall with Advanced Security is a very complex tool that most home and small office users will probably never fully explore. However, if you do have an interest to read more about the tool, the Resources section provides a plethora of information to do just that. You can read about the topics covered in Getting Started and more about diagnostics and troubleshooting. The Documentation review link takes you to the Microsoft Windows Vista TechCenter that I mention earlier. This is a great resource if you want to get more sophisticated with your Firewall security settings and if you want information beyond the scope of this book. There is also a link so that you can understand more about server and domain isolation. I suggest taking a little time and digging into the tool. It will help you understand a bit more about network-related security.

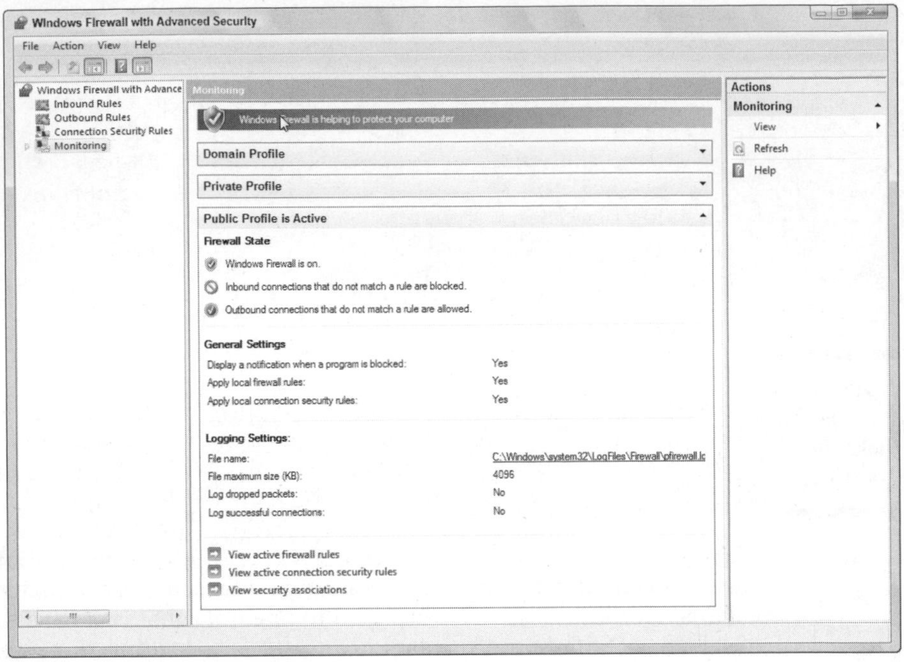

Figure 11-14:
Monitor
your current
policy
settings.

What Do I Do Now?

As you can see, the Vista Windows Firewall is a very complex tool that you can use to fine-tune and batten down the hatches. The problem is that you could also easily lock your system down too tight so that you can't perform particular functions that you need. Because everyone uses their systems differently, it is difficult for me to tell you exactly what to block. A program that I might want to block might just be a program that you use daily to be productive. I can, however, provide you some general guidelines that you should use when configuring your firewall no matter whether you use the Vista Windows Firewall or a firewall from another software provider.

- ✔ **Review your settings regularly.** Review the programs and ports you're permitting through the firewall often to ensure that changes are not being made, allowing communication to occur without your knowledge.

- ✔ **Allow only those programs that need access.** Don't get in the habit of allowing every program to have access. You will be prompted (configured by default) to be notified when a connection needs to talk to the outside world. In that way, you can better determine what access is needed, and what is not. Many users often get into the habit of just allowing access to any program that requests it, without first investigating what that program is doing. This defeats the purpose of the security that the firewall provides.

✔ **Use Caution.** Many tales are out there of people that enabled the Vista Firewall, or a firewall from another vendor for that matter, and suddenly found that the programs they relied upon were no longer working. Locking your system down with the firewall certainly takes some trial and error. You are bound at some point to break something. If you keep track of what changes you are making with the firewall settings, you can likely backtrack and get things fixed again. More important, you will understand the effects of the changes that you are making.

Other Firewalls

Although the Vista Windows Firewall provides adequate protection for most home or small office users, some users might want to use another product. A lot of good firewall products are available — some good, and some not so good. If you're going to use another product, I suggest that you do a little homework and make sure that it's compatible with Vista. Some vendors are Microsoft participating Independent Software Vendors (ISVs), which means they meet certain Microsoft standards. The products from these vendors are more likely to be recognized by the Windows Security Center so that you can dispense security from that interface.

Chapter 12

Locking Down Wireless

*W*ireless networking saved the day! Well, it did for me. I had the drill out, the tool to pull the cable through the wall, a few hundred feet of network cabling, and the weekend free. I was ready to go. Then it struck me: Go wireless! Not necessarily a difficult decision because I really wasn't looking forward to drilling and pulling cable through the floors and walls of my 100-year-old house. So I went out and purchased the wireless equipment. About two hours after arriving home with it in hand, I had every system in my house connected wirelessly.

My experience isn't unique. Wireless connectivity is picking up steam because it's so convenient, providing users with longed-after flexibility. Wireless devices are so easy to set up that even the most novice users can install a wireless network within minutes — certainly within an hour. That, however, is where the problem lies. Because manufacturers of these devices develop their systems to be so easy to use that any Joe Schmoe can do it, little security exists for the default settings. The average user plugs in the device, performs a few steps, and walks away with a wireless network, never to return to implement any type of security. As a result, bits and bytes of possibly very personal data flies around their home or small office with little or no protection.

In this chapter, you get the basics about wireless security and the new Vista-wireless-related security features. You see how to configure your wireless connections in Vista so that you can maintain a responsive, yet secure, wireless connection. I also go a step farther and provide you with the information that you need to secure your wireless network, regardless of the manufacturer of your device, so you can be reasonably sure that your wireless network is not placing you — or your data — in harm's way.

Wireless Network Basic Training

Wireless networking (Wi-Fi) has been around for a little while now, and chances are that you or someone you know uses it. Although this chapter is less about setting up a wireless network in Vista than it is about securing one, I take a few minutes to discuss some basic principles of wireless networking that might help you better understand the rest of this chapter.

Wireless networks offer some advantages over wired networks. However, some disadvantages also exist. Table 12-1 provides you with advantages and disadvantages to both wired and wireless networks.

Table 12-1	Pros and Cons of Wireless and Wired Networking	
Network Type	*Pros*	*Cons*
Wired	Cost-effective, easy to configure, fastest speeds, more secure	Clutter, difficult-to-run wiring, difficult to upgrade
Wireless	Flexibility, easy to upgrade, easy installation, less clutter	Less secure, slower speeds

A wireless network transmits your digital data through the air using either radio signals or microwaves instead of traversing a cable, thus providing you an easy way to connect your computers and peripherals to your network wirelessly. This connectivity is gained via a wireless access point (WAP) that sometimes also serves as a router (or vice versa) and a wireless network card that's installed in your system. The range of these devices varies from manufacturer to manufacturer, but consistently grows with each new generation of products. Some have a range of a few hundred feet, and some boast a few thousand feet. These ranges are affected by obstructions, such as furniture, walls, weather, and how much you're willing to spend on your wireless equipment. Among the equipment that those of us in the home or small office are likely to purchase for a wireless local area network (WLAN), you can realistically see a connectivity range of 100–150 feet. So, although a manufacturer might make all sorts of distance claims, the actual range of wireless connectivity is largely dependent upon perfect conditions. You're likely to realize a range that's far less.

As I discuss securing your wireless network, I want to begin by going over a few key concepts of wireless networking that I discuss later in this chapter:

✔ **Network discovery/broadcasting:** Wireless networks use a *discovery process* in which the WAP and the client both broadcast information. In a nutshell, this means the access point (AP) sends a broadcast that tells those clients within range, "Hey, I'm here. This is my name." Any client can respond, which begins the configuration of the communication process. (I am oversimplifying it a bit.) In addition, clients also send out probe requests of their own, looking for that elusive wireless network they can start talking to. Even if a network is set to *nonbroadcast mode* (a setting to stop the device from sending its network information to the neighborhood), the client continues to probe and broadcast the network-related information, sometimes even disclosing some of the client's secret network configuration information. Vista has taken a few steps to mitigate this risk. In fact, Vista is designed to be much more passive than Windows XP in this regard.

✔ **Unsecure network versus protected network:** An *unsecure network* is one that is not security enabled and protected by security protocols such as Wi-Fi Protected Access (WPA), WPA2, and so on. Vista goes out of its way to let you know if you try to connect to an unsecure network. Vista won't automatically make a connection, but will instead alert you and ask whether you want to connect to this unsecure network or choose a different network.

✔ **Ad hoc networking:** *Ad hoc networks* make it possible for users to quickly set up a wireless network with their own devices so that they can share and collaborate. Each system forwards the "radio waves" of the other systems in the ad hoc network. This type of network provides the ability for wireless devices to communicate directly with one another in a peer-to-peer fashion as long they are, of course, in sufficient range of each other. Typically, this type of networking is less secure.

✔ **Service set identifier (SSID):** The *service set identifier* is essentially the identity of the wireless network to which you are trying to connect. It is configurable in both the wireless network AP interface and on each client. Although the client will automatically recognize an SSID if it discovers the wireless network, you might need to manually configure the client under certain circumstances. *Note:* Both the client and the network must have the same SSID to complete a connection.

✔ **Network location types:** Windows Vista provides three different types of network locations, as follows:

- *Public:* A *public* network location is an unidentified network, such as a hotspot. The Vista Windows Firewall blocks all unrequested incoming traffic unless you specifically create exceptions. Network discovery is also disabled. By default, Vista sets a higher level of security on public networks.

- *Private:* *Private* networks are the networks typically found in the home or small office. Vista Firewall exceptions, as well as network discovery, are enabled.

- *Domain:* A *domain* network is a network in which Vista is connecting and authenticating to an Active Directory (AD) domain controller. Vista Firewall exceptions and network discovery is enabled by default, and many group policy settings can be applied.

What's New for Wireless Security in Vista

Holding true to the promise that Vista is a more secure operating system (OS), Microsoft added some additional security around wireless connectivity:

- ✔ **netsh command line:** Although not strictly a security feature, the `netsh` command line is an enhanced network command line interface (CLI) that enables automation and scripting and helps troubleshoot network connections. Using this CLI, administrators can verify, change, or remove a PC's wireless configuration profiles, some of which are security related.

- ✔ **Improved wireless configuration functionality:** The Network and Sharing Center provides easier and more intuitive security functionality for configuring your wireless connection securely. The user receives alerts when connecting to unsecure networks.

- ✔ **Protocol support:** Vista provides support of the latest security protocols, such as WPA and WPA2, that are more secure than WEP. Vista also supports PEAP, PEAP-MS-CHAPv2 (used in an enterprise environment with AD), EAP-TLS (used with certificates), and WEP. Some of these protocols are used in larger environments, but this chapter covers the protocols that are applicable to the home and small office user.

- ✔ **Network discovery broadcasting:** Vista provides more passive discovery broadcasting so that the amount of information broadcast prior to connecting to a network is reduced. Previous to Vista, wireless clients had to issue communications or broadcast as part of an understanding network information so they could make a connection, especially if an AP was configured to have the network hidden or set to a nonbroadcast mode. This behavior can be exploited in a variety of ways, and the more-passive Vista approach helps alleviate these problems. A Vista client will not broadcast the network name when searching for available networks when the network name isn't hidden. If you configure the network to be hidden or nonbroadcast, Vista broadcasts only the names of the preferred networks that are configured as hidden or nonbroadcast.

- ✔ **Temporary network name generated by client:** Previous Windows clients generate a temporary network name when no preferred network is available. Attackers could exploit this by connecting to the temporary network and performing a variety of malicious tasks. Vista reduces this vulnerability by parking the wireless adapter in a passive listening mode without generating a temporary network name. Although a temporary network is generated if a legacy driver is installed, Vista provides security functionality that essentially eliminates the risk for the legacy driver, too. Particularly, Vista creates a random key for the temporary network, making it essentially impossible for an attacker to connect to the temporary network.

✔ **Protection against unprotected wireless networks:** Vista improved alerting and prompting for connection to wireless networks that are unencrypted. Vista also uses wireless network profiling to prevent automatic connection to a spoofed wireless network.

✔ **Ad hoc security improvements:** Vista uses WPA2-Personal ad hoc networking, which is the most secure ad hoc wireless networking. After all the users disconnect from the network, Vista deletes the network unless the user specifically designated it as a permanent network. This mitigates risks associated if a user mistakenly leaves an ad hoc network open. Additionally, if the users were sharing an Internet connection across an ad hoc network, Vista disables Internet Connection Sharing when the user disconnects from the network.

✔ **Network profiles:** Vista allows for the differentiation between different types of networks, such as public, private, and domain. This allows for different levels of security to be applied to each of the types of network so that risks associated with each type can be addressed.

Configuring Wireless Security in Vista

Vista offers a variety of security options that can help you get on your way to having a secure wireless network. Some of them you will like; perhaps others you won't. However, understanding all these options enables you develop the security configuration that makes sense for you.

Connecting to a network

Like in previous versions of Windows, connecting to a wireless network is relatively transparent to an end user. Vista automatically connects to a secure network and requires very little interaction from the user. Depending on your security settings, however, some configurations might require more manual configuration on the client. For example, if you choose to disable Dynamic Host Configuration Protocol (DHCP) and assign static Internet Protocol (IP) addresses to each client, manual client configuration is necessary. In addition, Vista won't allow an automatic connection to an *unsecure wireless network* — that is, a wireless network not protected with encryption. Even in that instance, though, the user is required to do little more than acknowledge that he is connecting to an unsecure network.

A few words about unsecure networks

Connecting to unsecure networks presents a certain amount of risk to your system and any personal data. When something is represented as an unsecure network, no protection is in place for all those bits and bytes flying around in air in your home or small office. The problem is that those bits and bytes can contain your personal information.

I often hear people at home or in a small office contemplate whether this is really a big deal, often taking a position that no one would ever target them — that big corporations with more money, more employees, and so on make more likely targets. That argument seems logical, but it isn't always true. People drive around all the time looking for unsecure wireless networks. They publish the results of their findings on the Internet or elsewhere for others to see so that (at best) others can use these unsecure wireless networks for a free Internet connection. At worst, others can attempt to hack into these unsecure networks and carouse or steal personal information. Literally driving around and looking for these unsecure wireless connections is *war-driving* and has become almost sportlike among the more technical crowd.

Your personal information traversing your wireless networks is more at risk than ever before — that is, if you blatantly choose to not protect it. The fact that there are people that are purposefully driving around neighborhoods just like yours and mine — with beefed-up wireless antennas, special software, and a keen eye for spotting unsecure networks — should bring you enough concern to spend the half hour it takes to secure your network with security protocols, such as WPA and WPA2. The tools and technologies are there — you just need to use them.

With that said, you must wonder why Vista warns you about connecting to unsecure networks instead of forbidding it altogether? Unfortunately, many people don't secure their wireless network: hence, the popularity of war-driving. Certainly, your local coffee shop doesn't have the time nor the inclination to configure your laptop at the door so you have a secure connection. From time to time, most users will want or need to make such a connection. If Vista didn't allow you to connect to an unsecure wireless connection, many users would lose productivity.

To connect to a wireless network, perform the following steps:

1. **Choose Start⇨Connect To.**

   The Connect to a Network screen is displayed (as shown in Figure 12-1).

2. **Highlight the listed connection that you wish to connect to and then click elect the Connect button.**

   In Figure 12-1, the network is shown as an *Unsecured network*. I purposely configured the network this way so that you can see how the Vista Network and Sharing Center will indicate that a network isn't secured.

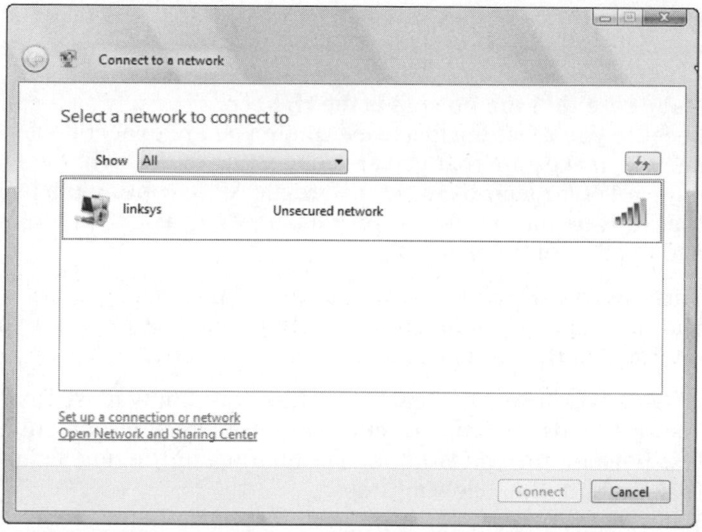

Figure 12-1:
Select a
network to
connect to.

Unsecure networks pose a substantial security risk to your systems or data. Intruders will often carouse unsecure networks to probe systems for weaknesses so that they can harvest sensitive information. Although not all networks will be secured that you will likely need to connect to, do so with caution.

Accessing wireless hotspots or other unsecure wireless networks

Many of us like to run down to the local coffee shop, sip our favorite latté, and grab a wireless connection to the Internet — after all, we're connected! I, too, find myself always wanting to be connected. If I don't have my laptop with me, I will have a cellphone that doubles as a Pocket PC. I can't imagine going a few hours without being able to read and respond to my e-mail or otherwise traverse the Internet. Therefore, that local coffee shop that offers free Wi-Fi service strikes a chord with me. I can sit back, relax, and be productive.

Unfortunately, others are lurking at these hotspots. People who aren't exactly like you and me. People that aren't there to be productive — at least not in the same way you are. They're looking — not to read and respond to their e-mail — but instead to snoop at ours. They're not there to work on their budget or complete their monthly reports. They're there to watch us do it — or, perhaps worse, steal our sensitive information to perpetrate identity theft or other fraud crimes. Make no mistake: These friendly hotspots aren't always so friendly. And though I don't recommend you drop by your nearest java joint pretending to be T.J. Hooker and arrest a few crooks, I do hope that you'll be cognizant that they do exist and that you need to take steps to protect your data.

If you frequent these wireless hotspots, I suggest that you take the following precautions:

- **Make sure that the hotspot is the right spot.** As silly as it sounds, just because you're sitting in a place where you are expecting a wireless connection, make sure that you are connecting to the right one. It isn't unheard of for a crook to set up a rogue AP to capture unsuspecting victims' private information as they unknowingly use the crook's network and not that of the real hotspot.

- **Turn on your Firewall.** Make sure that you are using Windows Firewall and that it's configured appropriately. Chapter 11 provides you all the information that you need to do that.

- **Disable Windows File Sharing.** Unless you simply must share files among friends in an open, very-risky unsecure environment like a wireless hotspot, turn off Windows File Sharing for the time being. To do this, perform the following steps:

    a. *Choose Start⇨Control Panel.*

    b. *Depending on the view that is set in Control Panel, choose one of the following:*

    - *Default view:* Choose Network and Internet⇨Network and Sharing Center.

    - *Classic view:* Choose Network and Sharing Center.

    c. *In the Sharing and Discovery section, expand File Sharing.*

    d. *Select the Turn Off File Sharing radio button and then click Apply.*

- **Pay attention to your surroundings.** Sometimes the best security is as simple as paying attention to those things around you. Many times, you will have an intuitive feeling that something is wrong. It might be body language, a look, or perhaps something someone says. Whatever it is, you might not be able to put your finger on it, but you get the feeling that something is wrong. Admittedly a little more art than science, pay attention to your surroundings. Never leave your laptop or personal data unattended.

Restricting use to specific wireless networks

Although most users want the ability to decide whether they connect to an unsecure network, Vista allows you to prohibit connectivity to unapproved networks via group policy. However, using group policy isn't something that applies to most home or small office users, so I don't cover it in this book.

Still, some technical controls — such as group policy — can help you set this. Chapter 11 covers Windows Firewall configuration; you can also use Firewall to control different aspects of a network connection, especially as they relate to public, private, and domain profiles that can be applied to unsecure network connections.

Network and Sharing Center

Network and Sharing Center provides an intuitive dashboard for your network and sharing configurations. The sharing configurations are covered in Chapter 6 of this book, and I focus on the network-related settings here.

To open the Network and Sharing Center, perform the following steps:

1. **Choose ⇨Control Panel.**

2. **Depending on the view you set in Control Panel, choose one of the following:**

    - *Default View:* Choose Network and Internet⇨Network and Sharing Center.

    - *Classic View:* Choose Network and Sharing Center.

The Networking and Sharing Center window (see Figure 12-2) provides the following:

- ✔ **Network connections view:** Here, view your network connections. You can see all your connections and their status.

- ✔ **Network map:** This is an intuitive illustration of how your system is connected to the Internet.

- ✔ **Sharing and Discovery:** In this area, you can view the status of a variety of configurations, such as network discovery, file sharing, public folder sharing, printer sharing, password-protected sharing, and media sharing. These settings are covered in more detail in Chapter 6 of this book.

- ✔ **Network-related links:** In the left pane of Networking and Sharing Center are links with which you can view, manage, set up, manage, and diagnose your network connections.

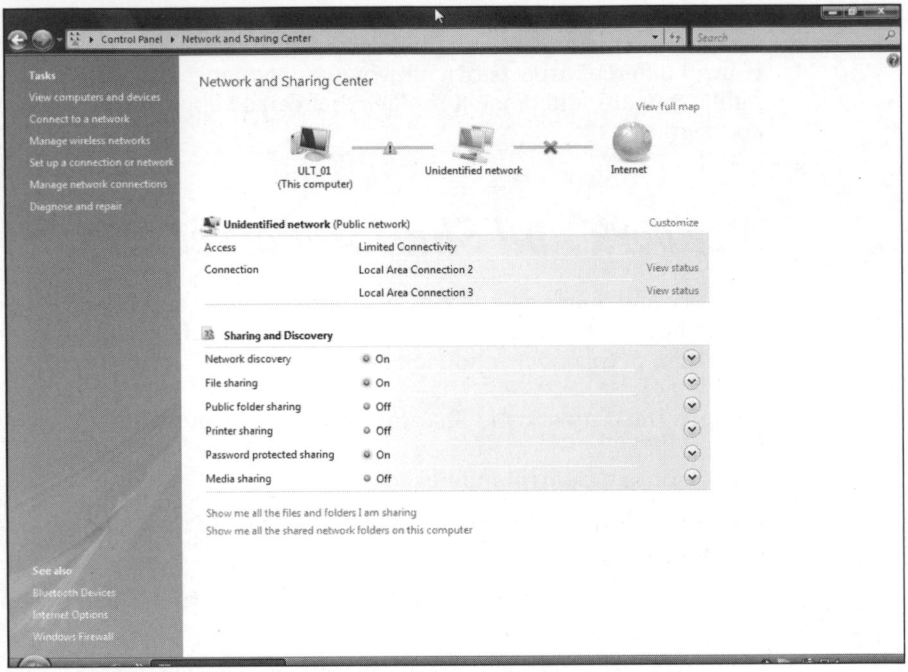

Figure 12-2:
The
Network
and Sharing
Center
interface.

Modifying your network connection

You might want to modify your network connection properties for a variety of reasons, such as configuring your wireless connection for security, modifying connection behavior, or assigning your client a static IP address instead of using DHCP.

To modify your wireless network connection, perform the following steps:

1. **Choose Start➪Control Panel.**

2. **Depending on the view that is set in Control Panel, choose one of the following:**

   • *Default View:* Choose Network and Internet➪Network and Sharing Center.

   • *Classic View:* Choose Network and Sharing Center.

3. **In the left pane of the Network and Sharing Center (refer to Figure 12-2), click the Manage Wireless Networks link.**

4. **In the Manage Wireless Networks dialog box (as shown in Figure 12-3), double-click the network whose properties you want to modify.**

5. **In the Wireless Network properties box of your selected network, you are presented with a dialog box (as shown in Figure 12-4).**

On the Connection tab, the Connect Automatically When This Network Is in Range and the Connect to a More Preferred Network If Available settings are selected by default.

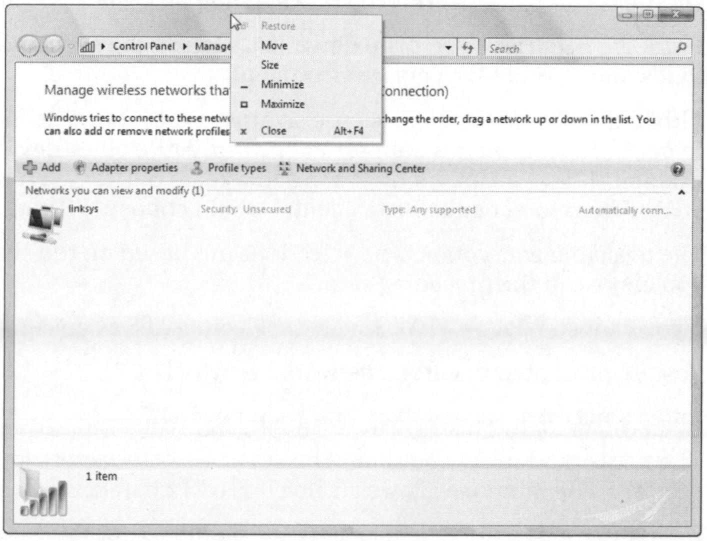

Figure 12-3:
Manage
wireless
networks
here.

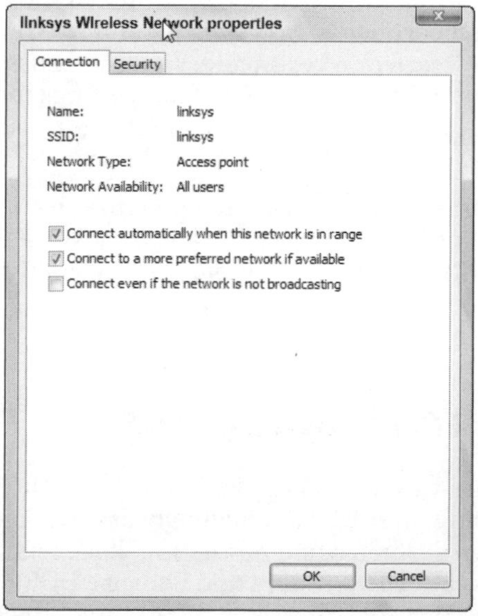

Figure 12-4:
The
Wireless
Network
properties
dialog box.

6. **(Optional) Modify these settings as you want.**

The default settings are suitable for your home or small office.

From here, to modify the security on the selected wireless network connection, perform the following steps:

1. **On the Wireless Network Properties dialog box, click the Security tab.**

2. **From the Security Type drop-down list, choose the security setting that's appropriate for your environment.**

Although WPA2 is the most secure security type, your selection here has to coincide with what is supported on your WAP/router device. For example, I have a Linksys AP that's a few years old; it's WPA but not WPA2. Therefore, on the Vista client, I would choose WPA and not WPA2.

The available encryption type selections are based on the security type you choose in the preceding step.

If you choose WPA or WPA2, I suggest selecting AES as an encryption type.

You are prompted to enter a network security key.

3. **Enter a network security key and then click OK.**

The network security key should be at least 14 characters for added security. The interface allows a value up to 27 characters.

Do not use a passphrase that's easy for others to guess.

If you're in a larger environment and choose WPA or WPA2-Enterprise as a security type, you have to choose a network authentication method, such as a smart card or a certificate. However, most home or small office users won't have a smart card or a certificate, so PEAP is usually the most appropriate choice. Additionally, the default settings for the network authentication method are likely to be sufficient for your environment.

Don't forget the passphrase that you used to configure the network properties on the client because you need to know these values when you configure the security on your WAP interface. The configuration on the client and the network device must match.

Configuring static IP addresses

Later in this chapter, I discuss why you might want to turn off DHCP to secure your wireless network. Turning off DHCP and manually assigning network addresses to each client provides you some protection. If a client can't get an IP address, it can't communicate on your network. Because DHCP automatically hands out IP addresses to clients, disabling it certainly provides some security benefit. However, prior to assigning static IP addresses, you need to understand your network-related information, such as default gateway, subnet mask, and so on. Your AP documentation should provide you some detail with regard to assigning static IP addresses. When you have a designated IP address for a client, assign it by performing the following steps:

1. **Choose Start⇨Control Panel.**

2. **Depending on the view that is set in Control Panel, choose one of the following:**

   • *Default View:* Choose Network and Internet⇨Network and Sharing Center.

   • *Classic View:* Choose Network and Sharing Center.

3. **In the left pane of the Network and Sharing Center interface (refer to Figure 12-2), click the Manage Wireless Networks link.**

4. **Click the Adapter Properties button.**

   The Wireless Network Connection Properties dialog box appears.

5. **Highlight Internet Protocol Version 6 (TCP/IPv6) and then click the Properties button.**

   The Internet Protocol Version 6 (TCP/IPv6) Properties dialog box appears. (See Figure 12-5.)

6. **Select the Use the Following IPv6 Address radio button.**

7. **Enter the appropriate IP address and network-related information into the fields. When finished, click OK.**

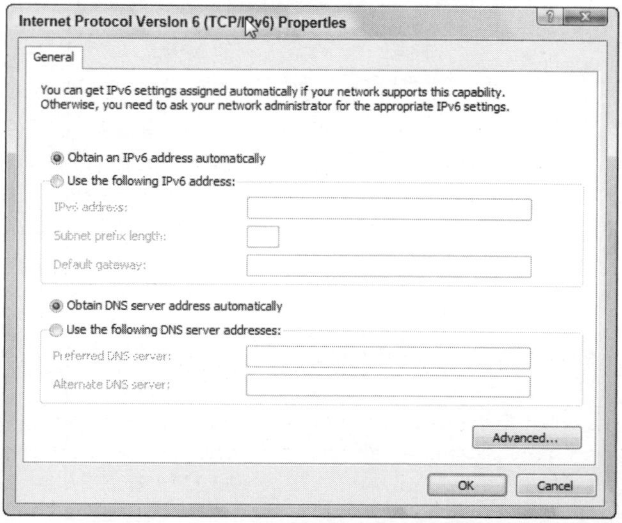

Figure 12-5:
IP and network address information.

Internet Protocol Version 6 (TCP/IPv6) Properties

General

You can get IPv6 settings assigned automatically if your network supports this capability. Otherwise, you need to ask your network administrator for the appropriate IPv6 settings.

⦿ Obtain an IPv6 address automatically
○ Use the following IPv6 address:
  IPv6 address:
  Subnet prefix length:
  Default gateway:

⦿ Obtain DNS server address automatically
○ Use the following DNS server addresses:
  Preferred DNS server:
  Alternate DNS server:

Advanced...

OK   Cancel

Setting up an ad hoc (peer-to-peer) wireless network

Certainly from time to time, you'll likely find yourself in situations where you need to share some files, but you don't have a USB thumb drive, and you don't even want to think about pulling out some old dusty cross-over cable. An ad hoc wireless network sure would look good right about then, but can you create one without breaking all the rules in that security book? Although ad hoc networks do pose a security risk, you will likely find yourself needing to partake in one now and again. Thanks to Vista, you can do so in a relatively secure manner. The Vista ad hoc wireless networking uses WPA2 (personal) to secure the connection. To set up an ad hoc network connection, perform the following steps:

1. **Choose Start⇨Control Panel.**

2. **Depending on the view that is set in Control Panel, choose one of the following:**

   • *Default View:* Choose Network and Internet⇨Network and Sharing Center.

   • *Classic View:* Choose Network and Sharing Center.

3. **In the left pane of the Network and Sharing Center interface (refer to Figure 12-2), click the Set Up a Connection or Network link.**

   The Set Up a Connection or Network window appears. (See Figure 12-6.)

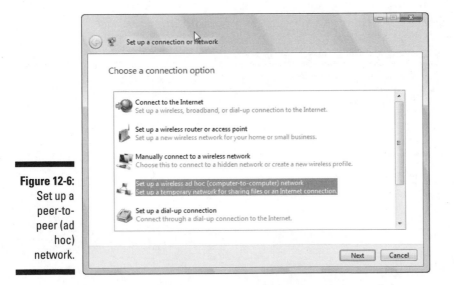

Figure 12-6: Set up a peer-to-peer (ad hoc) network.

4. **Highlight the Set Up a Wireless Ad Hoc Network choice and then click Next.**

   The next screen that appears doesn't have any settings; it just gives you some information about ad hoc networks. (See Figure 12-7.)

5. **Click Next.**

   The next window allows you to choose your security options. (See Figure 12-8.)

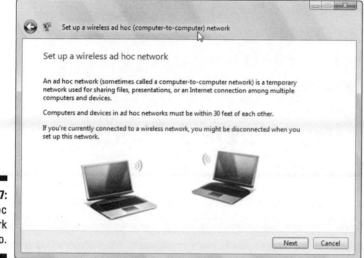

Figure 12-7: Ad hoc network info.

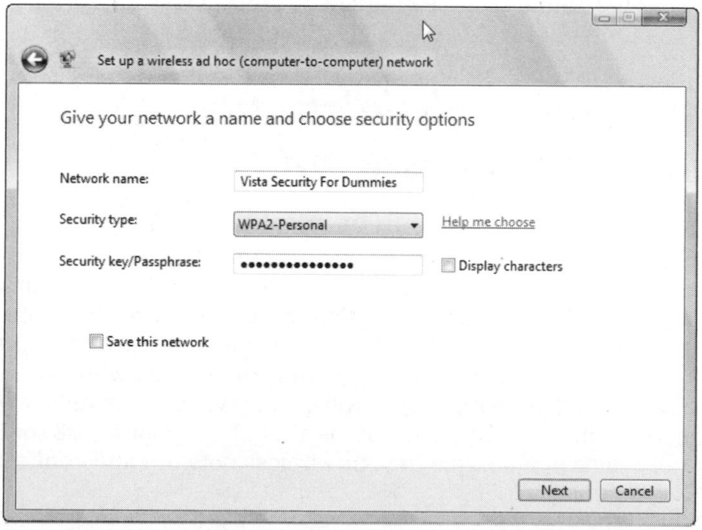

Figure 12-8: Ad hoc security options.

6. **Enter a network name.**

7. **Select WPA2-Personal as the security type and enter a security passphrase.**

I suggest using at least a 14-character passphrase.

8. **Click Next.**

When selecting the Security Type for the Ad Hoc network, you need to select something that will be compatible with all devices. If all the clients run Vista, WPA2 is supported and should be used because it offers the most security.

9. **Click Next.**

The resulting dialog tells you that the network is ready to use.

10. **Click Close.**

Securing Your Wireless Router or Access Point

You can't have a secure wireless network without making configuration changes to both your clients and to your WAP/router device on your network. Because your WAP is likely a different model then mine, I can't provide you exact steps to implement the necessary security changes. Therefore, I talk about these security configurations from a generic perspective. To implement these security configurations, you might need to consult your user's manual so that you can use the proper administrative interface to your device.

Change your administrative usernameand password

When you purchase a wireless device (AP or router), it comes configured with a default administrative username and password. This account is used to set up and control the configuration settings for the device and your wireless network. These default values are widely known. And even if an intruder to your network didn't know them, a simple 30-second Internet search with keywords — including the manufacturer/model of your device, along with the default admin password (or a slight variation) — will quickly yield the results any intruder is looking for. An intruder sitting down the street from your house (or in the house next door) can catch a signal to your wireless network and connect to your device's administrative interface by using the default account and password — and then they're well on their way to owning your network.

If, however, you take three minutes to change your device's administrative level account and password, you provide yourself a great deal of protection against an unauthorized person becoming able to connect to your device and alter the configuration and security settings. You can change this password by following your product documentation and selecting a username and password for the admin account that is not intuitive to anyone else and not easy to guess. Typically, an intruder attempting to gain access to your system will try the default admin username and password immediately. Because crooks are looking for an easy target, changing it just might keep them moving on to the next wireless network.

Change your service set identifier (SSID)

Your *service set identifier (SSID)* is used to identify your wireless network. If you don't change the SSID from the default name, an intruder trying to gain access to your network can easily guess it. Because there are only so many manufacturers of these devices, almost any intruder would be intimately familiar with the default SSID values of most — if not all — of these devices.

Changing the value is something that you can perform easily and is usually documented in your device user's manual or can also be found on the Internet. You access the device through the administrative interface — usually through a browser — and change the SSID name value to something that makes sense for you. I urge you, however, to not make it to intuitive, such as using your last name, your street number, the name of your company, or include any manufacturer or model information in the name. Don't offer any information to someone trying to compromise your system.

Enabling secure communication

Not long ago *Wireless Encryption Protocol (WEP)* was the security flavor of the day. WEP has fallen from favor perhaps because it has been cracked here and there and doesn't provide the level of protection once thought. Most devices support more-recent, wireless-security protocols: in particular, WPA protocol, or the even more recent WPA2. The point here, however, is that most devices ship with these protections disabled. Unfortunately, most of those devices in a home or small office also *remain* disabled.

If you have a wireless network and you don't have this secure communication protocols enabled, one thing is for certain: You are at risk. Such a wireless network is often called an *unprotected* or *unsecure wireless network,* even by the OS when it performs a wireless network discovery. There have been many publicized instances of *war-driving* and even *war-flying,* where people armed with homemade antennas connected to a laptop's wireless card and software hunt down wireless networks that are in an unprotected or unsecure state. These exercises typically find that over 50 percent of wireless networks don't have these security protocols enabled. Well, you can guess which wireless network a hacker is going to try to access: one that's enabled or one that isn't?

I admit right now that enabling this protocol isn't as easy as changing the default password or SSID values. Even still, it's not that difficult, and there is a great deal of documentation usually found on the Internet or even shipped with your device that will assist you. You wouldn't think of not having a lock on your front door, so don't think of not having a wireless network without having secure communications enabled. What traverses over those radio waves just might be data that you don't want others to get their hands on.

Consider disabling DHCP

Most wireless access points/routers also serve as DHCP servers to distribute IP addresses to clients so that they can connect to your network. Typically, a network adapter running on your Windows-based system periodically sends out a broadcast looking for a DHCP server. The DHCP server issues the client a unique IP address that is part of the DHCP pool and designated for distribution. At this time, the client also gets configured with other IP-related data, such as default gateway information, subnet mask information, and more. When the smoke clears and the client has an appropriately assigned IP address that coincides with your wireless network, that client can communicate on your network. If the client can't get an IP address and network related information, the client can't communicate on your network. As you probably can now imagine, controlling who gets an IP address and who does not certainly can help you secure your wireless network.

Understand, however, that disabling DHCP on your wireless network will require that you manually configure each system and the devices with a static IP address. Although beyond the scope of this book, you can find many resources online and perhaps even in your device documentation that will help you configure your wireless network with static IP addressing.

Disabling DHCP does make it more difficult for an unauthorized machine to get an IP address for your network, but it doesn't stop an intruder from configuring a static IP address. Restricting the address pool available on your router equal to the number of systems on your network will provide additional security for your network.

MAC address filtering

A *Media Access Control (MAC) address* is an address that uniquely identifies a system (or network card in that system) on your network. Your wireless AP/router device likely provides MAC Address filtering so that you can control which devices can and can't connect to your wireless network. Implementing this means that a system down the street, next door, or even in your house cannot access your wireless network without your permission. This, in my opinion, is a profound security control and is something that you should consider using even though it's a little more complex to implement than the previous security measures I discuss here.

Disabling SSID broadcasts

The *SSID* is the identification or name for your wireless network. For successful communication to take place between your system and your wireless AP, both must use the same SSID value. Your WAP/router device typically broadcasts this value, along with other information, so that clients within range of the signal can receive this information and start configuring themselves to communicate with your wireless network. Even though the broadcast of the SSID information is convenient so that such automatic configuration of the client can occur, it also introduces a level of risk in that it makes your wireless network visible to intruders. To mitigate this, most manufacturers of wireless access points/routers provide the ability for you to disable such broadcasting. However, doing so does mean that you have to manually configure each client to connect to your wireless network.

Disabling SSID broadcasts does provide additional security to your wireless network; however, it doesn't address the two main components of wireless security: encryption and authentication. Further, the downsides — such as the necessity of manual configuration for each client, the fact that the your WAP will transmit SSID information when a client requests it, and that this information can be seen by those eavesdropping on your network anyway — reduces the net value that you might get from disabling these broadcasts. If you have sensitive data traversing your wireless network, I suggest that you consider this setting, but understand that it only provides a certain amount of value. If you're in an environment where you use multiple APs, this is not a setting that you should implement.

Know your network's range and limit it if needed

I'll admit it. I am a techno-gadget geek. I like the latest cellphone/Pocket PC devices and other gadgets, just as much as my fellow propeller-heads. However, when it comes to a WAP, take a step back. You might not need the AP that carries a signal for a few miles when one that travels 300 feetwill suffice. In fact, I suggest that you avoid purchasing a device that carries a signal farther than you need it to. A signal that reaches beyond what you need only introduces more risk to you. Having a device that carries a signal a longer distance might ensure that you catch a good signal, but it also might provide a signal to the teenager two blocks down your street. And just when you're getting a good night's sleep, he's down in his basement trying to hack into your network. Some devices will allow you to adjust the signal, but others won't. My point is simple: Don't have a device with a range greater than what you need — it only puts your systems and precious data at greater risk.

Chapter 13

Implementing IE7 Security Features to Limit Your Exposure

In This Chapter

▶ Discovering how to reduce the risks associated with everyday Web browsing

▶ Looking behind the scenes at IE7

▶ Using the new features of IE7 that require Vista

*T*he release of Internet Explorer 7 (IE7) marks a substantial improvement in Web surfing safety compared with previous versions of IE. A Web browser is the most vulnerable method of exploiting the everyday user. Folks often don't realize the danger inherent with even the most common ways in which we surf the Web or otherwise use IE7. The Web world is plagued with threats: ActiveX controls operating with far too much privilege and access, cross-domain scripting attacks that can be launched with one simple click, and the ability to initiate remote scripts without the user having a clue about what's going on under the hood. Finally, Microsoft has seriously addressed these risks and more with IE7 and Vista.

This chapter guides you through the new features available in IE7 and provides recommendations to enhance your security without harassing you by asking your permission to do every little thing. The goal of IE7 is to enable you to achieve that balance between protection and productivity.

Configuring IE7 Internet Protected Mode Options

Prior to the release of IE7, the Windows operating system (OS) and the Web browsing functionality of IE were tightly coupled. Those days are gone. *Protected Mode* in IE7 employs three new technologies to separate the OS and the browser. In essence, the browser is quarantined from the system and forced to run at a low-privilege level. Even if IE7 is run from the administrator account, the IE7 process and subprocesses are still run as low privilege in Internet Protected Mode.

Two security mantras are *Least Privilege* and *Need to Know:* Both simply mean that an individual gets those privileges needed to accomplish his tasks, but nothing more. Microsoft seems to recognize that IE7 doesn't need the level of access to the computer that it enjoyed in the past to effectively accomplish its mission. As a result, IE7 now runs in a lower-privilege mode, which means that IE7 has the least amount of privileges needed and only "knows" what it needs to know about your system.

To run IE7 in Internet Protected Mode, you must be running Windows Vista. Protected Mode is part of the new Vista security framework and is used by IE7.

Here are the three technologies that define Internet Protected Mode:

- **Mandatory Integrity Control (MIC):** The key function of MIC is to protect the integrity of the system and data. Mandatory Integrity Control interrogates the code being run to understand how much of the code should be trusted. Mandatory Integrity Control prevents the system's high-integrity files, such as critical system files, from being altered by just about anyone. Mandatory Integrity Control also protects the integrity of user data files classified at a medium level, from the vulnerability to code that is downloaded from the Internet. Mandatory Integrity Control and the associated integrity levels are key components of the Microsoft approach to Windows Vista security.

- **User Account Control (UAC):** Chapter 4 of this book discusses UAC in greater detail. In a nutshell, though, UAC forces all users to be logged on to the system as standard users. If configured, when those standard users need a higher level of authority to perform tasks, a process to escalate that privilege is initiated. In the security world, this is known as the Principle of Least Privilege. If UAC is disabled, Protected Mode is also disabled because many of the Protected Mode components rely on UAC to be enabled.

- **User Interface Privilege Isolation (UIPI):** The best way to understand UIPI is to think of a chain of command. In the armed forces academies, a Cadet should never directly speak to a General; instead, he should follow a chain of command by talking to his immediate superior. Similarly, low-privilege processes running under an account beneath an administrator are Cadets; and higher privilege process, such as those run by the administrator, are Generals. User Interface Privilege Isolation prevents Cadets from interacting with Generals. This feature is the main defense against *shatter attacks:* when a low-privilege process tries to elevate its privilege level by injecting code into a higher-privilege process by using standard DLLs and windows messages.

Table 13-1 outlines common integrity levels and typical consumers — namely, an application, a service, or a user — at each level. Both MIC and UIPI rely heavily on the levels outlined here when making security decisions within the Windows Vista framework.

Table 13-1	Vista Base Integrity Levels
Integrity Level	*Consumers at This Level*
400 (System)	Operating system
300 (High)	Administrator/All local and network services
200 (Medium)	Standard authenticated users
100 (Low)	World (everyone)/IE7 in Protected Mode
0 (Untrusted)	Anonymous users

By default, Protected Mode is enabled for Internet, Local Intranet, and Restricted Sites security Zones; and is turned off for trusted sites and the local machine Zones. Here's how to change these defaults:

1. **Choose Internet Protected Mode via Tools⇨Internet Options.**

2. **Click the Security tab on the Internet Options dialog box that appears; see Figure 13-1.**

   In the Select a Zone to View or Change Security Settings area, you see all the Zones available.

3. **Select a Zone.**

   Protected Mode can be turned on or off per Zone by enabling or disabling the Internet Protected Mode check box within the properties of each zone.

I recommend keeping Protected Mode enabled in the default manner. However, remember how to enable or disable Protected Mode to troubleshoot Internet connectivity issues or local machine application issues.

To verify that Protected Mode is enabled, look at the status bar at the bottom right of the browser window, as shown in Figure 13-2. Here, you can see what Zone you're in: When Web browsing, you're typically in the Internet Zone. Next to the Web content Zone display are the words `Protected Mode: On` — that is, if Protected Mode is enabled.

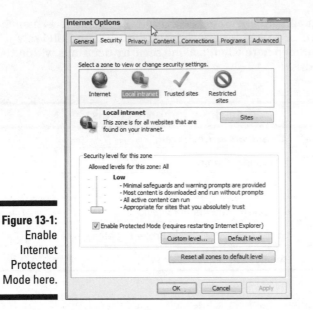

Figure 13-1:
Enable
Internet
Protected
Mode here.

On the system shown in Figure 13-2, Internet Protected Mode is Off.

Figure 13-2:
View
Internet
Protected
Mode status
here.

Status of Internet Protected Mode

Using Protected Mode undoubtedly affords the user much more security. However, security doesn't come without cost in the form of change. Here's a quick test. Say you use Notepad to view the Web page source code. What's not secure with this scenario?

As you can see in Table 13-1, IE7 in Protected Mode runs at a low integrity level of 100. Notepad is run at the standard integrity level of 200. So you now have to allow IE7 to use Notepad explicitly. Within Windows Security Center (WSC), you can change the Protected Modes Elevation policy, which allows IE7 to use the ranking Notepad software.

At this point, you allowed your browser to elevate its privilege when viewing Web page source code. And I see the potential for a lovely Notepad exploit in your future. Notepad still can open, read, and write to nearly any file on the system.

As a workaround, I recommend using Microsoft Visual Web Developer 2005 Express to view Web page source code and not allow IE7 to use Notepad.

Working Safely with ActiveX

The classic struggle between security and functionality cannot be better illustrated than with ActiveX and the Internet. In simple terms, *ActiveX* allows Web developers to enhance Web pages with application add-ins not natively supported by HTML. An *ActiveX control* is a small, single-purpose, standalone piece of software that can be called from Web pages. A typical example of an ActiveX control is a Web page that uses Windows Media Player to show a short commercial clip on the Web page. Writing HTML code to show this clip would be a tremendous undertaking, if it were even possible. But with a few lines of HTML, you can call upon the Windows Media Player ActiveX control and pass it parameters to play the commercial clip.

By design, ActiveX is a powerful tool and has the ability to interact with virtually all aspects of the computer to which it's downloaded. Enter the struggle between a very powerful tool of ActiveX on one side and the persistent danger of the Internet on the other side. So what protects you? Prior to IE7, your only protection was the few seconds that you spent reading a warning message before clicking an OK button. If you actually take the time to read this message before clicking, you'd see a question posed to you that's often nearly impossible to answer.

Figure 13-3 illustrates one of these questions. Most users simply do not know how to answer this.

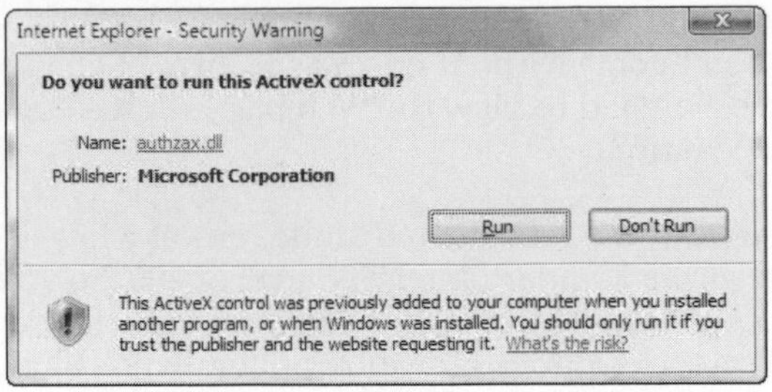

Figure 13-3:
ActiveX
security
warning.

So when is it fair to force an individual to make a snap decision of trust without any background information? The example in Figure 13-3 isn't even a worst-case scenario. When an ActiveX control hasn't been created by a large, well-known company, the citation in the warning of Publisher *XYZ company* is replaced with *Unknown*. You can see how the ActiveX control might hold the potential to destroy your computer's data in seconds. Buying a new house or a new car — or both at once — seems like an easier decision.

IE7 helps protect you with a new feature called ActiveX Opt-In, which attempts to limit the amount of ActiveX controls available to only well-known and supported ones. This reduces the security threat posed by not executing all ActiveX controls that it comes in contact with, but it does not eliminate the risk. ActiveX Opt-In can be configured on a per-Zone basis and is enabled for Internet, Local Intranet, and Restricted Sites security Zones by default. This setting will serve well in most situations, but Web sites running custom ActiveX will need their components approved.

To change the ActiveX Opt-In settings, perform the following steps:

1. **Open Internet Explorer.**

2. **Choose Tools⇨Internet Options.**

3. **When the Internet options dialog box appears, click the Security tab.**

4. **On the Security tab, under the Select a Zone to View or Change Security Settings section, choose a Zone (typically Internet), and highlight it.**

5. **Click the Custom Level button.**

6. **Scroll down to the ActiveX Controls and Plug-ins section.**

   Figure 13-4 illustrates the security options — in particular, ActiveX control options — that are available to configure for the Internet Zone.

   The first ActiveX configuration setting, Allow Previously Unused ActiveX Controls to Run without Prompt, enables or disables ActiveX Opt-In. By default, IE7 is configured to use ActiveX Opt-In, and this setting will be disabled.

7. **To disable ActiveX Opt-in, select this check box and then click OK to save your settings.**

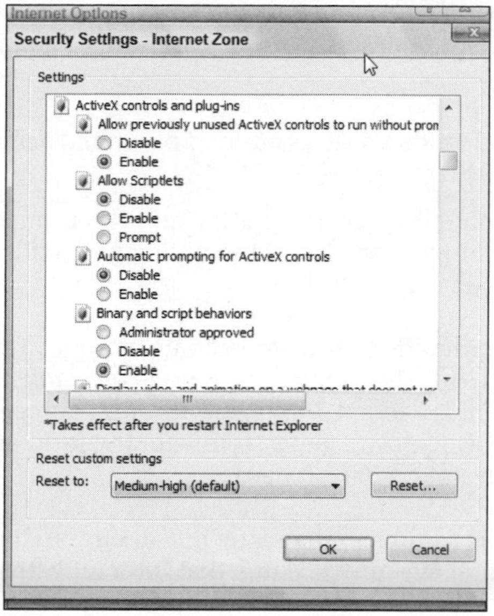

Figure 13-4:
ActiveX
control
options.

ActiveX Opt-In won't solve the security risk presented by ActiveX controls. You still will be faced with the snap decision of trust, but using ActiveX Opt-In reduces the frequency of having to make this decision.

ActiveX can pose a serious security threat, but if the average user has some street smarts, most dangers can be averted. The Internet is very much like a big city, with good areas and bad areas. Most people try to stay in the good parts of town, but we all sometimes get lost and end up in a bad area. This holds true for Internet surfing. Just like how your street smarts urge you to leave a bad part of town, so, too, should you leave the darker corners of the Internet. Stick to the mainstream Web sites because they are feature-and-content rich and very unlikely to do your computer harm.

Protecting against Cross-Domain Scripting Attacks

Microsoft took strong measures with IE7 to prevent cross-domain scripting attacks, also known as cross-site attacks. Cross-domain scripting attacks can take many forms. The fundamental tactic of this attack is to trick the user into believing that he's on a reputable site when he is not. Here's a good example of this attack. You receive an e-mail containing an advertisement saying that Some Big Department Store will give you a $200 credit if you visit its site and create an account. That offer sounds great, so you're tempted to click the link to learn more. If this were a cross-domain attack, two things can occur when you click the link:

- ✔ You could execute a script that scans your computer and sends personal information to the attacker.
- ✔ You could connect to the Web site of the attacker, who is impersonating Some Big Department Store in an attempt to entice you to fill out a form and provide your personal information.

Many of the features of Internet Protected Mode come into play to protect the user from the first scenario. The second scenario is *phishing,* which I cover in more detail in the next section. Perhaps both of the preceding scenarios would occur. Either way, all you get is trouble in the form of identity theft — and most decidedly not a $200 gift card.

This is more of a human error problem than a technical one, so how can IE7 help? IE7 has a more watchful eye for Web sites that interact with other Web sites by displaying the domain name where each script originates in the IE7 status bar. The user can see that he's not at the Some Big Department Store Web site. IE7 also limits the script to only interacting with content in the same domain: If some measure of the Some Big Department Store Web site is presented but the sign-up form ultimately resides on Joe Hacker's Web site, IE7 will notice and prevent further action by the user. This feature helps ensure that user provide information only to whom they intend.

IE7 has one configurable parameter in regards to cross-domain scripting attacks. To view it, do the following:

1. **Choose Tools⇨Internet Options.**

2. **Click the Security tab.**

3. **Choose the Internet Zone.**

4. **Click the Custom Level button to view the settings for this zone. Scroll down to the Miscellaneous heading.**

   The first parameter is Access Data Sources across Domains. This should be disabled by default. If enabled, chances are that your overall security level for this Zone is Medium or lower. The Internet Zone security level should be Medium-high or higher to reap the security benefits of IE7.

Configuring Phishing Filters

In the preceding section of this chapter, I outline a typical phishing scam. The Phishing Filter in IE7 provides further protection against this attack. When you browse to a Web site, the Phishing Filter intercedes to interrogate the target Web site. At this point, two tasks are executed:

1. IE7 compares the target Web site against a Microsoft-provided list of known phishing sites.

   If a match is found, you're notified, by a red warning icon, that the target Web site is harmful. Figure 13-5 illustrates a notification of a known phishing Web site.

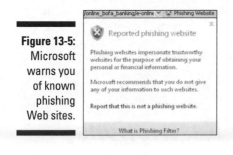

Figure 13-5: Microsoft warns you of known phishing Web sites.

2. If the target Web site isn't on the phishing list, the Web site is scanned for common characteristics of phishing sites.

   If these characteristics are discovered, you're notified, with a yellow warning icon, to proceed with caution. Figure 13-6 illustrates a notification of a potential phishing Web site.

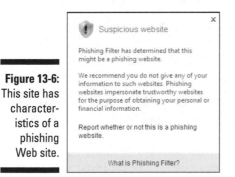

Figure 13-6: This site has characteristics of a phishing Web site.

In the Internet Explorer Tools menu is a new menu item named Phishing Filter. The four choices within this menu are

- ✔ **Check this Web Site:** Forces the querying of the Web site you're at against the Microsoft list.
- ✔ **Turn Off Automatic Web Site Checking:** Allows the user to turn the Phishing Filter on and off.

> ✓ **Report This Web Site:** Connects to a Microsoft site to allow the user to report suspicious activity.
>
> ✓ **Phishing Filter Settings:** Allows the user to turn phishing-characteristic scanning on or off. With this turned off, the target Web site is still checked against the Microsoft list.

IE7 uses a color-coding scheme to identify Web sites that have gone through an identity-verification process. These sites, which have obtained high-assurance certificates, cause the Address bar to change to green. Known phishing sites turn the Address bar red, and potential phishing sites turn the Address bar yellow.

A noticeable performance hit in Web page response time will occur when the Phishing Filter is active, but it's worth it.

Setting Binary Behavior Restrictions

Another change in IE7 is setting the default configuration for Binary Behaviors to be disabled instead of enabled. *Binary behaviors* are an advanced programming concept typically associated with Dynamic HTML (DHTML) to allow more user interaction with Web pages. As such, a close link exists between DHTML and ActiveX controls. By restricting the interaction between dynamic Web code and ActiveX, you can close another possible attack path that has been a favorite of viruses and worms.

To enable Binary Behavior restrictions, perform the following steps:

1. **Choose Start⇨All Programs⇨Internet Explorer.**

2. **Choose Tools⇨Internet Options.**

3. **When the Internet Options dialog box appears, click the Security tab.**

4. **Change Binary and Script Behaviors to Enable.**

Keeping Binary Behaviors disabled, as is the new default in IE7, is a safe bet. However, some very-hard-to-identify issues might arise for those using some of the features of advanced Web sites. Voice over IP (VoIP) Web sites and services (such as Google Phone) might be affected, and advanced graphics Web sites might be affected. I doubt that common Web surfers will be affected by disabling this feature.

Understanding Local Machine Zone Restrictions

In IE7 and recent prior releases of IE, the use of built-in security Zones is used to classify and group Web sites into categories based on risk. After a Web site is categorized, IE7 limits each Zone's permissions accordingly. The Zones in IE7 are as follows, from highest risk to lowest: Internet, Local Intranet, and Trusted Sites. One additional Zone — Restricted Sites — is a bucket for Web sites that might damage your computer. The most significant changes in IE7 are to the Internet and the Trusted Sites Zones:

- **Internet Zone:** The Internet Zone, where the majority of Web browsing occurs, has been updated with two very significant changes. The Internet Zone runs in Protected Mode on Windows Vista (as I mention earlier in this chapter), and ActiveX Opt-In also helps reduce the number of ActiveX controls available in the Internet Zone.

- **Trusted Sites Zone:** The Trusted Sites Zone in IE6 was a very powerful feature. If a user added a Web site to the Trusted Sites list, it could automatically install signed ActiveX controls on the user's machine. In IE7, the default setting for the Trusted Sites Zone is Medium, which is the same level as the Internet Zone in IE6. This change lowers the Trusted Sites Zone's effect on the computer by restricting access to the system.

Another key change is the on-demand use of the Local Intranet Zone. IE7 now checks whether your computer is connected to a domain. If it is, the Local Intranet Zone will be available. Conversely, if you're not part of a domain, Local Intranet Zone isn't available. The main reason for this change is that the Local Intranet Zone has been a haven for malicious Web sites to execute with fewer restrictions.

A common security risk to all releases of IE is Zone-spoofing attacks. Attackers employing this technique manage to fool IE into treating an outside site in the low-privilege Internet Zone as a high-privilege Trusted site. In doing so, they forgo the burden of restrictive security measures and have more access to the computer. In IE7, Zone restrictions are strongly enforced through the use of Protected Mode and stronger internal code to prevent Zone spoofing and Zone hopping.

- *Zone spoofing* happens when a Web site pretends to be a Web site that is a member of a higher-privileged Zone.

- *Zone hopping* happens when a Web site tries to have part of itself run at a higher privilege, meaning that the Web site is a member of multiple Zones at the same time.

Intranet, schmintranet

A summer intern at Microsoft pointed out to the geniuses there that most home users don't have intranets. Therefore, the additional Zone is nothing more than a security risk. Can you imagine the look on their faces? Kudos to Microsoft for listening and implementing this change.

However, there is good with the bad. Figure 13-7 illustrates a message from IE7 notifying the user that another window must be opened. Be prepared to see this message at first when you're training your IE7 on the Zone assignments for your frequented Web sites.

Figure 13-7:
IE7 new window warning message.

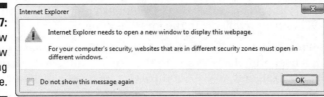

And just when we got accustomed to tabbed browsing, it's gone. Note that the warning message in Figure 13-7 reads, `Open a new window` — not open *a new tab*. This might carry a high annoyance factor for some, but it's worth the added security. It will not take the average user more than a few acknowledgements of this message to properly train his IE7.

The Local Machine Zone is not a real Zone; rather, it contains all the data content of the computer except IE cache files. All data in the Local Machine Zone bears a high level of trust. This Zone can't be configured through IE and can be altered only through Registry changes. By default, the security zone settings are stored in the HKEY_CURRENT_USER subtree.

Direct Registry editing is not a recommended action.

The only typical task that would involve this course of action is assigning a local HTML file to the Internet Zone. This HTML file would contain all the ActiveX controls, Java, or scripts you would use to interact with an external site. Fortunately, you can accomplish this task without accessing or modifying the Registry directly. By inserting the following line into the local HTML file between the <HEAD> </HEAD> tags, you can assign your local file to the Internet Zone:

```
<!-- saved from url=(0020)http://www.jlccc.com/ -->
```

The `saved from url` section instructs IE to apply the Internet Zone security level to this file. The number `20` represents how many characters follow the equal sign. The Web address used is the target Web location where this page resides.

The preceding method for assigning a local file to the Internet Zone is one you should be aware of. It is commonly called Mark of the Web (MOTW). Any page that contains the MOTW won't trigger the security warning in IE6 and IE7 because they won't cross Zones or be under the scrutiny of the Local Machine Zone security.

AUTHOR'S PICK

Keep the following line handy because it may save your computer. If you ever come across a Web page that you have to run locally but you're not sure that you trust, simply insert the following MOTW line into the HTML file:

- The comment must start with the following:

  ```
  <!-- saved from url=
  ```
- The comment must end with the following:

  ```
  -->
  ```
- The full line will look like

  ```
  <!-- saved from url=(0013)about:internet -->
  ```

After this line is inserted, the Web page can run in the restrictive Internet Zone and is far less likely to damage your system.

Adding more security with MIME safety and MK protocol restriction settings

Multipurpose Internet Mail Extension (MIME) is the standard format for virtually all e-mail transmissions. Also included in the MIME format are mechanisms to transmit file attachments and support non-English language character encoding. A little-known fact about MIME is that it's also a fundamental component of transmission protocols, such as HyperText Transfer Protocol (HTTP). The MIME format plays a key role in Web surfing by mapping the file type to a viewing program. For example, when a JPEG image is received via IE, MIME maps this extension to display the image in IE. If an MP3 file is received, MIME maps this extension to Windows Media Player. The MK protocol still plays a role in some older Web applications to retrieve information from compressed files.

Both MIME and MK have been used recently to compromise systems. The MK protocol has been used to gain remote access to a system, and MIME typically facilitates phishing attacks. Within 24 hours of the release of IE7, a vulnerability was reported in how IE7 MIME handles the MHTML file type.

Exploiting this vulnerability, a attacker was able to move an executable file into the Local Machine Zone and execute it.

In IE7, significant work was done behind the scenes to minimize the use of both MIME and MK to penetrate systems. The MK protocol is now turned off by default and can be activated only through the use of group policy or the installation of add-in software to support it. Multipurpose Internet Mail Extension continues to be a security headache, but additional Zone restrictions and Internet Protected Mode reduce the exposed surface area of a computer. This brings us back to using your street smarts while Web browsing. Know what type of Internet "neighborhood" you're in and know what you're clicking. For example, if a Web site is enticing you with a great offer, realize that the site might actually be enticing you to become the next victim of identity theft.

To further combat MIME vulnerabilities, I recommend that all home users disable ActiveX scripting in the Internet Zone. This change won't affect using ActiveX and other functionality on nearly all mainstream Web sites. Another key configuration change for the Internet Zone is to enable the Open Files Based on Content, Not File Extension option. This makes use of IE7's ability to read the beginning of a file and determine the best program to use. If you allow files to be open based on file type, you're trusting the file author to truthfully tell you what type of file this is. You may just come across a wolf in sheep's clothing in the form of an executable script posing as a JPEG image file.

1. **Choose Start⇨All Programs⇨Open Internet Explorer.**

2. **Choose Tools⇨Internet Options.**

3. **When the Internet Options dialog box appears, click the Security tab.**

4. **Click the Custom Level button.**

5. **Under the Scripting section, change Active Scripting to Disable (as shown in Figure 13-8).**

6. **Click OK.**

Locking down network protocols to prevent exposures

Network protocols were a key component in some Web-based applications. Their use now has declined to almost nonexistence with the onset of eXtensible Markup Language (XML), Active Server Pages (ASP), and similar Web technologies. IE7 has a configuration setting to catch and disable all network protocols in one fell swoop. By default, this option is set to Prompt User, but I suspect that the average user will never see this prompt. The only legitimate use for network protocols comes in the form of older client server applications. Examples of these include the IPX and SPX protocols. If you don't use older Web applications, try changing this setting to Disable. In the past, this has been an attack vector for malicious code, so it's fundamental for today's user to obey the tenet, *Disabled until Needed.* Figure 13-9 illustrates the options to lock down network protocols.

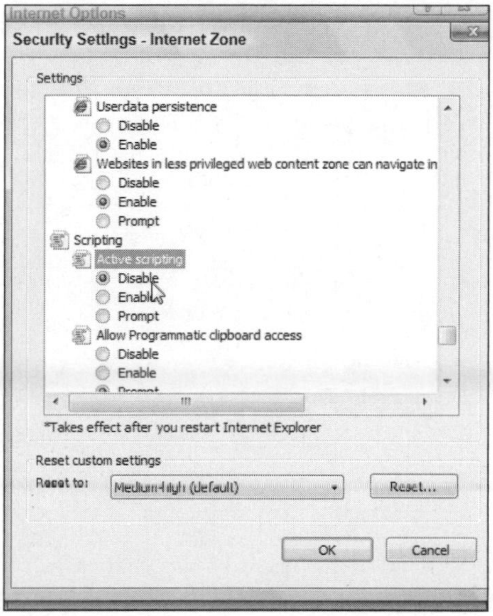

Figure 13-8:
Change
Active
Scripting to
Disable.

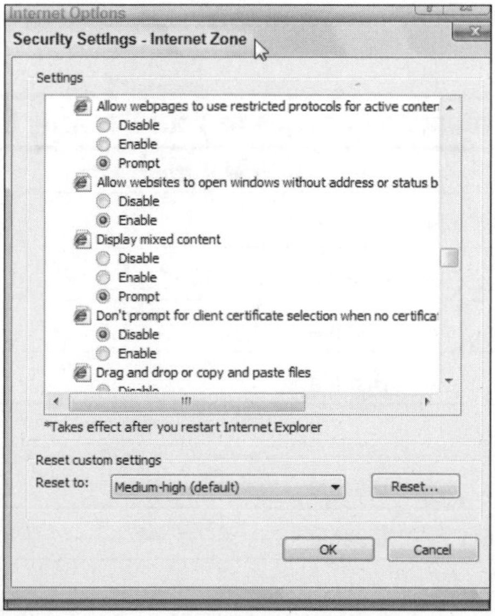

Figure 13-9:
Network
Protocol
Lockdown
Options.

In addition to network protocols, you can further minimize your exposure and provide greater security by disabling more seldom-used features in IE7. Navigate to the Internet Options dialog box and select the Internet Zone. Starting at the top, modify your settings to reflect those in Table 13-2. Figure 13-10 illustrates these additional options.

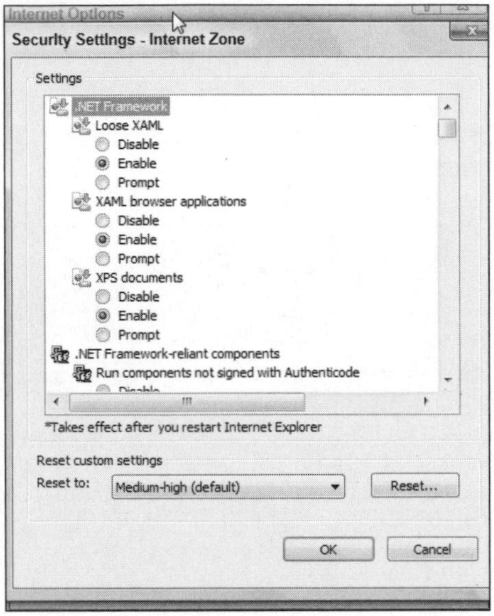

Figure 13-10: Lock down additional protocols.

Table 13-2 shows you the recommended setting for each option.

Table 13-2	Recommended Changes to Your Security Settings
Configuration Item	*Recommended Setting*
.NET Framework	
Loose XAML*	Disable
XAML Browser Applications	Disable
XPS Documents	Disable
Downloads	
Font Download	Disable
Enable .NET Framework Setup	Disable
Miscellaneous	
Allow META REFRESH	Disable

Configuration Item	Recommended Setting
Allow Web pages to Use Restricted Protocols for Active Content	Disable
Display Mixed Content	Disable
Drag and Drop or Copy and Paste File	Disable
Installation of Desktop Items	Disable
Launching Applications and Unsafe Files	Disable
Launching Programs and Files in an IFRAME*	Disable
Software Channel Permissions	Maximum Safety
Submit Non-Encrypted Form Data	Disable
User-data Persistence	Disable

The preceding steps are the equivalent to my nightly house check. Every night, I tour my home, verifying that not only are my doors locked and the garage doors are down, but also that the kids haven't opened the seldom-used windows in the guest room or other areas of the house. Think of the settings in Table 13-2 as seldom-used windows in your house. By keeping these closed, you drastically minimize the chance of being burglarized. The same holds true in the computer world.

Controlling object caching

Object caching comprises storing Internet objects, which are ActiveX controls, for later use. Why download an ActiveX control on every visit to a Web site when you can download it the first time and save it for faster future use? Examples of these controls are

- ✔ Windows Genuine Advantage Validation Tool
- ✔ Microsoft Office Update Engine
- ✔ Shockwave Flash Object

To view the objects installed on your computer, perform the following steps

1. **Choose Start⇨All Programs ⇨Open Internet Explorer.**

2. **From the menu, choose Tools⇨Internet Options.**

3. **When the Internet Options Window appears, click the Settings button in the Browsing History section.**

4. **Click the View Objects button.**

   Figure 13-11 illustrates the objects installed on my test system after performing these steps.

This interface doesn't allow you to delete an object. You have to uninstall via Control Panel.

From time to time, you might want to delete your browsing history to recover disk space. Here's how:

1. **Open Internet Explorer and choose Tools⇨Internet Options.**

2. **When the Internet Options window appears, under the Browsing History section, click the Delete button.**

   Figure 13-12 shows the options available to delete your browsing history.

Program File	Status	Total Size	Creation Date	Last Accessed	Version
QuickTime Object	Installed	4 KB	2/23/2007 9:36 PM	2/23/2007	7,1,5,58
Shockwave ActiveX Control	Installed	4 KB	4/9/2007 10:53 PM	4/9/2007	10,1,4,20
Shockwave Flash Object	Installed	8 KB	11/9/2006 3:46 PM	11/9/2006	9,0,28,0

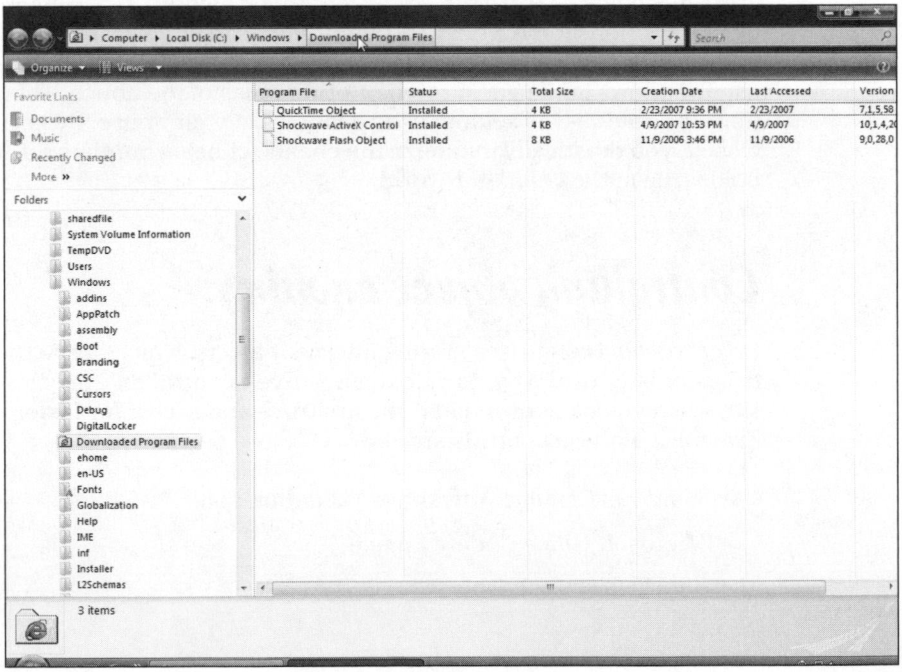

Figure 13-11:
View
installed
objects
here.

Figure 13-12:
Delete
browser
history here.

Earlier in this section, I list three typical ActiveX controls that are installed: Microsoft Genuine Advantage Validation Tool, Microsoft Office Update Engine, and Shockwave Flash Object. By name alone, you can guess that these are likely legitimate tools, so leave them installed. If you have doubts, right-click the control and view its properties. Figure 13-13 illustrates the properties of active control objects.

Figure 13-13:
Viewing
object
properties.

The properties of an ActiveX control tell you a few important facts:

- ✔ The last-accessed date
- ✔ Version number
- ✔ The company who created the control

The mantra to remember for object caching is *Delete if Not Needed.* If you don't recognize a control by name, open its properties and view the last-accessed date, version, and creating company. If you don't recognize the company, remove the control. Removing is synonymous with uninstalling. If you recognize the company but have a last-accessed date of over two months, remove the control. If the hairs on the back of your neck stand up when seeing any control, remove it. The beauty of this approach is that ActiveX controls are transient in nature. If you remove a critical ActiveX control that supports your online banking, for example, that control will be downloaded, approved, and installed again upon your next visit to that site. No harm, no foul.

The last-accessed date is by far the most important because all the fields *except the last-accessed date can be forged.* The last-accessed date is controlled and updated by IE7.

A typical two-hour Web browsing session with a modest amount of time spent at each site can accumulate between 5 and 25 new ActiveX controls.

Controlling automatic downloads and scripts

Thoughout this chapter, I discuss how individual features work and benefit you. This section begins to pull all aspects of Web browsing security together in battlefield conditions. At the heart of your Web browsing safety is the ability to exercise control over your experience and retain control of what is downloaded to your computers.

If your goal is to exercise and retain control of your experience, how do you combat automated threats? One key piece of new technology is Internet Protected Mode, which prevents most scripted actions or automatic processes from downloading data or affecting the system because of the integrity levels. Next, consider the new Zone restrictions and safeguards to better protect higher-privilege Zones. Finally, you have ActiveX Opt-In to only allow specific controls to function. To a lesser degree, you can benefit from the Phishing Filter to identify both known and potential phishing sites. These sites carry a high likelihood of attempting automated attacks on arrival to the site. The best news is that all these new technologies are available in IE7.

Bringing It All Together

Consider every Web browsing session to be a battle. Like in every battle, the front line wavers back and forth as opposing sides gain territory against their opponents. The Internet is no different, and the battle is primarily waged within your Web browser. With the new arsenal provided in IE7, though, you are surely better equipped for a safer Web browsing experience.

If you're not a Vista user, you still can install and use IE7. The drawback is that you can't benefit from Internet Protected Mode that Vista offers. Still, there are plenty of great reasons to move from IE6 to IE7 on a non-Vista platform. The following reason is by far the best as it summarizes the state of your Web browsing union: Install IE7 to protect yourself from IE6. As pervasive as security threats are these days, you must make use of the very latest software. To not use IE7 in place of IE6 is akin to showing up to a gunfight with a stick.

Here is a hot list that summarizes the security improvements in IE7:

- **Internet Protected Mode:** This provides integrity levels throughout the system to prevent malicious code from taking up residence in the system.

- **ActiveX Opt-In:** ActiveX controls that haven't been checked out and verified as safe no longer run automatically by default; instead, they're automatically disabled by ActiveX Opt-In.

- **Cross-domain security:** Cross-domain scripting attacks are prevented by forcing scripts to run in their original security domain even if they attempt to redirect to a different security domain.

- **Protection against phishing:** IE7 introduces the Phishing Filter, which helps protect users from being misled into entering personal information that can be used for identity theft. The Phishing Filter automatically checks the Web sites you're visiting against a dynamically updated list of known phishing sites to identify potential phishing sites.

- **Zone protection:** ActiveX controls are locked into a specific site or into a specific security Zone.

- **Stronger security Zone restrictions:** Security Zones in IE7 are locked down with higher default security settings. Removing the Local Intranet Zone on nondomain computers reduces the potential of malicious code to find a hiding spot.

- **Address bars:** All browser windows in IE7 contain Address bars, so it's harder for a malicious site to conceal its identity by hiding the URL of the site.

- **IE7 SSL improvements:** IE7 will disable SSLv2 and enable TLSv1. This will not allow unsecure HTTP content in secure HTTPS pages. Another SSL improvement in IE7 is the ability to block navigation to sites that have SSL certificate errors.

Chapter 14

Avoiding Invasion (By Malware, Spyware, Viruses, and the Other Usual Suspects)

- -

In This Chapter

▶ Running new Windows Defender features

▶ Protecting your system

▶ Avoiding risky behavior

- -

*S*pyware is insidious, unsanctioned software that intrudes upon not only the performance of your systems but also upon your time, your patience — and ultimately, your pocketbook. As your productivity comes to a screeching halt, or at best a slow drip, you are then forced to turn your attention to your arsenal of security tools to partake in the often-painful mission of ridding your system of this invasive pest. Spyware is arguably the most significant and costly computer-support issue today — by many reports, even occurring at more than twice the amount of computer virus infections. Add to this the issues encountered from other unapproved software, and you can see that invasion by malware, spyware, viruses, and their ilk is a matter of epidemic proportion.

In this chapter, you can read how spyware, viruses, and other unapproved software can affect your systems. You then see how to use Vista Windows Defender to protect and respond to spyware and when you might need to turn to other tools to help. I also discuss what you can do to protect your system from other approved programs that also affect your systems and could place your personal or sensitive information security at risk.

The 411 on Unsanctioned Software

Unsanctioned software is not approved by the user or those who set policies for when and how a system can be used in the home, small office, or a large corporate network. Unsanctioned software comes in many flavors. As you begin to understand how to defend against these threats, you need to understand the subtle differences between the different types.

- **Virus:** For the purpose of this discussion, a *virus* is a malicious computer code that replicates itself. A virus can be delivered as part of file-sharing programs, e-mail attachments, and more. They are often sent by unsuspecting friends who have you in their e-mail address book. There are several types of viruses, such as those that attach themselves to programs, boot-sector viruses, macro-viruses, and more.

- **Malware:** *Malware* is essentially any electronic program that is harmful to a computer system. Malware can include viruses, worms, Trojan horses, and also spyware.

- **Greynet applications:** These applications perhaps have a legitimate use but aren't sanctioned by your business or small office for use on the corporate network. Users install these applications, usually contrary to corporate policy (or your rules at home), and security issues and risks are introduced into the environment.

  These applications might use proprietary protocols, encapsulate packets inside other protocols, or use other techniques that make them difficult to detect and track. Examples of these applications might be instant-messaging programs, peer-to-peer file sharing programs, and search toolbar plug-ins (and more) that contain spyware.

- **Spyware:** *Spyware* is a program that gathers information about a system or user without consent. The information that is gathered is often shared with Internet marketers on the user's surfing and other computing habits.

  Typically, these programs are installed by the end user under false pretenses: either by a misleading popup or by being packaged in another program that the user installs, or even entirely without the user's consent. It's not the data-collection traits of the software that defines it as spyware, but rather the deceptiveness of its installation and the fact that the user is unaware of the information being gathered and who this information is being shared with.

- **Adware:** This type of software typically delivers advertisements to the end user. If this is done by the user downloading an application and being aware of what it contains, this isn't usually a problem. However, adware crosses the line and becomes spyware when deceptive installation tactics and covert user behavior tracking (such as Internet surfing habits) are used. This information is often shared with third parties.

- **Trojan:** A *Trojan,* or *Trojan horse,* program is an application with a hidden purpose. The program contains manipulative or malicious code, yet hidden or disguised to the user as something entirely different.

Reducing Spyware, Malware, and More with Windows Defender

As the threat of spyware and other malicious software grew, so did the expectation that Microsoft needed to address it. Speculation grew that Microsoft was going to offer a tool based on a product offered by a company that Microsoft announced in 2004 that it was going to acquire: namely, GIANT Company Software Inc., which makes GIANT Antispyware.

In 2005, Microsoft confirmed what everyone had hoped — that it would make available a tool to assist in fighting malware for those with fully licensed versions of Windows 2000, XP, and Server 2003. This tool, Microsoft AntiSpyware, made its debut in a beta 1 version in January of 2005 and largely resembled the GIANT anti-spyware product. It had no new features and no real improvements: just a repackaged version of the product that Microsoft acquired. Even still, it was a step in the right direction, and the user community was excited.

In February of 2006, the beta 2 version of the product was released. This version, however, did not resemble the GIANT product. The new sheriff in town was named Windows Defender. With the new name, a greatly improved interface, and some redesign under the hood, Windows Defender offered some promise in fighting a problem that plagued users for quite some time.

When Microsoft was developing Vista, it continued to improve Windows Defender. Amidst all the hype of Vista, so, too, was a considerable amount of hype around the improvements that the Vista version of Windows Defender had. In fact, it was even said that with the comprehensive security features of Vista (including Windows Defender), there would be no need for any third-party antivirus tools. Since that bold and much-disputed statement, Microsoft has backed off. Still, Windows Defender is a moderately robust, easy-to-use tool that comes bundled with the Vista operating system (OS).

What's New

Here is a list of what's new with Windows Defender:

- **Spyware detection and removal:** Windows Defender is a hunter of sorts. It hunts for that vicious spyware software. It can detect spyware and those unsanctioned programs as defined in the up-to-date detection files from Microsoft.

- **Internet browsing integration:** Windows Defender integrates with Internet Explorer (IE), providing a great level of safety while browsing the Internet. When IE downloads files, Windows Defender lurks in the background, checking any malicious code at the door (so to speak).

✔ **Software Explorer:** This new feature offered in Windows Defender provides a bird's-eye view of startup programs and other software on your Vista system.

✔ **Up-to-date information on the latest threats:** You have at your disposal the Microsoft SpyNet community, where you can get the latest information on even unclassified threats and find out what others are doing about them.

Defending Your System

Defending your system against spyware or other malicious software isn't something that you do only from time to time. Although you won't win every battle, you can win the war with a strong commitment, persistence, and an arsenal of security tools. Windows Defender should be part of your arsenal.

With your diligence and the right tools, you can minimize the effect that malicious software can have on you.

Getting to know the Windows Defender interface

Windows Defender is a moderately capable and easy-to-use tool. You will likely find the Defender interface intuitive. See Figure 14-1. With the help of this chapter, you can easily figure out how to perform almost any task of your choosing.

Updating Windows Defender definition files

Windows Defender *definition files* are the baseline for which the application determines whether your system is infected by spyware or other malicious code. These definition files are updated as new threats emerge.

Keep Windows Defender up to date so that it can appropriately scan your system for even the newest spyware threats.

To update your definition files, perform the following steps:

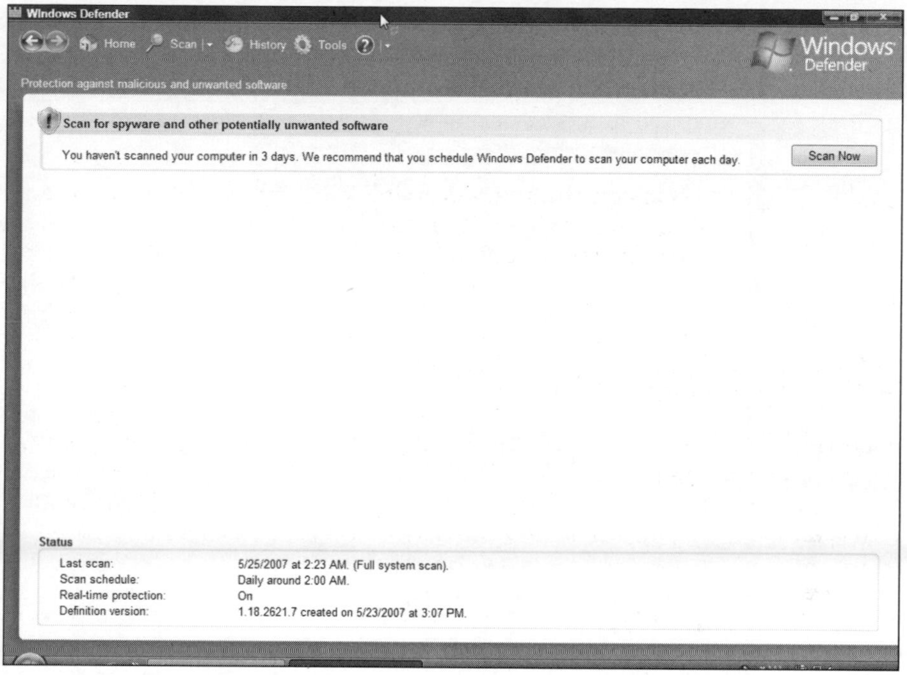

Figure 14-1:
The
Windows
Defender
interface.

1. **Start Windows Defender by choosing Start⇨Control Panel.**

   In the default view, choose Security⇨Windows Defender. In Classic view, choose Windows Defender.

2. **Open the ? icon drop-down menu at the top of the Windows Defender window.**

3. **Choose Check for Updates (as shown in Figure 14-2).**

Real-time protection

Real-time protection occurs when Windows Defender (and perhaps other tools) run in the background and defend your system from any threats when they occur. Real-time protection is most often referred to in antivirus programs; however, Windows Defender and other anti-spyware programs offer the same level of functionality. If these tools detect spyware when it's infiltrating your system, action can be taken to stop it.

This is most evident in the Windows Defender integration with IE. When you surf the Internet and download files, Windows Defender is scanning in the background. It pokes and prods these files and compares them against known definitions of spyware. If spyware is detected, it takes action, keeping the invasive pest at arm's length — and your system, data, and information safe.

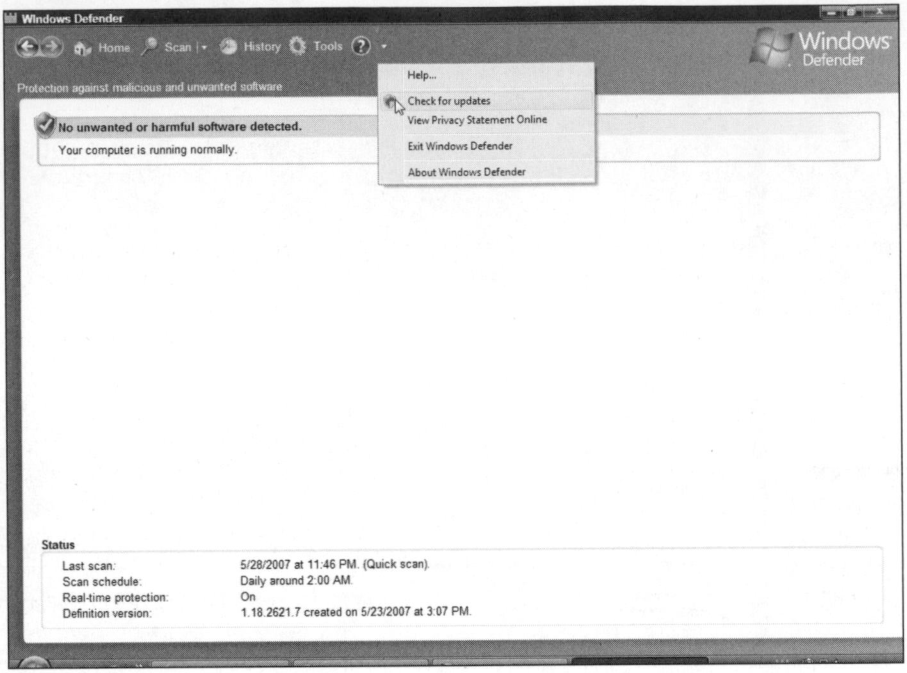

Figure 14-2:
Let
Windows
Defender
check for
updates.

There is no needed interaction from the user when real-time protection is doing its job. And the user only needs to take a simple configuration step to enable real-time protection. Even better news: In Windows Vista, this protection is automatically enabled by default. You can turn real-time protection on or off with the Use Real-Time Protection setting via Windows Defender configuration options.

To view or modify these settings, perform the following steps.

1. **Start Windows Defender by choosing Start⇨Control Panel.**

   In the default view, choose Security⇨Windows Defender. In Classic view, choose Windows Defender.

2. **Choose elect Tools from the menu at the top of the Windows Defender window.**

3. **Under the Settings section, select Options.**

4. **At the Options window, scroll down to the Real-Time Protection Options section (as shown in Figure 14-3).**

By default, the Use Real-Time Protection (Recommended) check box is enabled. Also, by default, all the real-time security agents are enabled.

I want to talk a little here about the security agents. What you will likely notice is that these areas are those that malicious code, such as spyware, most often gravitate toward:

✔ **Auto Start:** When this setting is enabled, Windows Defender monitors your list of programs that start automatically when you run your computer. This is essential because many malicious programs are configured to run when your system starts up.

By keeping a watchful eye on this common hangout in your system's Registry, Windows Defender can detect spyware programs as they configure themselves to start up automatically.

✔ **System Configuration (Settings):** Your system configuration contains a wealth of information about your system; this is where the configuration of your system can be set and modified. Your OS, hardware information, information on components, and certain types of software loaded on your system are contained here.

Much like you find system configuration information helpful, so might malicious code. In fact, spyware and other malicious code often try to either read or change security-related configuration settings. By watching this particular area on your system, Windows Defender can detect spyware prior to it making modifications that could change the overall security of your system.

✔ **Internet Explorer Add-ons:** Often, malicious software impersonates Web browser add-ons and runs without the user's knowledge. By integrating with IE, spyware can easily be detected when it tries to achieve this.

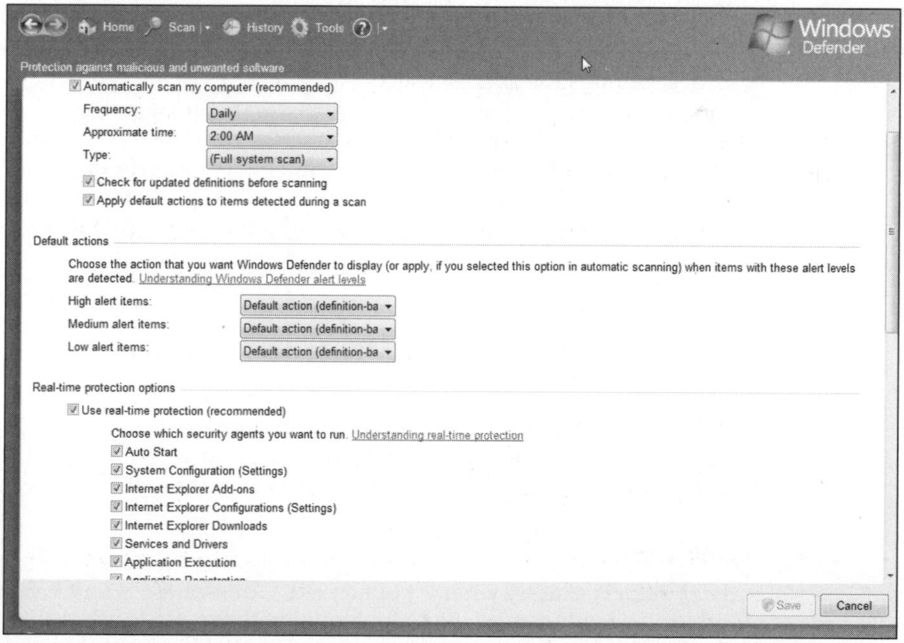

Figure 14-3:
Set real-
time
protection
options
here.

- ✔ **Internet Explorer Configurations (Settings):** You configure your IE settings a certain way, much of which is about protecting your system from malicious activity (as you can discover in Chapter 13). Knowing that, it then makes sense that spyware or other malicious code will try to get their pesky hands on these settings and change them to make your system more vulnerable. Windows Defender must monitor these settings so those changes can be detected and fixed early on.

- ✔ **Internet Explorer Downloads:** When you surf the Internet, certain programs — such as ActiveX controls — are downloaded by the browser. Enabling this setting is essential so that Windows Defender can be on the lookout for malicious code taking advantage of this functionality.

- ✔ **Services and Drivers:** Services and drivers provide an interesting attack vector for malicious code. Because services and drivers have unique access into the OS, they should be monitored for any exploitation by malicious code.

- ✔ **Application Execution:** By watching when applications start — and even more important, what they're doing when they're running — Windows Defender can get early warning when spyware or other malicious code attempts to exploit a legitimate application.

- ✔ **Application Registration:** By watching the tools and files that are used and accessed by programs to register to run, Windows Defender can be alerted to malicious code.

- ✔ **Windows Add-ons:** Add-on programs can contain snippets of code that collect information about you that would classify them as spyware. Therefore, it's imperative that real-time scanning monitors these types of programs for such activity.

These settings can be enabled or disabled at your discretion. Because these are areas that malicious programs are most likely to attempt to exploit, I suggest that you enable real-time monitoring and all these sub-settings. Doing so is essential to protecting your system and personal information.

Invoking on-demand scans

An *on-demand scan* is one that you initiate. Perhaps you run a scan as part of a daily or weekly routine, or when you suspect that your system might be infected with spyware or other malicious programs. Whatever the case, Windows Defender makes it easy for you to run a scan whenever you see fit.

Quick scan

A *quick scan* is exactly what it sounds like. You initiate a quick scan from the Windows Defender interface to look only in those places that these pests are known to hang out. It provides you the ability to run a scan quickly and get back to what you need to do.

To perform a quick scan, perform the following steps:

1. **Start Windows Defender by choosing Start⇨Control Panel.**

   In the default view, choose Security⇨Windows Defender. In Classic view, choose Windows Defender.

2. **Choose Scan from the menu at the top of the Windows Defender application window.**

3. **Choose Quick Scan, as shown in Figure 14-4.**

Full scan

A *full scan* scans all the disks on your system as well as any applications that are running when the scan is initiated.

To perform a full scan, perform the following steps:

1. **Start Windows Defender by choosing Start⇨Control Panel.**

   In the default view, choose Security⇨Windows Defender. In Classic view, choose Windows Defender.

2. **Choose Scan from the menu at the top of the Windows Defender application window.**

3. **Choose Full Scan (as shown in Figure 14-5).**

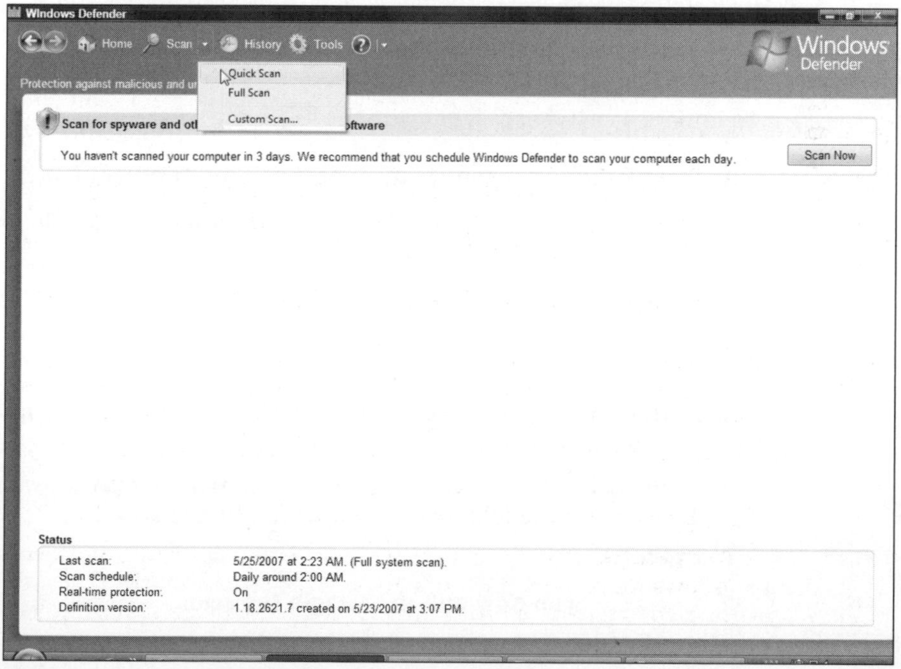

Figure 14-4: Initiate a quick scan here.

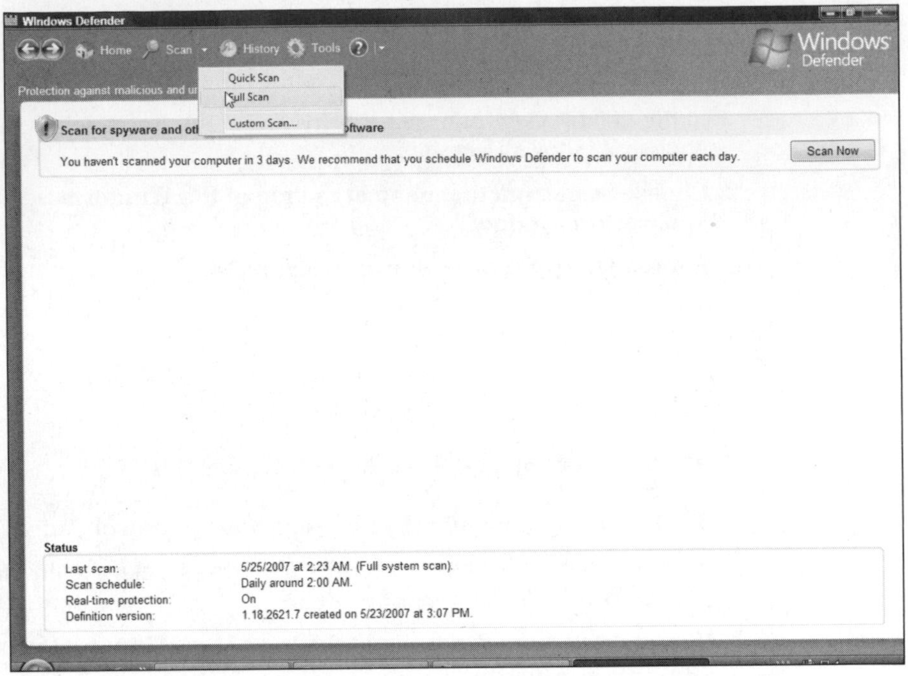

Figure 14-5:
Initiate a full
scan here.

Custom scan

A *custom scan* scans a particular area of your system that you suspect might be infected with spyware. This is a very handy feature because you can focus your attention on a particular trouble-spot of your choosing.

To initiate a custom scan, perform the following steps:

1. **Start Windows Defender by choosing Start⇨Control Panel.**

   In the default view, choose Security⇨Windows Defender. In Classic view, choose Windows Defender.

2. **Choose Scan from the menu at the top of the Windows Defender application window.**

3. **Choose Custom Scan.**

4. **In the Select Scan Options window, click the Select button, as shown in Figure 14-6.**

5. **In the Select Drives and Folders to Scan window (as shown in Figure 14-7), select the folders that you would like to scan.**

6. **Click OK.**

7. **Click the Scan Now button to begin the scan.**

No matter what scan you select, understand that when Windows Defender scans your system, it compares your system against the Windows Defender definitions that it currently has. If these definitions are out of date, spyware could reside on your system but not be detected by Windows Defender. To update your Windows Definition, see the section, "Updating Windows Defender definition files," earlier in this chapter.

Responding to threats

From automatic (scheduled scans) to how Defender reacts to a high-alert item, a variety of settings essentially tell Windows Defender how to respond to threats.

Automatically scan my computer (scheduled scan)

By default, automatic (or scheduled) scanning is enabled in Windows Defender. This is a great thing because if it weren't set by default, many users would forget to enable it themselves. However, the fact that it is set at a 2 default time might not be so great. If your system is turned off at 2:00 a.m., your system might never gets its much-needed automatic scan.

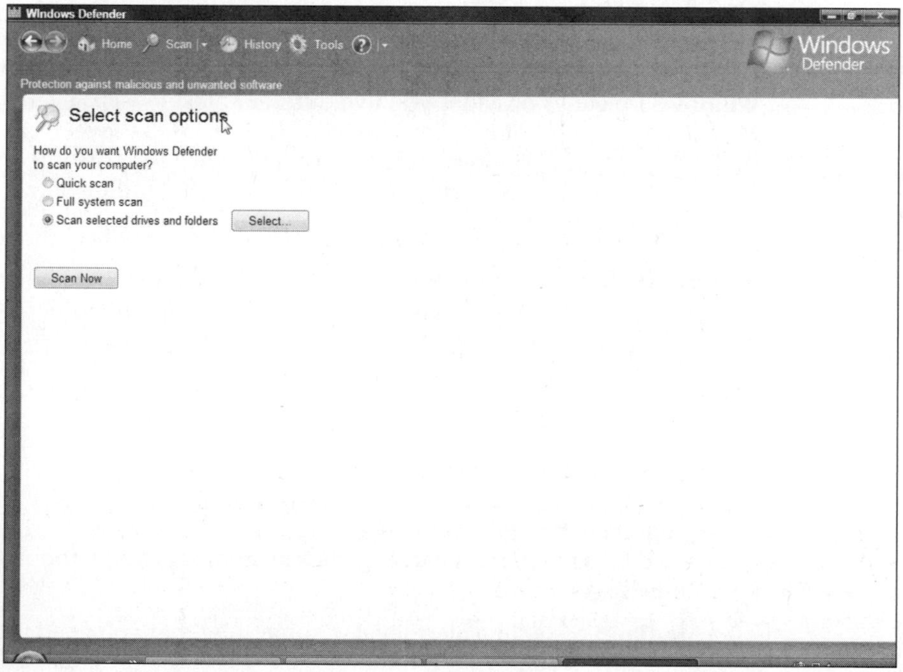

Figure 14-6:
Windows
Defender
scan
options.

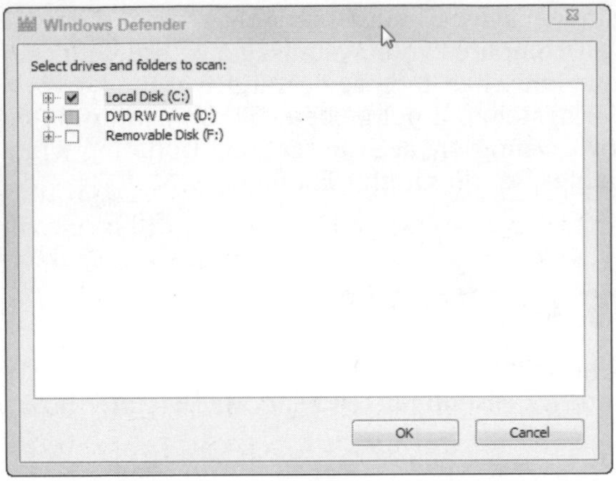

Select drives and folders to scan:

☐☑ Local Disk (C:)
☐☐ DVD RW Drive (D:)
☐☐ Removable Disk (F:)

OK   Cancel

Figure 14-7:
Select
drives and
folders to
scan.

Keep automatic scan enabled. This is an important feature that allows you to scan your system at a predetermined interval. I suggest that you consider modifying the default 2 a.m. time to when you might not be using your system heavily but when the system is turned on. For the scan type, I think that a full scan is most appropriate and that you select these check boxes from the Options window (refer to Figure 14-3): Check for Updated Definitions Before Scanning; and Apply Default Actions to Items Detected During a Scan.

Knowing what alerts really mean

Windows Defender provides you five different alert levels: Severe, High, Medium, Low, and Not Yet Classified. For three of these levels, you can select default actions for Windows Defender to take when they are encountered. Before I get into that, however, start with an understanding of the alert levels and what they mean:

- ✔ **Severe:** A Severe alert level is serious. This means that you are at risk for widespread malicious programs that have the potential to significantly impact your security and privacy. If such an event is encountered, you want to remove the program immediately, regardless of what value you think it provides you.

- ✔ **High:** A High alert level is something that you should also consider as serious. These are programs that are reported to collect your personal information and could put your system and your privacy at risk. These programs often perform covert operations, such as collecting your personal information or changing your system settings without your knowledge.

- ✔ **Medium:** A Medium alert level is something that you need to look at but shouldn't assume that it requires removal of the program. This could be a program that might contain code monitoring or collect your information and change your system settings.

✔ **Low:** A Low alert level indicates that something might be amiss. This software might or might not be spyware, but it has some minor characteristics that alert Windows Defender to warn you. Usually, software at this level isn't something that you must remove, but you probably want to review it and understand how it behaves.

✔ **Not Yet Classified:** These programs are usually not a problem. However, every now and then, programs in this category will be classified in the Medium or higher categories when more information is determined about them.

Setting your threat levels

After you understand what the threat levels mean, you can configure Windows Defender to act in a way that makes sense for you when these alert levels are encountered.

Windows Defender allows you configure actions on High, Medium, and Low alert items. To configure how you want Windows Defender to react to these alert items, perform the following steps:

1. **Start Windows Defender by choosing Start⇔Control Panel.**

   In the default view, choose Security⇔Windows Defender. In Classic view, choose Windows Defender.

2. **Choose Tools from the menu at the top of the Windows Defender application window.**

3. **In the Tools and Settings window, under the Settings section, select Options.**

4. **Under the Default Actions section (as shown in Figure 14-8), you can select an option under each alert level.**

Your options are as follows:

✔ **Default Action (Definition-Based):** This option is set by default in Vista and means that the definition files will determine how a particular item needs to be treated. The definition files are put together by Microsoft and have the data that Defender needs to determine exactly how a particular threat should be handled.

✔ **Ignore:** This setting configures Defender to ignore a particular event that is labeled at a certain alert level, regardless of the recommendations put forth in the definition file.

✔ **Remove:** This setting configures Defender to remove the software that has been determined to be at a particular alert level, ignoring any recommendations put forth in the definition file.

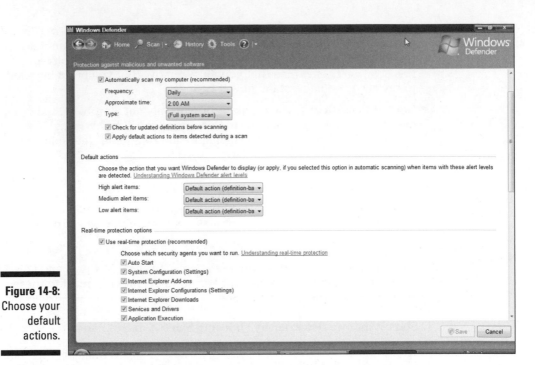

Figure 14-8:
Choose your
default
actions.

The default settings, Default Action (Definition-Based), are likely to be adequate because the definition files contain the needed information so that Defender can react appropriately. However, for those of you who don't want to rely on the definition files, I suggest changing the High alert items to Remove. The remaining items are fine at the default level. In fact, I recommend against changing them.

Putting Defender's tools to work

Windows Defender comes with a variety of tools that can help you with the daunting task of keeping your system clean from spyware and other malicious code. You can access these tools by performing the following steps:

1. **Start Windows Defender by choosing Start⇨Control Panel.**

   In the default view, choose Security⇨Windows Defender. In Classic view, choose Windows Defender.

2. **Choose Tools from the menu at the top of the Windows Defender application window.**

   In the Tools and Settings window (as shown in Figure 14-9), under the Tools section, is a list of the tools offered by Windows Defender.

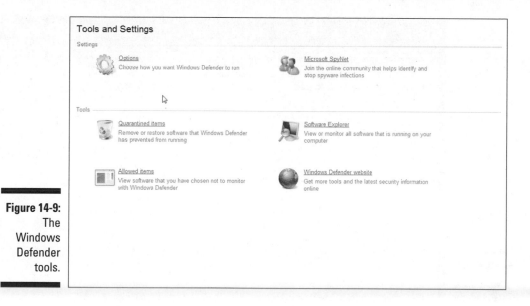

Figure 14-9:
The
Windows
Defender
tools.

Quarantined items

In much the same way a hospital quarantines very sick and contagious patients, Windows Defender quarantines those items that it deems to be spyware. These items are moved to a specific area of your system and are not allowed to run.

After these items are sequestered, your job is to decide what to do with them. You can remove the item. Or, if you find that you need or want to use the program, you can restore the item. To manage your quarantined items, perform the following steps:

1. **Start Windows Defender choose Start⇨Control Panel.**

   In the default view, choose Security⇨Windows Defender. In Classic view, choose Windows Defender.

2. **Choose Tools from the menu at the top of the Windows Defender application window.**

   In the Tools and Settings windows, under the Tools section, is a list of the tools offered by Windows Defender. (Refer to Figure 14-9.)

3. **Choose Quarantined Items.**

To remove or restore an item, perform the following steps:

1. **From the Quarantined Items window (as shown in Figure 14-10), select an item that you want to address.**

   Quarantined items are listed under the Select an Action to Apply section.

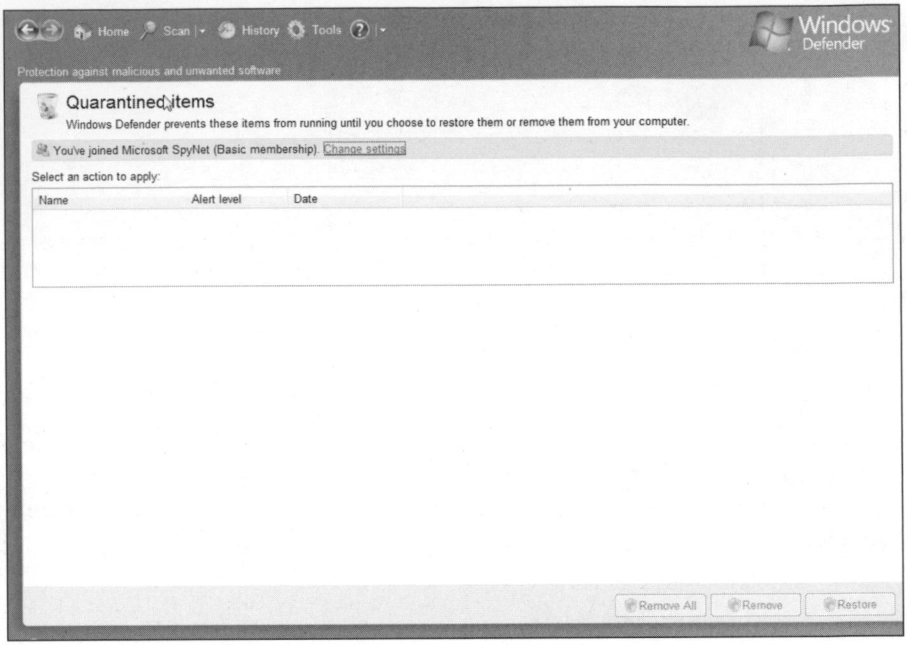

Figure 14-10:
View
quarantined
items here.

2. **Highlight the item and select to restore the item or remove the item by clicking the appropriate button (bottom right of window).**

Restoring an item puts the item back into an active state on your system. Windows Defender ignores that item in the future and will not quarantine it. Therefore, you must understand what you are restoring prior to actually doing so. Next to any item listed as quarantined is also an Alert Level column. Microsoft — nor anyone else — does not recommended restoring an item that has a Severe or High alert level: Doing so will place your system, privacy, and perhaps personal information at risk.

Using Allowed Items

Allowed Items is a tool that you can use when you want Windows Defender to ignore certain software. This probably isn't something that you want to get into a habit of doing, but here's the deal. Sometimes a particular piece of software is considered to contain snippets of code labeled as spyware, but you need to use it anyway. You can configure Windows Defender to ignore a particular item by performing the following steps:

1. **Start Windows Defender by choosing Start⇨Control Panel.**

   In the default view, choose Security⇨Windows Defender. In Classic view, choose Windows Defender.

2. **Choose Tools from the menu at the top of the Windows Defender application window.**

3. **Under the Tools setting, select Allowed Items (refer to Figure 14-9).**

4. **From the Allowed Items window (as shown in Figure 14-11), highlight the item that you want to allow.**

5. **Click the Remove From List button.**

Software Explorer

The Software Explorer tool gives you almost a dashboard view of the software loaded on your system — at least from a spyware perspective. With this tool, you can view detailed information about your software that could have an effect to your security and privacy well-being. Here's how to start Software Explorer:

1. **Start Windows Defender by choosing Start⇨Control Panel.**

   In the default view, choose Security⇨Windows Defender. In Classic view, choose Windows Defender.

2. **Choose Tools from the menu at the top of the Windows Defender application window.**

3. **Under the Tools setting, select Software Explorer.**

   The Software Explorer tool starts. See Figure 14-12.

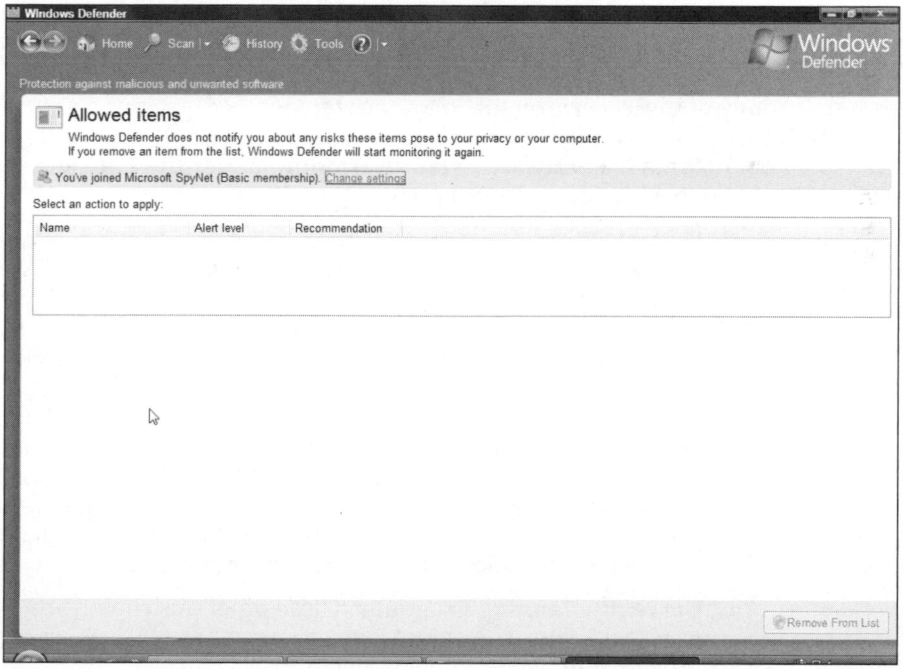

Figure 14-11: Set Allowed Items here.

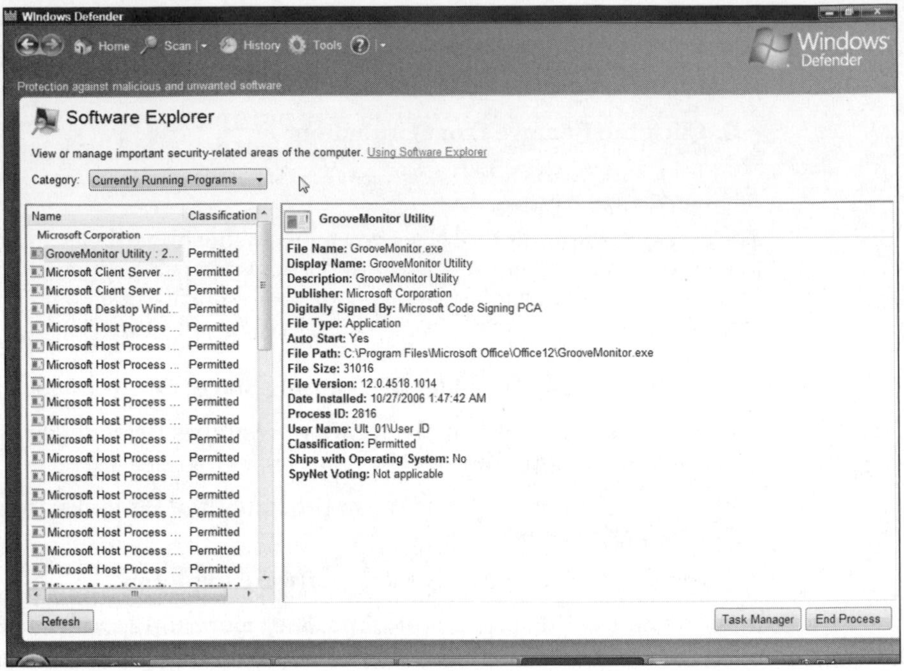

Figure 14-12:
The
Software
Explorer
interface.

From Software Explorer, you can monitor startup programs, running programs, network-connected programs, and Winsock service providers. To view any of these, perform the following steps:

1. **From the Software Explorer window, under the Category section, open the drop-down menu.**

2. **From the drop-down menu, choose what category you want to view, such as Startup programs, Currently Running Programs, Network-Connected Programs, and Winsock Service Providers.**

Select a category to perform particular functions related to it. Here are your choices:

✔ **Startup Programs:** These programs are designated to automatically start when your system starts. Spyware and other malicious software often modify your system's Registry so that they start automatically. This view provides you a list of programs that start automatically. You can remove, disable, or enable each program.

✔ **Currently Running Programs:** These programs run on your system with or without your knowledge. You can open Task Manager or end the process for each program selected.

- ✔ **Network-Connected Programs:** These programs connect to the Internet or to your home or small office network. You can end the process or block incoming connections for each program selected.

- ✔ **Winsock Service Providers:** These programs perform networking and communication-related functions for Windows and have unique access to your OS. You can't adjust any item from here.

Windows Defender Web site

In the Tools section is a link for the Windows Defender Web site (refer to Figure 14-9). At this site, you can find a plethora of information regarding Defender. I suggest taking the time to become familiar with the site and using the information there.

Lending a helping hand in classifying spyware

How well Microsoft can classify spyware threats largely depends on getting information from the user community. Because this participation is so critical, Windows Defender provides a way for you to become a member of that community — and thus help Microsoft help you (and others).

The Microsoft Spynet online community not only helps Microsoft help you better, but also helps you to understand how to better choose how you respond to threats, especially those that aren't yet classified. You can choose from two memberships: basic or advanced.

To configure your client to choose a Microsoft SpyNet membership, follow these steps:

1. **Start Windows Defender by choosing Start➪Control Panel.**

   In default view, choose Security➪Windows Defender. In Classic view, choose Windows Defender.

2. **Choose Tools from the menu at the top of the Windows Defender application window.**

3. **Under the Setting section, click the Microsoft Spynet link.**

   At the Microsoft SpyNet window, you are provided information on the SpyNet Community.

4. **Select the membership of your choosing (as shown in Figure 14-13) and then click Save.**

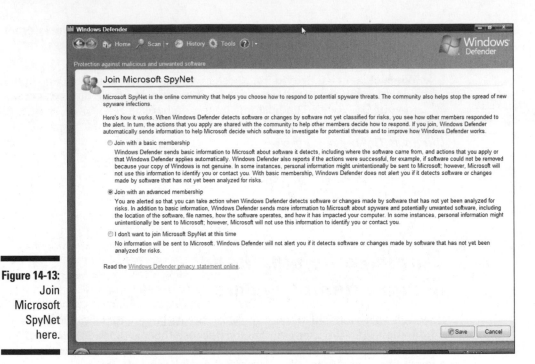

Figure 14-13:
Join
Microsoft
SpyNet
here.

Other ways to protect against spyware, viruses, and other malicious software

Although Windows Defender has been greatly improved, offering ways to protect your system from spyware and other malicious code, you should also have other tools at hand in your security arsenal to deal with this very real threat.

Implementing user best practices

Very often, user behavior contributes to a system becoming infected with spyware or other malicious code. If you're really ever going to adequately protect yourself from threat, you cannot ignore that fact — and must certainly address user behavior. The following are some things that you can do to help reduce the risks associated with spyware and other malicious code:

✔ **Be careful where you surf.** I cannot begin to tell you how many times I have seen a machine infected with spyware or other malicious code as the result of where a user travels in an Internet journey. I equate it to going to a bad part of town, late at night, by yourself, carrying a wad of cash. I think that you will agree that when you do that, bad things are likely to happen. In much the same way, traveling to those darker places on the Internet will place you at greater risk of being infected with spyware or other malicious code. Very often, those shady sites are running code aimed at harvesting your personal information and penetrating the security of your system. If you must go, go at your own risk!

✔ **Don't sign up for stuff.** Seems simple, right? Well, not really. My wife is a reformed contest chaser. She would traverse the Internet looking for that next thing that might be free. A phone, a free trip to Florida — if there was a chance she might be able to win something, she was there, providing her name, e-mail address, and who knows what else. She never won anything but gave away a ton of information — and now receives more junk e-mail than probably anyone on this planet. I couldn't convince her that this was a bad idea, until one day when she was scammed. She stopped signing up for things. Still, every now and again, I see her staring at a popup flashing on her screen, yelling out to her to join a contest. She looks at it, looks over at me, and then moves on. The problem is that a lot of users out there are just like her. Providing information — like when entering giveaways and contests — creates a great deal of risk. You provide information to those that shouldn't have it and end up being on every phisher's e-mail list. I'm not here to spoil the party, but giving away too much personal information is just a bad idea. I recommend that you find a less dangerous activity to pursue as a pastime because at some point, you will become a victim of identity theft or other crime of fraud.

✔ **Use caution when downloading.** I'm sure many of you can relate to this as well, especially if you have teenage children. Remember those free file-sharing sites? Lots of well-meaning folk used these sites to find free (cough, pirated) music, but many others used them to spread viruses and other malicious software like a wildfire. These sites essentially amounted to nothing more than a virus depot. Anyone I knew who used file-sharing sites needed to clean their system (at one point or another) of the many viruses that found their way into their system as a direct result.

Third-party software

As a user, you have many tools that are available to you to help you fight these threats. Some third-party tools might cost a few bucks but are well worth the investment. (As I talk about at length earlier in this chapter, Windows Defender can be downloaded for free from Microsoft for non-Vista systems.) Plenty of tools are at your disposal that cost little or no money and that can help you adequately protect your system. Chapter 18 provides you with the information that you need to select some of these third-party tools.

With the considerable hype of the security of Vista, speculation abounded whether — as a Microsoft executive claimed — Windows Defender and other capabilities of Vista would eliminate the need for antivirus software. Since then, Microsoft has backed off of that statement and now recommends — as do I — installing antivirus software in addition to using Windows Defender.

Part V
Establishing Advanced Security Practices

The 5th Wave   By Rich Tennant

"Yeah, these voice recognition systems can be tricky. Let me see if I can open your word processing program?"

In this part . . .

Vista provides a great deal of security features and functionality for all types of users and their data. I wager that you'll use some tools enthusiastically, but I'll caution you about some tool to avoid at every turn. For those of you who need more protection (or perhaps are a little paranoid, like me), have data on the move, or have an interest in more advanced security practices, this is the part for you.

In this part, read about protecting your removable media, using Windows Service Hardening, and implementing local security policies to further lock down your system.

Chapter 15

Restricting the Use of Removable Media (And More)

*R*emovable media is a general term that applies to all types of data storage mechanisms that you can easily remove from your computer, including recordable CD/DVDs, USB drives, iPods, and external hard drives. Vista is designed to protect your data from getting in the wrong hands through all the measures described in this book (and even some that aren't). However, Vista doesn't control removable media the same way it does your hard drive or other installed devices. Therefore, your responsibility is to figure out how to protect both your machine and your data when you use any type of removable media.

In this chapter, I describe the risks associated with using removable media and offer ways how you can protect yourself against these risks.

Removable Media and Associated Security Risks

Removable media allows you to transfer data easily from one device to another. Attaching removable media to your machine allows you to copy the data stored on that media but inherently brings risks associated with allowing data to come onto your computer. Detaching removable media from your machine allows you to store that data as a backup or to give it to someone else for their use; however, you now have to worry about how to protect that data.

Risks of attaching media

One of my favorite penetration-testing stories relates to removable media and how it can be used to attack another machine. According to the story, a security firm was hired to test how secure one company's network was. Instead of trying a direct attack on the network, the security firm decided to "use" the workers of the company to do the job.

The security firm put a Trojan virus on some USB thumb drives, and then one night, left them randomly around the parking lot. Workers found these USB drives in the morning, plugged the USB devices into their machines, and looked at the data to see whether they could find out who lost the drive. This infected the machines with the Trojan, and the penetration-testing firm was able to steal data from the machines without ever attacking the network.

The lesson in this story is that *removable* media is also *attachable* media. It doesn't only represent a way to take data off your machine, but also a way to put data on your machine. Therefore, you need to protect yourself against malicious code added to your computer through this method for the same reasons you do when surfing the Internet.

Risks of detaching media

Throughout this book, I talk about all the different ways how Vista can protect your data. However, after you take the data off your computer, Vista no longer has control over it. Generally, this isn't an issue if you're burning music CDs to play in your car or adding new MP3s to your iPod: That's not data that most people care to protect. If you're backing up your tax returns or data from an accounting software package, that's a completely different case. In that case, ensuring that the data that you have moved to removable media stays as secure as it was on your computer is vitally important.

Someone with access to your machine can also use removable media to steal your data in a way that can get around most Vista controls. I'm sure that you've seen this in movies or on TV time after time: Someone is tricked into walking away from their computer, and the good/bad guy uses removable media to steal the data that he wants. (You know, clever bandits hanging from a ceiling or going through a whole series of biometric sensors that they have to trick.) In reality, though, all it takes is someone plugging in a USB drive or dropping in a recordable CD when you walk away from your computer.

Protecting Yourself Against the Risks of Removable Media

To protect yourself against the risks associated with removable media, you must rely on a combination of software controls and secure work practices. Which ones you use — and to what extent — really depends upon various factors, such as who else has physical access to your computer and how secure you need to make your data. As always, security must be a balance between ease of use and defense against risk: This is especially true in regard to removable media.

Protecting against viruses and malware

The main concern when transferring data to your computer is ensuring that you don't introduce code that will attack your machine. This isn't only a concern when copying a spreadsheet from a USB drive but also when installing a piece of software from a CD. Here is a list of different ways that you can protect against malicious code being installed on your machine:

- **Scan removable media before use.** Most antivirus programs have an option for scanning removable media for viruses when you install or access the media; however, some people decide to not use this option because it can slow down your machine. Anti-malware or anti-spyware programs generally don't have this setting as an option. Therefore, before opening anything, you need to understand what data you'll access on the media and whether you're protected against the risks.

  If you execute software from the removable media, always perform a scan for both viruses and other malware before you begin. If you're just copying nonexecutable files from the removable media to your hard drive, you don't have to worry about malware — but you still need to ensure that the file itself doesn't contain a virus.

- **Turn off AutoPlay and AutoRun.** These two Vista features allow the operating system (OS) to automatically detect the removable media and begin executing or playing the files located on it. Although these features are convenient, they also can stop you from taking any actions that you want before the files on the removable media are accessed.

- **Enable User Account Control.** User Account Control (UAC) will alert you that something is trying to install on your machine because an installation requires administrative access. For example, if UAC pops up to ask for authorization when you just want to look at a Word document on the USB memory stick that someone just gave you, chances are that something is wrong. For more information about UAC, see Chapter 4.

  ✔ **Reformat unknown media before use.** If you're given or purchase removable media that doesn't contain any data that you're interested in, the best way to ensure that you're protected is to reformat the device prior to using it. Follow the manufacturer's instructions for how to reformat your particular device.

  ✔ **Use the Vista Device Control to control the use of removable media:** I discuss Device Control in detail in the upcoming section, "Using Device Control to Protect Data on the Move." Use this to control to find what you're allowed to do to a type of removable device — for example, read from a CD/DVD or a USB drive — or whether Vista is allowed to recognize the device at all.

Protection against removal of data from your machine

If your machine contains sensitive information and is in an area where others can easily get to it, you need to protect yourself against this risk. The real risk here is not that someone will compromise your password and be able to log on to your machine (unless you're not using a password or have it written down near the computer), but rather that someone will use the computer after you logged on. The following is a list of different ways how you can protect against data being stolen from your machine in this way:

  ✔ Always use password-protected accounts on your machine. This is the most basic security precaution that you can take, and none of the other items in this list will be of any value if your accounts aren't password-protected.

  ✔ **Lock your computer whenever you walk away.** If you're already logged on, Vista recognizes whomever sits at the keyboard as you. If you lock your computer, however, anyone later using the machine must reauthenticate himself to the machine before getting to your data.

  ✔ **Use a password-protected screen saver.** Use a screen saver as a security device. If your machine has no activity for the amount of time set for the screen saver to kick in, it essentially locks the machine when the screen saver becomes active. To set Vista to use this feature, do the following:

   a. *Right-click the desktop and choose Personalize.*

   b. *Click Screen Saver.*

     This brings up the Screen Saver Settings dialog box, as shown as Figure 15-1.

   c. *Select the On Resume, Display Logon Screen check box.*

This option is available regardless of which screen saver you use. You're not limited to the screen saver shown in the figure.

d. *Click OK to accept this change.*

✔ **Use the Vista Device Control to control the use of removable media.** Use Device Control (discussed in the upcoming section, "Using Device Control to Protect Data on the Move") to control what you're allowed to do to a type of removable device (say, write to a CD/DVD or a USB drive) or whether Vista will recognize the device.

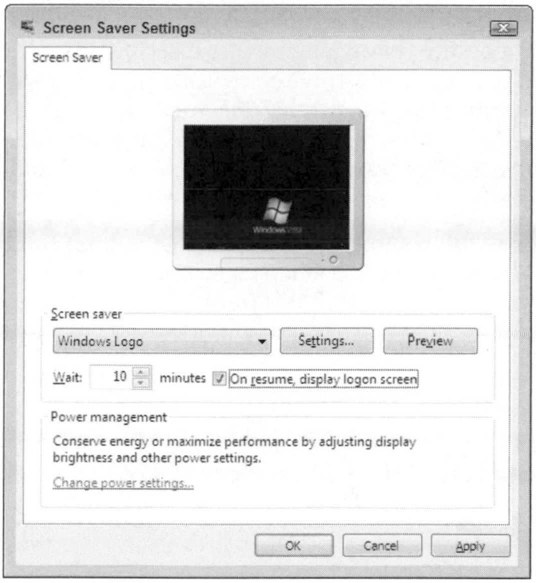

Figure 15-1: Set your screen saver settings here.

Protection of data on removable devices

After you place sensitive data onto a removable device, take the necessary steps to protect it for the life of the data. You can use either physical protection of the device itself or protections on the data within the device, but you also must think about destruction of the data after you no longer need it. The following is a list of different ways that you can protect your data after you place it on a removable device:

✔ **Physically secure the removable media.** If you copied sensitive data to some removable media, such as a recordable DVD, store that DVD securely. This could be something as simple as putting it in a locked file cabinet. Or, for a little more security, put it in a safe or in a safety deposit box.

✔ **Encrypt and access control the data on the device.** Although Vista has encryption options, BitLocker is mainly used in relation to hard drives.

Too, both BitLocker and EFS require an NT File System (NTFS). Therefore, you might need to use a third-party tool to encrypt and access-control the data. One option is to use a compression utility, such as WinZip, to compress, encrypt, and password-protect the data before copying it to the removable media.

Another option is to use a software encryption package to encrypt the removable media itself. That way, all data placed on it will always be encrypted. These tools have the options of setting up user accounts on the media or just using password protection, and can even be set so that computers other than yours cannot decrypt the data.

✔ **Electronically destroy no-longer-needed data:** After you no longer need the sensitive data on the removable media, deleting it is not enough to protect it. Deleting a file really only removes the pointers within the file system. A *data scrubber program,* however, goes to the place on the media where the file has been stored and actually overwrites the data with gibberish. *Note:* This technique is effective only on removable media that you can overwrite, such as a CD-RW or a USB drive.

✔ **Physically destroy the removable media when you no longer need it.** For write-once removable media, such as a CD-R, the only way to protect the data when you no longer need it is to destroy the disc itself.

I recommend using a document shredder rated for CD and DVD shredding.

Using Device Control to Protect Data on the Move

Device Control is a Vista feature that allows you to control removable media, such as USB storage drives and CD/DVD recorders. This feature allows you to make decisions that Vista enforces on all users. Unfortunately, Device Control isn't available on all versions of Vista. With Device Control, you can manage the installation settings for removable media or what users can do with them after it's installed. Device Control is implemented through Registry entries that you can manage through Group Policy.

Implementing Device Control installation settings

The best way to implement a device-control strategy is to use the Group Policy Editor within Vista. (For more information on this interface, see Chapter 16.) The settings for Device Control installation are included in the Device Installation Administrative Template in the Device Installation Restrictions section, as shown in Figure 15-2.

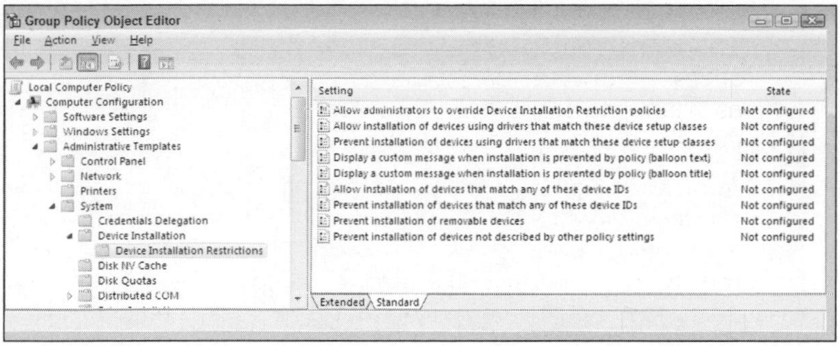

Figure 15-2:
Set Device
Control
installation
policies
here.

In the following sections, I cover the settings in more detail. In general, though, here's how to implement your Device Control installation strategy via the Group Policy Editor:

1. **Start the Group Policy Editor by choosing Start and then entering** gpedit.msc **into the Search field that appears.**

   If gpedit.msc isn't found or isn't available, you're probably using a version of Vista that doesn't includes the Device Control feature.

2. **Choose Local Computer Policy⇨Computer Configuration⇨ Administrative Templates⇨System⇨Device Installation⇨Device Installation Restrictions.**

   This gives you access to all the Device Control installation policies. For more information on which settings to use, see the upcoming section, "Controlling device installation."

3. **Double-click and configure each individual setting that you want to use.**

Implementing Device Control usage settings

The settings for the use of removable devices are located in the Removable Storage Administrative Template in the Access to Removable Devices section, as shown in Figure 15-3.

This policy section allows you to define what types of activities are allowed on different types of removable media.

1. **Start the Group Policy Editor by choosing Start and then entering** gpedit.msc **into the Search field that appears.**

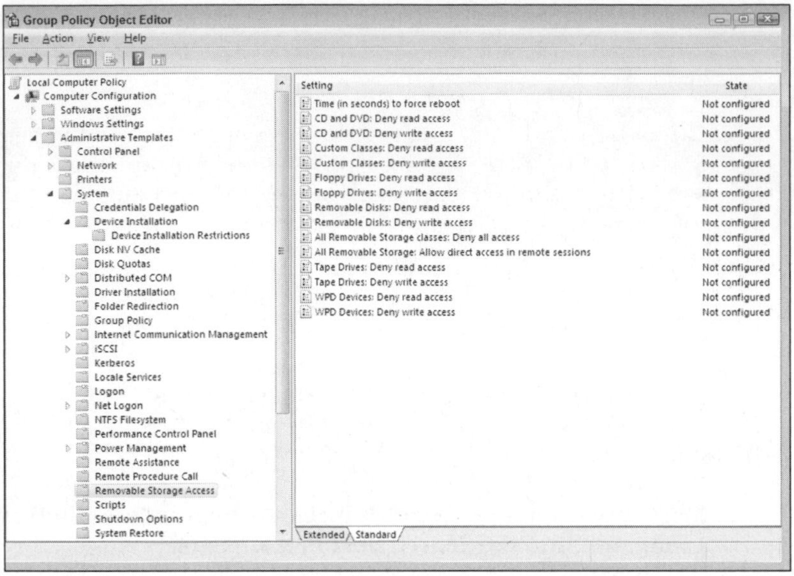

Figure 15-3:
Setting
removable
storage
access
policies.

2. **Choose Local Computer Policy⇨Computer Configuration⇨ Administrative Templates⇨System⇨Removable Storage Access.**

   This gives you access to all the device usage policies. For more information on which settings to use, see the upcoming, "Controlling device usage."

3. **Double-click and configure each individual setting that you want to use.**

For a more detailed description of implementing Device Control settings, I suggest that you read "Step-By-Step Guide to Controlling Device Installation and Usage with Group Policy," which is available from the Microsoft Web site at www.microsoft.com. This excellent guide takes you through every step of the configuration process, including a full explanation of device IDs and device classes.

Controlling device installation

The device installation options work together to allow you to craft an overall strategy for the installation of removable storage devices on your computer. This can be complicated because it requires a combination of settings to accomplish the strategy that you choose and might even require that you know the IDs of specific devices or device classes. However, the advantage of device-installation policies is that you can specify whether administrators have the rights to add removable storage instead of the policy applying to everyone who uses the machine.

Here are some strategies that you can employ by using the device control installation policies (as described earlier in "Implementing Device Control installation settings"):

✔ **Allow installation of all devices by all users.** This is the default setting within Vista. You don't have to do anything to implement this strategy. If you tried a different strategy — and therefore changed from the default settings — reverting is easy: Just reset all the policies to Not Configured.

✔ **Allow users to install only specific devices.** This strategy prevents the installation of all devices except those devices or device classes you specify. To implement this, you need to find out the specific device IDs or device classes of those devices that you want to allow to be installed. Choose the Prevent Installation of Devices Not Described by Other Policy Settings and Allow Administrators to override Device Installation policy, along with either the Allow Installation of Devices That Match Any of These Device IDs *or* Allow Installation of Devices Using Drivers That Match These Device Setup Classes setting.

✔ **Prevent installation of all devices.** This strategy prevents anyone from installing any removable devices to the machine regardless of their rights. Use the Prevent Installation of Removable Devices setting to implement this strategy.

✔ **Prevent installation of all devices by users.** This strategy allows administrators to install removable devices but prevents all standard user accounts from being able to do so. Use the Prevent Installation of Devices Not Described by Other Policy Settings *and* the Allow Administrators to Override Device Installation Policy settings to implement this strategy — but no others.

✔ **Prevent installation of specific devices.** This strategy ensures that no one can install specific devices, or even types of devices, that you specify. To implement this, you need to find out the specific device IDs or device classes of those devices that you want to prevent from installing and then use either the Prevent Installation of Devices That Match Any of These Device IDs *or* the Prevent Installation of Devices Using Drivers That Match These Device Setup Classes setting.

For a detailed description of how to find specific device or class IDs, read the "Step-By-Step Guide to Controlling Device Installation and Usage with Group Policy," available online at the Microsoft Web site.

✔ **Prevent installation of specific devices by users.** This strategy requires administrator permissions to install the devices, or types of devices, that you specify. To implement this, you need to find out the specific device IDs or device classes of those devices that you want to control. Use the Allow Administrators to Override Device Installation Policy *and* either the Prevent Installation of Devices That Match Any of These Device IDs *or* the Prevent Installation of Devices Using Drivers That Match These Device Setup Classes setting.

Controlling device usage

The removable storage access settings don't prevent Vista from installing the device and are either enabled or disabled for every user of the entire machine. However, settings worded something like *CD and DVD: Deny write access* are very easy to understand. You can deny all access to all removable storage devices or can configure CD/DVD, floppy drives, removable disks (such as USB drives), tape drives, Windows portable devices, and even specific devices or device classes to deny Read or Write access through these settings.

By default, Vista allows access to all devices. Therefore, using any devices that you don't specifically deny will be allowed after they are installed. The one setting within Removable Storage Access that is different is the All Removable Storage: Allow Direct Access in Remote Sessions setting. This setting affects remote users, such as those using a remote desktop, and not someone who is physically sitting in front of your computer. It allows that person to access the removable media that you have on your machine. By default, Vista does not allow this type of access.

Chapter 16

Working with Vista Security Policies

*T*he term *policy* in Microsoft-speak represents the interfaces that Microsoft provides for managing settings on a computer. Vista offers more than 2,600 different policy settings that cover how your desktop looks, how your firewall is configured, and practically everything in between. However, more policy setting options besides just those that come with the operating system (OS) are available. Microsoft has traditionally released new policy setting options with each Service Pack or new OS release, and you can even create custom templates to manage any Registry key or value that you want.

Microsoft allows you to manage almost any security-related setting through some kind of policy setting. Even if you're managing the security of only your own computer — not a whole network — the policy interfaces strive to provide you with a single place to define all your security settings.

In this chapter, I explain the different interfaces that you can use to manage policy settings, the different types of policy settings that are available, and how to choose the right policy settings for your security needs.

Managing your computer through policy is not possible on all versions of Vista. Local group policy is not available on the Starter, Home Basic, or Home Premium editions; you must have one of the Business editions of Vista or the Ultimate version to take advantage of the information in this chapter.

Implementing the Right Security Settings for You

Unfortunately, the simple truth is that security is the opposite of convenience and efficiency. Sure, it's more convenient to just open a door and go into a room, but that's obviously not as secure as locking the door. When designing the security for your house or apartment, you instinctively understand how people interact with the environment — and this affects your security decisions.

From a security perspective, nothing is wrong with locking every door and cabinet because such prudence increases the safety level in your house. As long as the right people have a key to all the things they need, everyone still has access. However, the flaw of this security plan becomes obvious when you wake up in the middle of the night to go to the bathroom and don't bring your key with you. Figuring out the right security settings for your computer follows the same basic principles.

To design a good security plan, you must understand how you — as well as others — interact with the computing environment. When you understand this, you'll know when you need to add security to your environment to protect it. Microsoft designed Vista to be secure at its core but left the user experience to be as convenient as possible by default.

For example, by default, you don't need a password attached to your user accounts on a Vista machine. Any security person will tell you that this is a bad idea, but Microsoft allows this because anyone can use the computer without having to worry about managing passwords. Other nonsecure password options might include setting a password that you never have to change or using a very short password that uses all lowercase characters. Security people (including me!) will tell you not to do this; however, if the only way that someone can remember a password is to make it that easy, these options are as secure as you can make your environment.

These examples are simple, and security questions can get a lot more complex. However, the basic answer to any of these questions is the same: Think about what the setting prevents and whether you (or your computer) need to be able to do it.

Why you should use policy to manage security settings

Microsoft built in thousands of settings to allow you to make security choices about which "doors" to lock within the system. Throughout this book, I show you many of the interfaces from where you can manage the security of the system. Policy provides an interface for the machine's security settings; however, the interfaces for managing policy have the added bonus of allowing you to manage the same settings as many of the other security interfaces. Examples of this include Firewall settings. In addition, if you use policy to configure these settings, you can capture this configuration and use it for other Vista machines that you want to have the same security.

Within Vista, the two main ways to manage policy settings are the Group Policy Object Editor and security templates. The *Group Policy Object Editor* allows you to change any policy setting that you desire on your machine. In a domain environment, this interface also allows you to set group policy for multiple machines. On the other hand, *security templates* are entire security designs for your computer that you can apply all at once. You can obtain these from many sources, including Microsoft, or you can custom design your own. I discuss both options in this chapter.

Managing policy with the Group Policy Object Editor

The Group Policy Object Editor interface is relatively straightforward in its design. Access the interface by choosing Start and then entering **gpedit.msc** in the Search field. Or, start a Microsoft Management Console (MMC) and add the Group Policy Object Editor snap-in. For a standalone Vista machine, the target of the interface is the local group policy of the machine.

As shown in Figure 16-1, you can open the Group Policy Object Editor to reveal the Computer Configuration or the User Configuration areas, and open those again to reveal the Software Settings, Windows Settings, or Administrative Template areas. A black down arrow shows that a path is expanded; and a white sideways arrow shows that settings in the path can be expanded (but aren't).

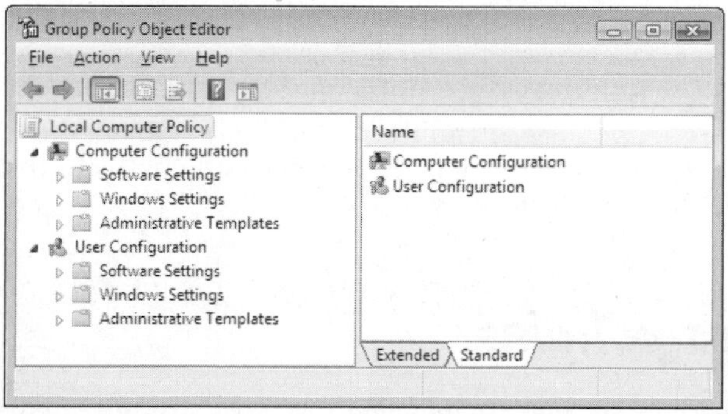

Figure 16-1:
The Group Policy Object Editor interface.

To manage a policy setting, follow the path to that setting and then double-click to bring up a popup with two tabs. Use the Local Security Setting tab to manage the options for that particular policy setting. This tab is different for each policy setting because it's specific to the settings that you can, or must, set to make that policy setting effective. The Explain tab provides detail about the particular policy setting that you're managing.

When you make a change to a local security policy setting from the Group Policy Object Editor interface, Vista makes that change to the security of the machine as soon as you click Apply or OK. However, the effects of the change might not be immediately effective because some security settings are loaded into active memory at boot or attached to the user during logon. To make those settings effective, either log off and log on, or reboot the machine.

Protecting Your System with Local Security Policy Settings

The policies that can be defined from the local security policy MMC snap-in (secpol.msc) are all considered security settings; as a group, these are known as the *local security policy* for the machine. These settings are only a fraction of the local group policy settings that you can manage through the Group Policy Object Editor (either locally or through group policy being applied from a domain) or by using security templates. However, the policy areas described in this section form the basic security environment for your computer.

All local security policies relate to the computer configuration area of local group policy rather than to the user configuration. (See the upcoming section, "Diving Deeper into Security Policy Settings," for details on the difference between these policy areas.) Also, in some cases (such as the password-policy settings), local group policy is the only Microsoft-provided method that you have to manage these settings.

The paths shown in the following sections are relevant to using the Group Policy Object Editor (gpedit.msc) only. Although both the Local Security Policy interface (secpol.msc) and the Group Policy Object Editor can be used to manage the local security policy settings, the paths to the settings are different in the two interfaces.

Password policies

Use password-policy settings to manage the security requirements for passwords stored on your Vista machine. Password requirements for domain accounts are controlled in Active Directory (AD) through a special group policy named Domain Policy. Password-policy settings control certain parameters (such as password age, length, and complexity) and ensure that all accounts on the machine meet your standards. You access these settings in the Group Policy Object Editor (gpedit.msc) via Computer Configuration⇨ Windows Settings⇨Account Policies⇨Password Policy.

The most important setting in the password policy area is the Minimum Password Length setting. By default, this is set to 0 (zero), which allows for no password being required.

Passwords are the most basic security precaution on your machine and should always be set. I recommend that Vista passwords be at least eight characters long, and you should set the security policy of your machine to enforce this.

Other important password policy settings are

- **Password Must Meet Complexity Requirements:** Requires that passwords use a combination of different types of characters, such as numbers and letters

- **Maximum Password Age:** Determines when you are required to change your password

- **Enforce Password History:** Sets whether you are allowed to reuse your old passwords

Account-lockout policies

Use account-lockout policy settings to manage the security for how and why Vista locks out an account, preventing a user from logging in. These policies can be used to protect against someone repeatedly trying to guess your password. Access these policy settings in the Group Policy Object Editor (gpedit.msc) via Computer Configuration⇨Windows Settings⇨Account Policies⇨Account Lockout Policy.

The most important of the account lockout policies is the Account Lockout threshold. This setting determines whether accounts will lock out at all, whereas the other settings determine _how_ a locked out account will be reset.

Be careful when setting lockout policies! The problem with locking out an account is, of course, that you can't use it while it's locked out. This means that if you enter your password incorrectly too many times, you may not be able to get back on your computer unless you have a different account you can use to log in.

Security best practice is that you should lock out accounts, but I recommend setting the limit to at least five failed attempts for home use. I also recommend allowing the lockout to expire without intervention after 30 minutes for a home user and 60 minutes in a business setting. You can control when a lockout expires with the Account Lockout Duration setting.

Audit policies

Use audit policy settings to determine what kind of events should be recorded within the Security Event log. In some cases, such as audit object access, enabling the policy setting only gives Vista the go-ahead to look at the auditing settings on the item to determine whether to record an event. Other audit policy settings, such as audit account logon events, tell Vista to record an event every time that event occurs. You access these policy settings in the Group Policy Object Editor (gpedit.msc) via Computer Configuration⇨Windows Settings⇨Local Group Policies⇨Audit Policy.

Within the 9 audit policy categories provided in the policy interfaces, Vista provides 50 subcategories of more detailed policy settings that allow you to specify exactly what activities in an area you want to audit. Using these subcategories can keep you from filling up your event logs with unnecessary data while still getting the critical data that you want. (See Chapter 7 for more information on auditing.) Unfortunately, these subcategories are currently only able to be managed through using a command line tool (AuditPol.exe) and not through the Group Policy Object Editor interface. (For more information on the use of AuditPol.exe, see the Microsoft Web site.) Therefore, if you set audit policy through a policy interface, Vista automatically overwrites all subcategory settings for that policy to the setting you specified for the entire policy.

User rights assignment

User rights are systemwide authorities used to perform certain types of actions. These rights and privileges manage different groups' abilities to log on to the machine, perform different tasks, or even do some programmatic tasks related to low-level OS functions (such as providing the ability for a program to impersonate a different user account in order to complete some action), among other things. You access these policy settings in the Group Policy Object Editor (gpedit.msc) via Computer Configuration⇨Windows Settings⇨Local Group Policies⇨User Rights Assignment.

Generally, leave these settings at their Windows defaults for home and small business usage. Some applications require additional user rights that they assign to themselves during installation. Changing user rights without fully understanding everything to do with your environment and computer can have some unintended and disastrous effects.

Security options

Security options comprise a wide range of optional settings related to the security of your system. Approximately 80 different security options are available, broken down into many different categories in the first release of Vista, although some of the security options are specific to managing security on servers instead of Vista. You access these policy settings in the Group Policy Object Editor (gpedit.msc) via Computer Configuration⇨Windows Settings⇨Local Group Policies⇨Security Options.

The default Microsoft settings for security options are pretty sound; however, this is one area where understanding how you use your computer can have a positive effect on your security environment. Some security options you should consider are

- **Devices: Restrict CD-ROM Access to Locally Logged-on User Only:** By default, this option is disabled. In most environments, however, there is no reason for a user to access your CD-ROM drive across the network. The only exception is if you set your backup to do Volume shadow copies. (For more information on this, see Chapter 8.) However, if you're not using this backup technique, enable this setting.

- **Devices: Restrict Floppy Access to Locally Logged-on User Only:** Like the previous bullet point, enable this setting unless you need to allow a user to access your floppy drive across the network. (Volume shadow copies are too large to fit on a floppy disk.)

- **Network Access: Do Not Allow Anonymous Enumeration of SAM Accounts and Shares:** By default, Vista allows this access. This allows users on your network to view the accounts on your computer or any file shares that you set up on the machine without authenticating to the machine first. Although this doesn't provide any direct access to data, it can allow a malicious user to plan a more effective attack on your shares.

For this reason, I recommend that you enable this policy with the understanding that it means that anyone who wants to see your shares will have to have a valid account on your Vista machine.

- **Recovery Console: Allow Floppy Copy and Access to All Drives and All Folders:** By default, Vista disallows this access. Microsoft believes that this is the proper setting for more secure environments but actually doesn't set it for a business environment because this can be used for troubleshooting when you have issues.

As long as you do not enable the Recovery Console: Allow Automatic Administrative Logon option, I recommend that you enable this in a home or small business environment even though it's less secure. In those situations, the risk of not being able to fix your computer or copy certain critical data will probably outweigh the chance that someone malicious will physically get to your computer with proper credentials and steal your data.

✔ **System Settings: Optional Subsystems:** By default, Vista allows the Posix subsystem through this setting. This enables Linux/Unix tools (as well as the Oracle call interface) to be run on Vista. If you're not using these types of tools, the Posix subsystem is unnecessary, and this check box can be deselected.

✔ **User Account Control: Admin Approval Mode for the Built-in Administrator Account:** By default, Vista sets this to be disabled so that the built-in administrator account (which is also disabled by default) does not have to use User Account Control (UAC).

My belief is that unless you have a specific reason to use the built-in administrator account to do something that can't handle UAC involvement, this should be set to the same as all other administrators; therefore, you should enable this setting. (For more information about UAC, see Chapter 4).

Event log

The event log policy settings determine how Vista manages the Application, Security, and System Event logs. These settings control items, such as log size, as well as Vista retention methods and settings. You access these policy settings in the Group Policy Object Editor (gpedit.msc) via the Computer Configuration⇨Windows Settings⇨Security Settings⇨Event Log.

Microsoft sets the default sizes of the log files relatively low: Most people don't need a long history of events, and extensive logging eats up extra hard drive space. If you're doing a lot of security auditing, you should definitely change the setting for the Maximum Security Log Size from the default of 20,480K (approximately 20MB) to something larger.

How large you want the log files to be depends upon how limited your hard drive space is, how extensive your security logging will be, and how much you value the data. Therefore, I recommend that you begin by leaving the setting at the default value and raise it as necessary.

Diving Deeper into Security Policy Settings

Local security policy controls the security of the core components of the operating system; however, this isn't the limit of local group policy settings with security implications. Local group policy settings can be used to manage security components (such as Windows Firewall) or to control the user environment so that it runs in a secure manner. Vista separates the policy settings available to manage into two types of configurations based on how and when they apply to the computer: computer configuration and user configuration.

Computer configuration policy settings

Vista applies computer-based security policy settings during the initial boot-up of the OS. As the name implies, you use these policy settings to control the security configuration of the computer itself. If a conflict ever happens between computer and user configuration settings, Vista applies the computer configuration policy setting and ignores the one set in the user configuration area.

Local security policy is a subset of the policy settings available in the computer configuration area of the Group Policy Object Editor interface, but it's not the only item available in the computer configuration area. In addition to the account and local group policies that make up local security policy, the following additional policy areas are available in the Group Policy Object Editor (gpedit.msc) within the Computer Configuration⇨Windows Settings⇨ Security Settings area of the policy-editing interfaces:

- ✔ **Windows Firewall with Advanced Security:** This area is used to manage the settings for Windows Firewall.

- ✔ **Public Key Policies:** This area is used to manage many different items related to certificates as well as adding Encrypting File System (EFS) recovery agents. For more details on EFS, see Chapter 9.

- ✔ **Software Restriction Policies:** These policies are used to manage whether certain pieces of software are allowed to run on your computer based on the rules you set in the policy setting.

- ✔ **IP Security Policies:** These policies can be used to manage the security of communications that use Internet Protocol (IP).

Your ability to use the computer-configuration policy settings to enhance and control the security of your machine extends beyond security-related settings. Through computer policies, you can also apply scripts that run at the startup or shutdown of the machine (available in the Group Policy Object Editor (gpedit.msc) via Computer Configuration⇨Windows Settings⇨Scripts) for tasks such as automatically running a program at that time. If you're in a domain environment, group policy can even be used to deploy software, such as antivirus updates or security patches, through the Software Settings area of computer policy.

User-configuration policy settings

Vista applies user-configuration policy settings when a user logs on instead of when the OS starts and can be used to control the security configuration of the user environment. The settings in the user configuration area for controlling the security of the environments are generally a subset of the ones available through computer policies. These user-configuration policy areas include software deployment, logon and logoff scripts, and public key policies.

For those policy settings that exist in both the computer and user configuration policy area, you might wonder why you would use the user policy settings instead of the computer type. The answer depends on how and when you want the setting to be applied. However, these are really only considerations within a domain environment. For a standalone machine, there is really no functional difference between setting a policy for a user versus for a computer.

Security options within user configuration policies do have one main difference from those in the computer configuration area: Internet Explorer (IE) security. You can manage and control IE through group policy settings, and this control extends to the security settings available in local group policy. You access these settings in the Group Policy Object Editor (gpedit.msc) via User Configuration⇨Windows Settings⇨Internet Explorer Maintenance⇨ Security. Use policy settings to manage the settings for security zones and privacy, content ratings, and Authenticode. For more details on these security options within IE, please see Chapter 13.

Administrative templates

Administrative templates provide interfaces for a series of settings related to a specific topic. The settings within the administrative templates all write values to the machine Registry, so they're not the only way to improve the security of your environment.

For more information on editing the Registry, see Chapter 7; however, keep in mind that making a mistake when editing the Registry can create major issues for your machine. Therefore, I highly recommend that you always use a Microsoft-provided interface if you have the option.

In addition, the administrative templates do provide important details for each setting on the explain tab for that setting, as shown in Figure 16-2 (the particular setting in the figure determines the encryption algorithm and key size used by BitLocker).

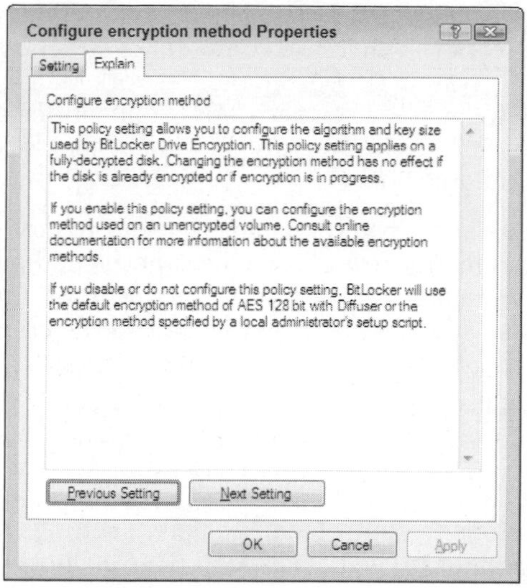

Configure encryption method Properties

Setting | Explain

Configure encryption method

This policy setting allows you to configure the algorithm and key size used by BitLocker Drive Encryption. This policy setting applies on a fully-decrypted disk. Changing the encryption method has no effect if the disk is already encrypted or if encryption is in progress.

If you enable this policy setting, you can configure the encryption method used on an unencrypted volume. Consult online documentation for more information about the available encryption methods.

If you disable or do not configure this policy setting, BitLocker will use the default encryption method of AES 128 bit with Diffuser or the encryption method specified by a local administrator's setup script.

Previous Setting | Next Setting

OK | Cancel | Apply

Figure 16-2:
An example Explain tab for an administrative template setting.

In addition to the current templates that come with Vista, you can create your own administrative templates so that you can easily control Registry settings without having to go into the Registry Editor. You do this through the creation and application of .admx files. Details about creating these files is beyond the scope of this book; however, instructions can easily be found on the Microsoft Web site as well as other places on the Internet.

Administrative template settings are available in both the computer and user configuration areas. In some cases, the same settings are available in both places and which one you should use depends upon when you want the settings to be applied. If there is a conflict between a computer and user policy setting that is invoked through an administrative template, the computer setting takes precedence.

Although Microsoft provides about 125 different administrative templates with Vista, the interface for these templates groups the settings in more general categories. These include, but are not limited to, the following:

- **Control Panel:** These options allow you to manage how Control Panel can be used on the machine, including whether it is even allowed to be viewed. Settings in this category are available for both the computer and user configuration.

- **Desktop:** These options allow you to manage all items related to the desktop, including which icons appear and whether new items can be added. In addition, you can use this category to disable active content on the desktop, which can be a security risk. This category of settings is available only inside the user configuration area.

✔ **Network:** These options allow you to manage how the system or user interacts with the network to which the computer is attached. This includes Domain Name System (DNS), Simple Network Management Protocol (SNMP), and local area network (LAN) connections as well as the use of offline files. Settings in this category are available for both the computer and user configuration.

✔ **Printers:** These options allow you to manage settings related to printers, although they're generally not related to a locally attached printer unless you use your Vista machine as a print server for other machines on your network. These settings are available only in the computer configuration area.

✔ **Start Menu and Taskbar:** These options allow you to manage how the Start menu and taskbar appear as well as how they behave. These settings are available only in the user configuration area.

✔ **System:** Use these options to control many different settings related to how Vista actually operates in the background. This includes things such as removable storage access (see Chapter 15 for more information), disk quotas, power management, and Windows file protection. Settings in this category are available for both computer and user configuration.

✔ **Windows Components:** These options allow you to manage how components of Vista operate. Examples of the types of Windows components and settings that you can manage include (but are not limited to) the following:

- *AutoPlay Policies:* This can be used to define the behavior for AutoPlay and AutoRun from either the computer or user configuration areas.

- *BitLocker Drive Encryption:* Settings that can be managed from this interface include configuring the BitLocker encryption method and recovery options, but these settings are available only from the computer configuration area.

- *Internet Explorer:* This can be used to control the entire configuration of IE, from the title bar to whether a user is allowed to run ActiveX controls. Different options exist in the computer and user configuration areas.

- *Windows Defender:* Settings include turning Windows Defender off and how Windows Defender signature files are handled, but these settings are available only from the computer configuration area.

- *Windows Explorer:* This can be used to control the entire configuration of Windows Explorer from the maximum size of the Recycle Bin to whether the shell runs in Classic mode. Different options exist in the computer and user configuration areas.

Managing Policy by Using Security Templates

Security templates are collections of policy settings that are designed for setting a specific level of security on your machine; however, this interface displays only the local security policy settings and won't show administrative template settings (although it will apply those settings if they are within the template itself). Working with security templates requires both the Security Templates and the Security Configuration and Analysis snap-ins. You can add both snap-ins to a single MMC, as shown in Figure 16-3.

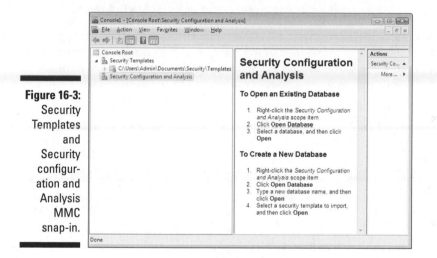

Figure 16-3:
Security
Templates
and
Security
configur-
ation and
Analysis
MMC
snap-in.

Creating your own custom security template

Although the Security Templates plug-in shows the default path for templates, Vista doesn't have any on the machine by default. You can create your own template through this interface by right-clicking the template path, choosing New Template, and then entering a name in the Template Name text box. This new template will then show under the default path (as shown in Figure 16-3), and you can then define any settings you want.

The purpose of creating your own security template is so that you can easily transfer the customized security that you set on your Vista machine to another machine. The security configuration and analysis tool can't scan your machine and pull the security settings from your machine into a template. However, with a little work, you can do it yourself. Here's how to create a new template:

1. **Open the Security Templates area and right-click the default template path shown.**

2. **Choose New Template from the pop-up menu and type in a name for the new template.**

3. **Create a new database by right-clicking Security Configuration and Analysis and choosing Open Database from the pop-up menu.**

4. **Type a name for the new database and then click Open.**

5. **Select the security template that you just created and then click Open.**

6. **Have Vista analyze your computer settings by right-clicking Security Configuration and Analysis and choosing Analyze Computer Now.**

7. **Click OK to accept the default path for the error log file.**

   A pop-up appears, showing Vista analyzing the different policy areas, and then it publishes the computer settings to the MMC.

8. **Review the computer settings.**

   Figure 16-4 shows the MMC display for settings after an analysis has taken place. The Computer Setting column shows the settings for the current configuration of the computer. Review this information and decide which settings you want to export to a template that can be applied to other computers.

   Now you need to configure the new database with the settings you want to export.

9. **Double-click each setting to change the value in the database.**

   The pop-up for each setting tells you the current computer and the database settings.

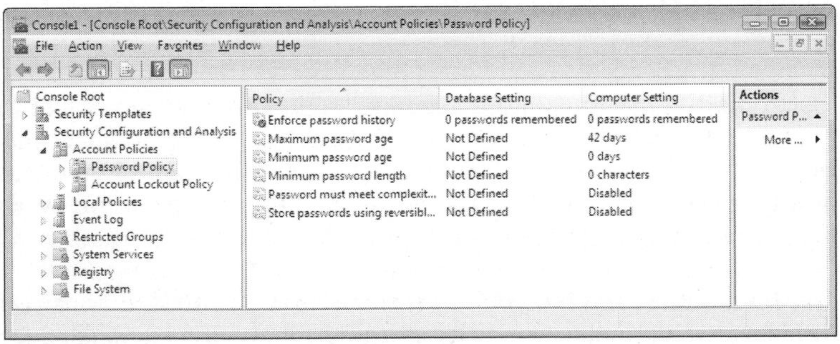

Figure 16-4: Display of Security Configuration and Analysis MMC after computer analysis.

Although the display of the setting changes immediately, Vista doesn't immediately update the database itself with the changes you specify in Step 9. Therefore, wait a minute or so after completing all of your changes before you attempt to export the template, or you run the risk of some settings not actually being exported to the template.

10. **Export the template by right-clicking Security Configuration and Analysis and choosing Export Template.**

11. **Choose the template you created earlier or type in a new name to create a new one, and then click Save.**

Windows Vista Security Guide templates

In addition to creating your own security template, you can obtain predefined ones from Microsoft or other sources. One of the best sources of predefined security templates for Vista, as well as the best explanation of policy settings, is the Windows Vista Security Guide, which is available for download at the Microsoft Web site.

When you install the Windows Vista Security Guide to your machine, it creates a set of folders. The security templates that you can apply to your Vista machine are located at Windows Vista Security Guide⇨GPOAccelerator Tool⇨Security Templates. There are seven templates and two security databases that you can use in conjunction with the Security Configuration and Analysis MMC interface to secure your machine. However, these are really broken down into three major categories:

 ✔ **VSG EC:** Vista Security Guide Enterprise Client. Microsoft designed the security settings in this template for use in a business environment that has a mix of both Windows XP and Vista clients, which log on to a domain consisting of Windows 2003 servers.

 ✔ **VSG SSLF:** Vista Security Guide Specialized Security – Limited Functionality. Microsoft designed the security settings in this template for use in a highly secured environment where a loss of functionality is acceptable to make the environment more secure.

 ✔ **Vista Default Security:** This template resets the security of the system back to the default configuration of Vista.

Neither of the VSG templates is truly applicable to the home user because many of the settings are used to control the local environment so that the end user can't mess up the machine. However, the settings in these templates do provide a very good guide to settings that you should consider when customizing the security of your machine. In what may seem like a strange twist, the higher-security SSLF settings might actually be more applicable to your standalone machine than the EC settings because many of the differences between the two relate to allowing connections with other machines. However, this is not the case if your machine is on a small home network.

The best way to leverage the VSG templates is to go through the steps outlined in the preceding section, "Creating your own custom security template." Instead of creating a new template and database, as you do in the first four steps of those instructions, start with Step 5 and choose the VSG template and database that you're interested in using as your base. You can then analyze and compare the settings, and then choose to configure your computer now or to export the settings to a new template.

Applying a security template to your machine

After you create a custom security template, or make the decision to use a template provided from another source, you're ready to apply the template to a machine. You accomplish this through the same Security Configuration and Analysis MMC interface, using many of the same steps described throughout this chapter.

1. **Open a database with your preconfigured settings by right-clicking Security Configuration and Analysis and choosing Open Database from the pop-up menu that appears.**

   If you have the database that contains the settings you want to apply, choose that database. If you only have the security template that contains the settings, create a new database by typing in a name and then choose the template with the settings in them when prompted.

2. **Have Vista analyze your computer settings by right-clicking Security Configuration and Analysis and choosing Analyze Computer Now.**

3. **Click OK to accept the default path for the error log file.**

   A pop-up appears showing Vista analyzing the different policy areas, and then it publishes the computer settings to the MMC.

4. **Review the computer settings.**

   Refer to Figure 16-4 to see the MMC display for settings after an analysis has taken place. The Computer Setting column displays the settings for the current configuration of the computer. Review this information to ensure that the settings in your database are the settings that you want to apply to the machine.

5. **Apply the settings to the computer by right-clicking Security Configuration and Analysis and choosing Configure Computer Now.**

6. **Accept the error log file path by clicking OK.**

   Vista displays a pop-up that shows the progress of applying settings to the different policy areas, the same way it did for the analysis of the settings. After this is complete, the screen reverts to the how it looked in Step 1.

7. **Have Vista analyze your computer settings again, and then review to make sure that the computer settings all match the database settings that you wanted to apply.**

   I admit that this step is just paranoia because if you did Steps 2 and 3, it should be unnecessary. However, you are changing the basic security of your system through a tool, so making sure that everything is set correctly is a very important precaution.

   After the analysis, you should have a green check mark next to each setting you wanted to make through applying the template settings (refer to the Enforce Password History setting in Figure 16-4). If this is not the case, reapply the settings.

Part VI
The Part of Tens

"A centralized security management system sounds fine, but then what would we do with all the dogs?"

In this part . . .

If you're like me, you look forward to the infamous Part of Tens of a *For Dummies* book.

In this part, read about ten common security risks that you're likely to encounter as well as what you can do to protect yourself against them. You can also discover ten security tools that you shouldn't compute without — including why you should use them and how to get them immediately.

And for good measure, see the glossary and a short chapter on the Vista flavors and their security features.

Chapter 17

Nine Security Risks and How to Thwart Them

In This Chapter

▶ Understanding the inherent dangers of Internet use

▶ Protecting yourself from e-mail threats

▶ Expanding your security to include PDAs and other mobile devices

· ·

*T*he release of Vista is akin to throwing down the gauntlet to all hackers, identity thieves, and other technical crooks. It is a challenge that undoubtedly will be responded to by the darker technical community with enthusiasm and passion. Vista is not only the new kid on the block but is also being lauded as the most secure Windows operating system (OS) to date, making it a difficult target for crooks to resist. In this chapter, you find out about the most likely types of attacks you might encounter and what you can do to defend your computer from them. Although I don't cover specific code vulnerabilities in this chapter, I do talk about those general risks that Vista brings to the table, as well as other risks that might be inherent in your computing environment and those that you might introduce yourself.

Always Being Connected

Without a doubt, a broadband connection brings you a speedy and more reliable Internet connection than its clunky predecessor (pokey ol' dial-up). You don't have to wait for the modem to dial, you don't have to worry about busy signals, and you have a connection that is always on and ready to go. Most of us cannot imagine how we ever lived with dial-up. Although I could never imagine going back to that archaic Internet connection, I will tell you that security risks are associated with broadband — in particular, having a constantly open connection. Having a broadband Internet service provider (ISP) is similar to having a corporate network or Internet connection albeit with a critical piece missing: security. A corporate network is protected by firewalls, intrusion detection systems, and a plethora of other security controls that help keep crooks at arm's length. Most ISPs, however, have little (if any) of these security controls, making it ultimately your responsibility to adequately protect your systems and personal data.

As a home or small office user, placed on the Internet via an IP address assignment from your ISP, your system is available to the entire world for a little poking and prodding. Crooks from across the globe can scan your system and run all kinds of neat tools in attempt to compromise your system's security. Now more than ever before, our systems hold or process sensitive information. It might be our income tax files and banking information; or perhaps even our financial records, including our budget, credit card numbers, and other sensitive information. This information can be the keys to the kingdom for a crook. The following are some things that you can do to further secure your broadband Internet connection. Chapter 12 also provides direction on securing your broadband wireless network:

- ✔ **Use a broadband router.** Home routers provide an inexpensive way to shield your computer from the Internet. Newer models come with firewall features that provide even more stringent security functionality. (If you use a wireless router, see Chapter 12 for guidelines on locking down the device.) Even a regular broadband router provides a large degree of protection by intercepting incoming data and looking for a user configured rule to allow that data through. For example, the average broadband connected computer will receive, on average, one Web server attack every two hours. If you don't have your router configured to allow that traffic through (which you likely do not), the router denies access to these attacks.

- ✔ **Use a personal firewall.** Whether you choose to use Vista Firewall or purchase a third-party firewall, protect your system with some sort of firewall when you're connected to a network. (For more information about Vista Firewall, see Chapter 11.)

- ✔ **Disable the network when not in use.** Many of us constantly keep our systems turned on. However, turning off your computer when you're not using it makes your computer unavailable for attack and helps reduce some of the risk of always being connected.

Taking Shortcuts with Security

Throughout this book, I provide you with a great deal of information so that you can appropriately use the features and functionality provided in Vista to protect your system and data. However, none of us are perfect. Undoubtedly, you'll likely do something that introduces a certain amount of risk. Maybe you use your system to perform certain tasks that might be considered riskier than others. Or, you choose to not implement certain security controls, ultimately accepting a greater level of risk in lieu of gaining more productivity. Whatever the case, one thing is for certain: Users introduce a certain amount of risk to their system and data. Understanding what risks you introduce is key to making the right decisions to either reduce or accept that risk. The following are common areas in which you, as a user, might introduce yourself to risk:

- **Lacking a security plan:** In much the same way that you wouldn't go on a cross-country trip without a map, you shouldn't travel through the digital world without a security plan. Not having a plan means that you can easily leave gaps in your security that can be exploited by attackers or lead to a loss of data that cannot be recovered. Chapter 2 provides the information that you need to develop a proper security plan so that you can be sure that you can protect your system and precious data.

- **Failing to identify your data:** Home, small office, or even enterprise users often don't identify what data is important. Failing to do so essentially guarantees that it's not protected because it's probably not backed up or protected by any other security controls. Take the time to continually identify the data that is important to you and organize it accordingly. That way, you can effectively protect it.

- **Unsafe surfing:** The Internet can be a strange and dangerous place. It's not regulated, and sites can contain viruses and other malware that can infect your systems — and, ultimately, put your data at risk. In addition to viruses and malware, many phony sites exist for the sole purpose of collecting your personal information and using it to perpetuate identity theft and other crimes of fraud. I urge you to use caution and travel to sites that you know are safe. Do not provide your Personally Identifiable Information (PII) to anyone unnecessarily.

- **Creating weak passwords:** Users in an enterprise environment are likely to have been instructed or forced to use *strong* passwords: those that are alphanumeric, contain upper- and lowercase letters, and are at least eight characters. However, those of us at home or a small office sometimes use passwords that don't rise to that level. We share them with family members, name them after our dog, or even write them down for everyone to see. Always exercise good judgment. Despite any possible inconvenience, always use strong passwords that meeting the following minimum criteria:

  - *At least eight characters:* Using passphrases that are up to 14 characters is even better.

  - *Not intuitive to others:* Don't name your password after your dog or something that can easily guessed by others. However, don't make it so difficult that you need to write it down to remember it, either.

  - *Alphanumeric:* Combine numbers, letters, and any other characters that you can use on the keyboard. The more complex the password, the more security it provides from someone guessing or running a tool designed to guess common words and phrases.

- *Case combination:* Passwords are case sensitive; therefore, use upper- and lowercase letters in your password to make it more complex and more secure.

- *No sequencing:* Avoid using sequential numbers or letters, such as 123 or abc, because these strings can be easily guessed by people or password-guessing/cracking tools.

✔ **Deliberately bypassing security:** This might seem to be a fundamental and obvious consideration, but it's really not. Novices and experts alike all too often turn off security features because they find them annoying. Often, they do this without just cause. Sometimes, you need to decide to accept some risk in lieu of being more productive because some security features are such a hindrance that they impede productivity. In those cases, measure your need to be protected against your need to be productive. Every now and then, it makes sense to opt for productivity. However, doing so can be habit forming. Before you know it, you're turning off any security feature that inhibits your behavior whether it makes sense or not. Do not fall into this trap. Measure the security value that it provides and make a conscious effort to use the security features provided to you *unless you must absolutely bypass them.*

Failing to Apply Software Patches

Software patches serve many purposes from bug fixes to security enhancements. Keeping the software on your computer up to date is critical to the security of your system. The good news is that more and more software these days can ability to "phone home" for these updates.

Everything from media-playing software to software used to display PDF files seems to be equipped to do this task. These updates can be annoying and typically come with a Remind Me Later choice that many people just click so that they can finish what they want to do. This is a great example of a tendency to place ourselves at risk because most people don't go back and run the updates later. Therefore, to avoid putting yourself in the position of running software that is unstable or has security vulnerabilities, I suggest the following:

✔ **Use automatic/schedule update features.** Most software packages that include the ability to check for updates allow you to configure when they should check for updates and whether they will automatically install. Typically, this feature is available within the configuration menus of the program and can be set to run at times that you're generally not using the machine (such as the middle of the night). Vista itself comes with Windows Update that allows for automatic updating of Vista as well as other software programs that have chosen to participate with Microsoft in the program. Chapter 3 provides more detail on Windows Update.

✔ **Accept updates when they are offered.** Train yourself to allow the software to update when first asked to instead of delaying it. This way, you avoid racking up many requests over time and will have a more stable and secure computer overall.

✔ **Create a maintenance schedule for your machine.** Just like changing the oil in your car or taking out the garbage, maintain the patches on your computer software as one of the things that just has to be done. For those software packages without automatic updates, set a specific time to ensure that they're not vulnerable in some way. This schedule can be as easy as checking for software patches every Sunday morning or as complicated as choosing which software you will update on a daily basis. However, the key thing to remember is that a schedule means nothing if you don't actually follow it.

Unwillingly Participating in Attacks

The media loves to hype stories of mass computer armies aligning to attack one another. Although the chances of your computer participating in one of these attacks is low, protecting yourself from such an attack is critical. After a computer has been found vulnerable and exploited, the attacker may use the compromised computers as launching pads for attacking other systems. This attack is generally referred to as *Distributed Denial-of-Service (DDoS)*. Here's how it works:

1. The attacker compromises a host and installs an agent program that will await further instructions.

2. When a number of agents are running on different computers, the attacker can remotely instruct all the compromised computers to launch an attack on a target system with their malicious program.

3. The entire group of systems then focus the attack on a particular target, typically bringing the target to its knees because it cannot handle all the requests coming from hundreds — and sometimes, thousands — of these zombie-like computers.

The end target of the attack is not your own computer, but instead a company's Web server, e-mail system, or some other target. If the idea of participating in this form of attack doesn't make you concerned, I simply do not know what will. The fact is that you have reason to be concerned. Often, these types of attacks will be traced back to your "zombie" system, and you will likely find yourself answering an investigator's questions as to why your system was involved in the incident.

Here is what you can do about it:

- ✔ Consistently update your OS and software patches.
- ✔ Check that no administrative level accounts exist that you, or some software that you installed, did not create.
- ✔ Change passwords on a regular basis.
- ✔ Make sure that your antivirus and anti-spyware software are updated with the latest signature and engine files.

Getting Careless with E-Mail Security

E-mail has so ingrained itself as a communication technique that anyone with a computer today cannot realistically live without it. The primary way how viruses are delivered to your system is through attachments to e-mail. Although antivirus companies are very aggressive to provide signature file updates so that their product can detect viruses, this typically occurs after a virus has already begun to spread, which may be too late for you.

However, this is not the only threat brought on by the use of e-mail. E-mails are also used by con men to entice people into falling for scams that can cost them a lot of money or even their entire identity. These scams can be clear text messages with a direct appeal for money to help a sick child or an "opportunity" to make lots of money for little investment. Or, you might see an official-looking link to a legitimate Web site that takes you to a site that asks for personal data or runs scripts and ActiveX controls against your machine to try to compromise it.

Therefore, once again, the responsibility for protecting your system and data falls primarily into your lap. Here are some important safety tips to remember:

- ✔ **Do not open e-mail from an unknown or unexpected sender.** This is akin to what our parents have always told us and what we tell our children: Don't talk to strangers! Often, your name might even be in the Subject line as a clever ploy to con you into thinking that they know you. Use caution. If you don't know the sender, or have any doubt that you do, do not open any attachment from that person.

- ✔ **Do not open suspicious e-mail attachments.** This tip is critical and the best way to avoid a computer virus. Don't open attachments that you're not expecting, even if they're from someone that you know. Instead, if the e-mail is from someone familiar, contact that person and ask what the contents of the attachment are. You might find that they didn't know that they sent it to you. This would be a clear indication that a virus or other malicious code is using their Address book and automatically sending malicious attachments.

✔ **Disable preview windows in e-mail programs.** Previewing an e-mail is the equivalent of opening it. Therefore, if you use the preview window, just getting the e-mail can activate viruses that normally would run when the e-mail is opened.

✔ **Permanently delete suspicious e-mail from your computer.** In most e-mail programs, if you hold down the Shift key while pressing the Delete button, you can permanently delete the message from your computer without sending it to the Recycle Bin or the Deleted Items folder. This will prevent you, or someone close to you, from opening it in the future.

✔ **Regularly update your virus protection software.** Most software can manually update with the latest virus-fighting definitions. When in doubt, update manually.

✔ **Set your virus protection software to automatically scan attachments and files before opening them.** Viruses can lie undetected in files and folders until something triggers them to act. Consequently, have your virus protection software constantly check and recheck files and folders.

✔ **Do not try to quarantine or repair infected e-mail data as some antivirus software can do.** No e-mail is worth it. Instead, delete the message if anything suspicious is discovered.

✔ **Don't let curiosity get the better of you.** Opening unexpected or suspicious attachments is the surest way of contracting a virus and putting your system and precious data at risk.

Mobile Code

By definition, mobile code includes ActiveX, Java, and scripts. Mobile implies that the code is small, standalone, and easily transported. The primary transport mechanism for mobile code is through the Web and e-mail. Mobile code in a perfect, benevolent world presents no danger. However, mobile code has been and will continue to be used for malicious purposes. Malicious mobile code are viruses, worms, Trojan horses, and script attacks that pose the greatest danger not only to the corporate environment, but also to the home and small office user. Entire books have been written on the threat of Malicious Mobile Code (MMC). In this book, I discuss techniques to protect the two primary avenues of MMC attacks: Web and e-mail. However, here are two, lesser-known avenues of attack to your system using MMC: instant messaging (IM) and mobile devices (such as PDAs and IP-enabled cellphones). Both of these are discussed in subsequent sections of this chapter, but here's a closer look at how the new security model in Vista provides protection against MMC.

✔ **Vista Firewall:** By default, Vista Firewall is configured to forbid all untrusted, third-party traffic unless the user explicitly permits the action. By itself, Firewall curtails MMC quite nicely. However, beware that malicious code can execute in the user's context to also permit such action.

✔ **Internet Explorer 7 (IE7):** IE7 running in Protected Mode can prevent installation of MMC by restricting IE7 to a lower-privilege level to further restrict access to the computer.

✔ **User Account Control (UAC):** Some consider this Vista security feature a pest, but it goes a long way toward preventing malicious code from executing without the user knowing about it. Chapter 4 of this book goes into great detail on how you can use UAC to protect your system and precious data.

Peer-to-Peer Networking

Vista is designed to deliver streamlined network connectivity via an automated network setup that performs all the tasks associated with connecting to a network, if able, in the background. Although Vista peer-to-peer networking provides users with greater opportunity to connect to each other and share files easier than ever before, this also introduces greater levels of risk. The following are some key components to Vista peer-to-peer networking, the risks that they introduce, and what you can do to reduce those risks:

✔ **Meeting Space:** The underlying technology in Vista networking is named People Near Me. The Microsoft Meeting Space application is integrated into Vista. Meeting Space lets people share and view files on computers connected to the network. Security measures are built in to ensure that all parties know what they're getting into and that they're willing participants. People can choose whether to be seen in the People Near Me feature, and they can also decline or accept any particular invitation. For those hosting a session, choices are available to make their meeting public or private, or to require participants to provide a password before entering.

✔ **Internet Connection Sharing (ICS):** The ICS tool in Vista allows users to give access to additional computers on the network via a single machine connected to the Internet. The ICS host computer routes all the Internet traffic of the other machines on the network.

✔ **Ad hoc networking:** Ad hoc networking allows users to set up a peer-to-peer type of network in which they can connect to each other's machine and share files. Any time you open a pipe to the outside world from your system, you introduce more risk that your system or data can be compromised. Ad hoc networking, if not done securely, can introduce a great deal of risk, especially if it's set up via a wireless connection. Chapter 12 discusses wireless ad hoc networking in greater detail, but essentially, Vista offers security functionality to help reduce these risks. Use the methods discussed in Chapter 12 to secure that connection and reduce these risks to an acceptable level.

Unsafe Instant Messaging

Quickly becoming the most popular form of communicating over the Internet, IM provides a real-time supplement to (and, in some cases, a replacement for) e-mail. Recent statistics indicate that nearly 12 billion IMs are sent daily. Unlike e-mail, IM allows users to see whether a chosen friend or co-worker is online, available, and ready to communicate. Another key difference between IM and e-mail is that messages are exchanged almost instantly, allowing two-way communication in real time. In this section, I don't cover the typical street smarts of communicating with strangers over IM, such as not divulging personal information to strangers or arranging to meet people you only know through IM. Instead, I focus on the increasing popularity of IM as an avenue of attack and transfer of MMC.

Instant messaging allows text message and file transfer. Consequently, IM can transfer all varieties of malicious code that can evade Vista security protections. Hackers can use IM to gain backdoor access to computers without opening a listening port, effectively bypassing Vista Firewall. Another benefit to the hacker — and risk to you — is that finding victims doesn't require scanning unknown IP addresses. Instead, a crook can simply select targets from a directory of IM participants that is freely available. All the major IM networks support peer-to-peer file sharing where one can share a directory or drive. This means that all the files on a computer can be shared using the IM client, leading to the spread of files that are infected with a virus or other MMC or increasing the risk that your data can be accessed by an unauthorized person.

You must understand the present state of IM security and exercise constant vigilance when using this medium. Antivirus software companies are just now incorporating IM file-scanning measures, and the IM vendors themselves employ very little security in their products. Here are several rules to help reduce the risk of IM:

- **Never send or receive files through IM.** Use e-mail instead; e-mail has more mature and robust file attachment-scanning security.

- **Where possible, operate your IM sessions through a Web browser and not via the desktop client.** This allows you to take advantage of Vista security features. The primary reason for this is to move your IM sessions operating at standard user privilege level to the lower privilege level of IE7.

- **Be wary when receiving a Web link over IM.** Hover over the link with your cursor before clicking it to check whether the Web address seems legitimate. It might be a Web site that on arrival infects your computer with the latest and greatest MMC.

Mobile Device Security

Like the honeymoon is over for IM, so, too, is it over for mobile devices (such as PDAs and smart phones). As much as folks like these devices, they introduce various security issues, some of which can be very significant. Enter the viruses, including Liberty Crack, Phage, and Vapor for starters. As hand-held devices develop more functionality that mimics a desktop PC, they develop the ability to become infected like a desktop PC. Handhelds might begin to face attack from malicious programs, such as Melissa and Love Letter, which sent themselves as e-mail attachments to people in victims' Address books. Antivirus and other security software are becoming as common for hand-held devices as they are for the PC. Some quick tips to provide more security on your mobile devices are

- ✔ **Update the device OS.** Like with your computer, keep your mobile device OS up-to-date via regular patching. This prevents attackers from taking advantage of known vulnerabilities.

- ✔ **Install both antivirus and firewall software.** These devices are now vulnerable to viruses and network attacks, but the good news is that tools are available to provide protection against such vulnerabilities. Windows Firewall can help protect you against network attacks and is explained in more detail in Chapter 11. Chapter 18 provides you the information that you need to select an antivirus tool. Also, Chapter 14 provides related information.

- ✔ **Use caution with e-mail and surfing the Internet.** Exercise the same caution when Web browsing or working with e-mail on your mobile device as you do on your computer.

- ✔ **Disable unnecessary Bluetooth or wireless services.** To prevent receiving MMC and other malicious activity, disable Bluetooth and other network connections (including infrared, 802.11, CDMA, and GPRS) when not being used. Keeping them enabled when not in use only widens your attack surface.

- ✔ **Encrypt your data.** By encrypting all personal data, you prevent unauthorized access even if someone else has physical access to the device. Encryption software is built into some PDAs and available for most. If you have sensitive data on your PDA device, you should encrypt it. In fact, legislation in some states requires that certain types of data must be encrypted. If such data is not encrypted, you might be required to make certain notifications and pay penalties.

✔ **Enable and configure both power on and desktop sync password protection.** Use a strong password in both cases — and not the same password for both.

✔ **Use password brute-force protections.** Often, devices have the ability to lock themselves out or even reset if an incorrect password is entered a certain number of times. If you have sensitive data on your device, consider implementing such controls. If you lose your device, these controls can reduce the likelihood that someone can guess your password and gain access to your data. After the threshold of guesses you set is reached, the device is reset, and the data is erased.

Chapter 18

Ten Additional Security Tools and Resources You Shouldn't Compute Without

*L*iterally dozens of nifty little security tools can help you batten down the hatches and secure your system from many of the ills of the digital world. In this chapter, I cover the security tools that I believe will give you the most bang for your buck, while balancing ease of use with the potential security risks that you likely will encounter on your journey.

Antivirus Software

Although Vista certainly reflects Microsoft's ambition to make a more secure operating system, it's not perfect. If you've heard the hype about not needing to use antivirus software protection with Vista, you need to dismiss that notion. You do need to purchase additional antivirus software protection instead of just relying on Vista's built-in tools. Even Microsoft backed off its original claims that you can safely compute without additional antivirus software. Microsoft, too, now recommends that you use it. Here are some things that you need to consider when selecting an antivirus software product for Vista:

▶ **Vista compatibility:** As you might have either guessed or experienced if you're already using Vista, not all applications are compatible with this new OS. When you select an antivirus software program that works for you, pay special attention to whether Vista is listed under the system requirements as a compatible OS. Microsoft currently lists its recommended compatible products at Web site

```
http://www.microsoft.com/athome/security/update/windowsvistaav.mspx
```

One of which is their own Windows Live OneCare product. In addition to these suggested products, several others that aren't listed also claim to be compatible with Vista and can likely provide you the features and functionality that you need.

✔ **Scanning features:** When selecting an antivirus program, I recommend that you select one with that offers real-time, on-demand, and on-access scanning capabilities. The product should allow you to set up scans on a schedule so you don't have to run them manually. The product should also be able to scan inside compressed files.

✔ **Ease of use:** The antivirus software that you select should also provide you an intuitive and easy-to-use interface. Otherwise, you might not use it as often as you should. You can often download a trial version that will last for 30 days so you can try it out and see whether you like it.

✔ **E-mail scanning:** Viruses are often propagated through e-mail attachments, so it's imperative that the product that you select can scan attachments within your e-mail program for viruses.

✔ **Frequent updates:** Because viruses and other malware are released into the wild on a daily basis, select an antivirus software provider that frequently updates its software to detect the latest viruses. Otherwise, when a new virus debuts, your antivirus program won't detect it, and your system might become infected.

Spyware Removal Tools

A variety of third-party spyware tools are available to help you keep that pesky spyware at bay. Don't forget that Windows Vista also provides a native spyware tool — Windows Defender — and many third-party antivirus tools on the market have some anti-spyware functionality as well. Even still, I suggest that you get a third-party, anti-spyware tool for optimal protection. Many anti-spyware tools are offered for free on the Internet.

Because the market changes daily, it's tough to recommend a specific product. I suggest that you look through the various products offered and choose one for yourself. For best results, use multiple spyware-detection tools because one tool will often detect spyware that another tool will not. You should also make it a point to run the tools on a regular basis to keep your system clean and free of spyware.

The following are some things that you might want to consider in your search for a third-party spyware product:

- ✔ **Easy-to-user interface:** If a spyware removal program isn't intuitive and easy to use, it simply won't be effective. If users can't quickly figure out how to use it, chances are they won't use it regularly, meaning that spyware eradication efforts won't be very effective. Don't underestimate the importance of selecting a spyware removal tool that is easy to use.

- ✔ **Frequent updates:** In much the same way how viruses change from day to day or even from hour to hour, so do these pesky spyware programs. When selecting a spyware removal tool, select one that offers frequent application updates so that it can detect the latest spyware programs and routines. Successful spyware-eradication efforts largely depend on the tool's ability to detect the latest spyware programs.

- ✔ **Blocking or immunizing features:** Selecting a third-party product that offers blocking or immunizing ability is important because it might prevent your system from being reinfected with some spyware programs. Although this feature won't likely prevent all reinfections, any assistance the tool can provide in this area is very important.

- ✔ **Back-out or restore functionality:** Not everything goes as planned. When a spyware-removal tool makes changes to your system to remove potential spyware or block your system from being reinfected, you always take the chance that something might go awry. When that happens, having a tool with a back-out feature is your saving grace. Plenty of third-party tools have a back-out or restore feature that allows you to revert your system to before the tool made changes.

One of my favorites at the time of this writing is Spyware Search and Destroy. This tool does a great job in detecting spyware. In my opinion, it has all the aforementioned features.

Third-Party Backup Software

You might wonder why I mention third-party backup software if the Vista backup and recovery tool is a moderately capable backup utility that can meet most ambitious home user's needs. The truth is that the Vista native backup and recovery tool won't meet everyone's needs. And if it doesn't meet your needs, you need to find a backup and recovery tool that does. Additionally, some features with the Vista backup and recovery tool are available only with certain versions of Vista. Take, for example, the CompletePC Backup feature, which is available with the Vista Business, Enterprise, and Ultimate editions, but not with Vista Home Basic and Home Premium. In Chapter 8, you can determine what your backup requirements are. You can also see what Vista backup and restore features can help you meet those requirements. If you require some functionality not provided with your Vista version, you need to change to an upgraded version of Vista, such as Ultimate, that provides more backup and restore functionality. Or, purchase a third-party tool that fits the bill.

Firewalls and Other Network Protection

Because your home or small office computer is likely connected to the Internet, having a software or hardware firewall is essential to your security well-being and something that you certainly shouldn't compute without. The good news is that the Vista Windows Firewall is an effective tool that you can use to protect your system. It offers both inbound and outbound filtering capabilities, with a familiar interface and smooth integration with the operating system. Truth be told, however, most average users probably won't find the advanced settings intuitive or easy to use. Many third-party personal firewall products come with additional features, such as spyware blocking, identity-theft protection, privacy protection, and more. You can see that some users may be eager to obtain a third-party personal firewall product.

Before you run out and spend additional money, however, I suggest that you evaluate your need for a third-party product. If you believe that those extra features are important to you, it might warrant such an investment. You should understand, however, that even some of the best third-party firewalls — such as ZoneAlarm Pro from CheckPoint (www.zonelabs.com) — have been known to conflict with software on a system and often require some effort on your part to get them to play nicely together with Vista.

Use a hardware-based firewall, such as a router or broadband gateway with firewall capabilities, for your home or small office. These devices are relatively inexpensive and can further help you secure your environment whether you have one or a few computers sitting on a home or small office network. Talk with your local computer shop or electronics retailer for the latest available options in selecting a hardware firewall. Some of the features that are available are

- **Antivirus features:** Some of these devices offer virus protection at the edge of your network, stopping viruses before they even hit your systems.

- **Remote access VPN:** This allows you to access your system via a *Virtual Private Network* (VPN) to encrypt communications so that your data can't be viewed during its transmission.

- **Secure wireless protocols:** Getting a device that supports the latest wireless secure protocols allows you to lock down your wireless network securely.

> ✔ **Advanced firewall capabilities:** A hardware-based firewall provides more advanced packet-inspection capabilities than those found in a software firewall, allowing you an even greater level of protection. Additionally, you can use a hardware-based firewall in addition to your software firewall, so this is a great addition to your security toolbox.

Online Security Newsletters

Newsletters are a great way to keep updated on the latest security issues and trends. Many online resources allow you to sign up for their newsletters and easily cancel them if you find that you aren't interested. To the end user and IT professional alike, the SANS (SysAdmin, Audit, Network, Security) organization offers several newsletters that might be of interest and provides an excellent resource on various information security topics, threats, and trends. SANS operates the Internet Storm Center and makes available one of the largest collections of documentation related to information security on its Web site at www.sans.org. You can locate these newsletters at www.sans.org/newsletters.

At the time of this writing, the following newsletters are available for you to subscribe to:

> ✔ **SANS NewsBites:** A semiweekly summary of the most important computer security articles that hit the street in the past week. This newsletter not only provides you the latest, breaking computer security news but also provides some valuable insight into the issues that might affect your computer's security on a day-to-day basis. I strongly recommend that you sign up for this newsletter.

> ✔ **@RISK: The Consensus Security Alert:** A weekly newsletter that summarizes the vulnerabilities that you need to be concerned about the most. Also added to the list is a complete catalog of all the new security vulnerabilities found in the past week. This newsletter gives you the information that you need to understand what vulnerabilities exist — and what others are doing about them.

> ✔ **Ouch!:** Considered to be a very informative and effective security-awareness newsletter. This newsletter provides users with the information they need to understand certain threats and how their behavior can either protect them or hurt them. This is a must-read.

In addition to the SANS newsletters, Microsoft offers a free monthly e-mail newsletter packed with information to help you protect your home computer system. It includes how-to articles and security tips, security bulletins and critical updates, answers to frequently asked questions (FAQs) on security topics, and more. You can sign up for this newsletter at

`www.microsoft.com/technet/security/secnews/newsletter.htm`

The About.com Identity-Theft Web Site

I am a contributor to this site, so I admit that I might be a bit partial to it. Still, I can tell you that the About.com identity-theft site will be around long after I stop contributing to it, helping people just like you and me protect ourselves from identity theft and other fraud crimes. Much of why you need to secure your system is to protect yourself from those crooks who want to gain access to your system and the data that resides on it. The site, found at `http://id theft.about.com`, provides tips and guidance related to identity-theft statistics and basic information for those just finding out about it. The site provides information on scams and consumer alerts, data breaches, legislation, and other information related to privacy and security. Although this book provides you the information that you need to use the security features and functionality of Vista, you need to understand more. I urge you to spend time finding out how to protect your Personally Identifiable Information (PII) so you aren't the next victim of identity theft.

Microsoft Security Baseline Analyzer

The Microsoft Baseline Security Analyzer (MBSA) is an easy-to-use, stand-alone tool designed to help you make a determination as to the security state of your system. You can download this tool at the Microsoft Web site at `www.microsoft.com`. The tool can detect common security misconfigurations and will indicate that certain Microsoft security updates have not been applied to the system. Using this tool to scan your system on a weekly basis and performing the necessary remediation will increase the security stature of your system significantly. Here are some features that the MBSA provides that are most relevant to you:

- ✔ **Checks for weak passwords:** You can configure the tool to scan for weak passwords. This checks your computer for blank or weak passwords of local accounts on the system that you are scanning.

- ✔ **Checks for Windows administrative vulnerabilities:** This feature, if selected, checks your system for vulnerabilities, such as account password expiration, the Auto logon feature being enabled, the Guest account being enabled, simple or blank passwords of any local accounts on the computer, the type of file system on the hard drive, certain risky firewall settings, and more.

- ✔ **Checks for IIS administrative vulnerabilities:** If IIS is installed on the system, the tool will check the IIS configuration. The tool will check whether the parent paths are enabled, whether logging is enabled, and a few other IIS-related configurations to determine whether your system is vulnerable.

- ✔ **Checks for security updates:** You can make a selection for the tool to scan your system for any OS or office application security updates.

- ✔ **Provides a score report:** After the scan is completed, the tool provides a report on those vulnerabilities that were discovered. Particularly, it displays a report that easily identifies problems that the scan found and which problems are more serious and need attention first.

- ✔ **Checks desktop application configuration:** The tool checks the configuration of various applications, such as Microsoft Office and Internet Explorer (IE), to make sure that they're up to date and configured securely.

- ✔ **Provides a remediation path:** After you scan your system, the report contains a link named How to Correct This. Whether the problem is a security update or weak password on an account, clicking that link provides you all the information you need to fix that particular vulnerability.

Vista Security Sidebar Gadgets

Sidebar gadgets are software add-ons, downloadable from Microsoft, that allow you to customize the *Sidebar* (the right side of the desktop) on your Vista desktop. Luckily, one of the categories offered for the gadgets is Safety and Security. Some of these gadgets are excellent and can provide you some features and functionality that can make securing your system easier and even more fun.

For example, in the Safety and Security category is a password-safe utility named PWSafe, which allows you to manage all your passwords in one central location in a safe and easy way. Or, how about the Windows Firewall Profile gadget that displays the current profile of your Windows Firewall so that at a glance you know which firewall policy is being enforced? Under the Tools and Utilities category is the Wireless Network Controller gadget that displays your wireless network's current status and details. When opened, the gadget displays the service set identifier (SSID) and signal strength and security information.

As time goes on, these gadgets are only going to get better and better. You're likely to have a plethora of small, fun, and effective gadgets to help you manage your security. You can look at these gadgets at

```
http://gallery.microsoft.com/vista/SideBar.aspx?mkt=en-us
```

and download the security gadgets that are of interest to you.

Sysinternals Tools

Sysinternals, the creation of Mark Russinovich and Bryce Cogswell in 1996, was acquired by Microsoft in 2006. Sysinternals offers a variety of advanced system utilities and technical information that can help you manage, troubleshoot, diagnose, and — yes, you guessed it — secure your Windows systems and applications. These tools are advanced technical tools, but there is plenty here for the ambitious home or small office user. Take a look at the Sysinternals site at

```
www.microsoft.com/technet/sysinternals/default.mspx
```

You can look under the Security Utilities section and find a variety of tools to meet your security needs. Some of the tools have not yet been updated with a Vista-friendly version, so check back frequently. Sysinternals does a great job of getting their tools up-to-date quickly and releasing new tools as needs arise.

Secure File-Deletion Software

With identity theft and other fraud crimes making the news on a daily basis, more and more people are becoming cognizant that their computer can hold some PII that they just wouldn't want falling into the hands of a crook. What they might not completely understand, however, is the proper way to cleanse that information from their computer permanently so that a crook can't recover that data and use it against them. Perhaps an example better illustrates just how important this is.

I recall a conversation that I had with a colleague at a computer forensics training session. As part of her assignment for certification, she purchased two small hard disks on eBay for around $10 each. During her forensic examination of the drives, using sophisticated (and free) utilities that are widely available on the Internet, she was able to gather a great deal of personal information. Particularly, she was able to harvest several pictures of employees, their personal home addresses, phone numbers, and some Social Security numbers. The company that owned these drives thought that all this information was deleted.

Deleting a file on your Windows system doesn't permanently remove it; it just appears to the OS as though it's deleted. The truth, however, is that deleting removes the pointer to that file — but the file still remains on your disk until that particular space is overwritten with new data. This means that with data recovery software, your data can be resurrected. And, if that data includes some financial info or PII, this can used by a crook to commit identity theft or other fraud crimes.

When you sell, give away, or otherwise dispose of an old system, wipe the hard drive with an effective and secure software-deletion program to prevent your personal data from being resurrected. Here are a couple of the utilities that are available to do this:

- ✔ **BCWipe from Jetico:** BCWipe is a program that allows rapid secure file deletion and free space wiping. The program meets U.S. Department of Defense recommendations. BCWipe can be purchased for $39.99. You can download an evaluation version at www.jetico.com.

- ✔ **Wipe – Secure File Deletion:** Wipe is a file-deletion and free-space wiping utility that is OS independent. It's a bit more difficult to use than BCWipe, but it is effective — and free. You can get this utility by surfing to http://wipe.sourceforge.net and clicking the Download link at the bottom of the page.

Appendix A

Glossary of Vista and Security Terms

*a*ccess control model: The model for which access to certain tasks and functions are controlled.

ad hoc wireless network: A temporary network set up for collaborative sharing. Vista provides users the ability to set up this type of network via a peer-to-peer connection instead of using a wireless access point.

ActiveX: Microsoft object-oriented programming tools. An ActiveX control is a component program object that can be reused by applications within a computer.

Admin Approval mode: The default standard permission for all users logged into an administrative account.

asymmetric encryption: A cryptographic system that uses two keys: a public and private key. The *public key* is provided to anyone who wants to send an encrypted message to the person who holds the private key. The person holding the *private key* can then decrypt the message.

authentication: Determining whether someone (or something) is who he (it) says he (it) is. An example of this is the logon process, wherein a user supplies a username and password. If the user can provide the correct password, it's assumed that the user is valid.

authorization: The process for which a user is given access to certain data or to perform a certain function.

Backup and Restore Center: The Vista interface for tools used to perform backup and recovery of your system and data.

BitLocker: The Vista disk-encryption tool used to encrypt the system volume (that is, the C: drive) of the hard disk. The tool, if used with a Trusted Platform Module (TPM), can provide boot protection as well.

decryption: Converting data in an unreadable form *(cipher text)* into one that can be read. This is achieved by using a decryption key as part of encryption/decryption process.

digital certificate: An electronic document that establishes your credentials when performing a Web-based transaction.

digital signature: An electronic signature used to authenticate the identity of the sender of a particular message or document.

elevated privilege: When a user account has privileges greater than normal user privileges.

Encrypting File System (EFS): A feature that first appeared in previous Windows operating systems. The Vista EFS has been improved since its first incarnation. Encrypting File System provides users the ability to protect their sensitive information by encrypting those files or folders that they select. Encrypting File System uses both asymmetric and symmetric encryption methods to protect this data. *See also* asymmetric encryption, symmetric encryption.

encryption: Converting data into cipher text. This essentially makes the information unreadable to those who are not authorized to read it. *See also* decryption.

identity theft: A crime in which someone obtains key pieces of your Personally Identifiable Information (PII), such as your Social Security number or address, without your knowledge. The thief then uses that information to obtain credit or services by using your name or a false identity to obtain employment or otherwise impersonate you. *See also* Personally Identifiable Information.

Internet Explorer (IE) 7: As of the writing of this book, the latest browser from Microsoft used to surf the World Wide Web. It is bundled with Vista or can be obtained separately.

Internet Protected Mode: A feature in IE7 that separates the operating system and the browser by using User Account Control. In previous versions, browser functions had privilege in the operating system that was unnecessary. Protected mode addresses issues related to this unnecessary privilege and limits the operations that IE can conduct and the locations that it can write to.

Internet Protocol security (IPsec): A set of protocols for security at the network layer, particularly useful to secure communications as part of a Virtual Private Network (VPN) or other network communications.

Internet Protocol (IP) version 6 (IPv6): The latest level of IP, as of this writing. IPv6 lengthens IP addresses from 32 to 128 bits, which allows for future growth of the Internet. IPv6 was developed in large part to address the impending shortage of IP addresses.

malware: Any piece of software or digital file that's harmful to a computer system. Malware is a broad term that is often used to refer to viruses, worms, Trojan horses, or even spyware.

mobile device: Devices that are on the move, such as cellphones, PDAs, and so on.

NT File System (NTFS): The file system that made its debut in the Windows NT operating system and was also used as a foundation for later Windows operating systems. A *file system* is the area in which you create and store the data on your hard disk.

on-demand scanning: Scans that you set up on an as-needed basis when you use antivirus or anti-spyware tools.

Over-the-Shoulder Credentials (OTS): A feature in Windows Vista wherein a user is treated as a standard user until he needs to perform a task that requires elevated privilege. Then the user is prompted to enter the credentials to the account that has such privilege to perform the task.

Parental Controls: A Vista security feature that provides monitoring and restrictions related to Web browsing, file downloads, and more.

People Near Me: A Vista feature that allows the auto-detection of those connected to a local peer-to-peer network or subnet so that they can more easily collaborate.

Personally Identifiable Information (PII): Any information that can be used to help identify a person, such as Social Security number, date of birth, name, address, mother's maiden name, and so on.

phishing: A method that a crook uses to entice folks to provide PII or other sensitive data, usually via e-mail. The crook usually sends an e-mail that impersonates a legitimate source, such as eBay, your financial institution, and more. *See also* Personally Identifiable Information.

Phishing Filter: A security feature in IE7 that helps identify a suspicious site. The filter, if enabled, transmits data about the URL to Microsoft so that it can be compared against a known list of identified phishing sites. It also performs some internal checks that are common identifiers of a phishing site. The Phishing Filter helps users to be alerted to a site that might be impersonating an authentic site and attempting to collect PII of unsuspecting visitors. *See also* Uniform Resource Locator (URL).

principle of least privilege: A security principle that provides users the lowest privilege needed to perform the tasks that they need to perform their jobs, but nothing more.

Public Key Infrastructure (PKI): An infrastructure that pairs public keys with user identities via a certificate authority that allows for authentication of users and message encryption.

real-time scanning: A reference to scanning for viruses, worms, Trojans, or spyware while they occur. This type of scan doesn't need to be initiated by the user; if enabled, it operates in the background, scanning items while you work.

removable media: Media such as USB devices, thumb drives, DC/DVDs, floppy drives, and so on. This media "on the move" represents a significant security risk to home or small office users as well as users in a larger enterprise environment.

Rights Management Service (RMS): A feature in Vista and other Microsoft operating systems used to encrypt confidential documentation with policies. These policies can be used to prevent printing, coping, editing, forwarding, or deleting by unauthorized users.

risk: The potential negative impact to an information asset that might result from a present or future event.

Secure Desktop: A permission alert setting. When a user receives an elevation prompt from the Vista User Account Control (UAC) feature, the computer system's background is dimmed, and the user is restricted to only the prompt. The user cannot continue to work nor access anything on the desktop until the notification prompt is acted upon. *See also* User Account Control (UAC).

security controls: A protective measure or control prescribed to mitigate certain security risks or meet security requirements for a particular system.

Security Essentials: Refers to the Vista Windows Security Center (WSC) and the essential security features that it allows the user to configure.

sensitive information (data): A broad term that often means different things to different people and organizations. For the purposes of this discussion, this term can be used to describe information that might be considered corporate proprietary information; government classified information; or even PII, such as name, address, date of birth, Social Security number, and so on. Additionally, it could also include any information that one believes to be sensitive or private in nature. *See also* Personally Identifiable Information.

Service Isolation: A function of the Vista Windows Service Hardening in which system services are protected from actions of other applications.

spyware: Any software that gathers information about a user without his knowledge. Typically, this is an application installed on your system that gathers information about your surfing habits that is then relayed to online advertisers. Often, this software also is intrusive because it uses your valuable system resources and, over a period of time, may make your system run slower.

Standard User mode: The mode in which Vista places all users. This is similar to the regular Users group in previous versions of Windows, wherein users do not have any elevated privilege. Vista will run all users, even administrators, in this mode until they are actually executing a task that requires that elevated privilege.

symmetric encryption: A cryptographic message that uses a private key. Both the sender and receiver both know this private (secret) key and use it to encrypt and decrypt messages.

Trojan, or Trojan horse: A program that contains malicious or harmful code under the guise of a harmless, purposeful program. A Trojan program actually contains useful code or an application but also performs malicious functions.

Uniform Resource Locator (URL): A unique address located in the address bar of your browser: for example, `http://idtheft.about.com`.

User Account Control (UAC): A Vista security feature that essentially forces every user to run in a Standard user context without any elevated privilege. After a task is performed that requires an elevated privilege, the user is prompted to either continue (if he should be allowed to perform that task) or enter credentials to an account that has the authority to perform the task.

virus: A program or code that replicates itself to another program, document, file, or boot sector. Computer viruses are often propagated by e-mail attachments and come in many varieties, which can be most often categorized as file infectors, boot sector infectors, or macro viruses.

Vista Web Filter: A function of Parental Controls that allows you to block access to a specific Web site or specific types of Web content, such as those related to pornography, hate speech, drugs, alcohol, gambling, weapons, and more.

vulnerability: A particular weakness in your system, such as a patch that has not been applied, which a particular threat might take advantage of.

Wi-Fi Protected Access (WPA) and Wi-Fi Protected Access 2 (WPA2): A security standard used to secure wireless computer networks that was developed after weaknesses were discovered in Wired Equivalent Privacy (WEP). Vista supports WPA and WPA2, among other wireless protocols.

Windows Firewall: A personal firewall that made its debut in Windows XP Service Pack 2. The Vista Windows Firewall has several security-related enhancements, as described in Chapter 11. A personal firewall is an application that controls the inbound and outbound network traffic of a computer system. The user can configure security policy to permit or deny specific types of traffic.

Windows Meeting Space: A feature in Vista that uses peer-to-peer networking by which up to ten users can share files and collaborate.

Windows Security Center (WSC): A component that made its debut with Windows XP Service Pack 2 and is improved with Vista. This application provides users a single interface to manage a variety of security functions such as Windows Firewall, antivirus, spyware programs, and more.

Windows Service Hardening: A security control (or series of controls) provided in Vista that essentially mitigates the risk associated with the amount of damage that a service could do if it were to be compromised.

Wired Equivalent Privacy (WEP): A protocol used to encrypt wireless network traffic. After its release, WEP was discovered to have several weaknesses and isn't considered a very secure wireless standard. Although Vista supports WEP, I recommend that you use a stronger standard, such as WPA or WPA2. *See also* Wi-Fi Protected Access (WPA) and Wi-Fi Protected Access 2 (WPA2).

Appendix B

Getting to Know Vista Versions (And Related Security Features)

● ●

*L*ike all the great things in life, Vista comes in many shapes, sizes, and flavors. You can choose from Vista Home Basic, Home Premium, Business, and finally (you guessed it), the Ultimate version. The Home Basic version is not only the most affordable version but also the version with the fewest user and security features that ultimately provide you with the ability to protect your system and precious data.

Progressing from the Home Basic to the Ultimate version, each version becomes more expensive but also offers additional user and security features. To achieve the level of protection that meets your needs, select the Vista version that will provide you the tools that you need to get the job done. I urge you to take a close look at all the features and functionality that each version offers. That way, you can select a version that not only meets your security needs but also your functional needs.

Vista Home Basic

Vista Home Basic version — the entry-level version — is meant for those of you with very basic needs. This version is very light not only on user features but also the security features that will help you protect your system and data. If you use your system only to peruse the Internet and for the occasional e-mail, this version will certainly meet your needs. However, if you use your system to process financial transactions, healthcare-claim information, taxes, or other sensitive data, this version won't provide you the protection that you need. To appropriately protect or preserve more sensitive or irreplaceable data, I suggest that you select another version of Vista. At the time of this writing, Vista Home Basic is priced at about $89–$199 for the full release.

Vista Home Premium

This version of Vista is the most popular version for those with a home desktop or mobile computer. Although it provides more appealing user features and even a greater level of security than the Home Basic version, Home Premium won't provide adequate protection for any sensitive data or data that's hard to replace. This version doesn't come with any encryption capabilities or some of the important backup and restore features that the Vista Business and Vista Ultimate versions provide. However, if you don't use your system for financial transactions, medical claims, small business records, or other sensitive information, this version will likely meet your needs.

At the time of this writing, Home Premium is priced at $159–$229 for the full release. You can upgrade from Home Basic to Home Premium for $79.

Vista Business

Vista Business provides a great deal of features and functionality to meet the needs of a small business. This version is also very strong from a security perspective, offering a variety of protection capabilities for data preservation. However, if you hold or process sensitive data that might need to be encrypted, this version can't provide that capability, and you need to look toward the Vista Ultimate version.

At the time of this writing, Vista Business is priced at $279–$299 for the full release. You can upgrade from a lower version of Vista for $199.

Vista Ultimate

The name says it all. The Ultimate version offers not only all the user features and functionality but also all the security features that Vista has to offer. It is also the most expensive for home users and small business owners. However, if you have sensitive data that needs encryption, this is the version that I recommend.

At the time of this writing, Vista Ultimate is priced at $300–$399 for the full release. You can upgrade from Home Basic to Vista Ultimate for $199, from Home Premium to Ultimate for $159, or from Vista Business to Ultimate for $139.

Vista Enterprise

Vista Enterprise edition isn't available for retail purchase but can be purchased only with an agreement with Microsoft as part of its *Software Assurance Program,* which is the Microsoft software annuity licensing program. Vista Enterprise is designed for a large, complex IT infrastructure and offers capabilities of the Microsoft Desktop Optimization Pack to deploy and manage a large corporate PC environment. Vista Enterprise is not geared toward the small office user.

Comparing Versions of Vista

Table B-1 lays out the different security-related features in each Vista version.

Table B-1	Security Features of the Different Versions of Vista				
Security Features	Vista Versions				
	Home Basic	Home Premium	Business	Enterprise	Ultimate
Parental Controls (Helps monitor and control a child's activities)	X	X			X
User Account Control (UAC)	X	X	X	X	X
Windows Firewall	X	X	X	X	X
Windows Defender	X	X	X	X	X
Basic Backup and Recovery	X	X	X	X	X
Schedule and network backup		X	X	X	X
Shadow Copy (for restoring previous file versions)			X	X	X

(continued)

Table B-1 *(continued)*

Security Features			Vista Versions		
	Home Basic	Home Premium	Business	Enterprise	Ultimate
Incremental backups			X	X	X
Complete PC Backup (image backup)			X	X	X
Rights Management Services			X	X	X
Encrypting File System			X	X	X
BitLocker				X	X
IE7 (Phishing Filter and protected mode)	X	X	X	X	X
Windows Automatic Updates	X	X	X	X	X
Service hardening	X	X	X	X	X

Index

• *J* •

• *K* •